Wild women do

(and they *don't* regret it!)

The inspirational autobiography of Margaret Miles-Bramwell OBE, Slimming World's Founder and Chair.

Published in 2019 by Slimming World
Clover Nook Road, Somercotes,
Alfreton, Derbyshire DE55 4SW, UK
www.slimmingworld.co.uk

Created and designed by Slimming World's publications team and Sterling Creative

Publications manager: Deborah Charles
Editors: Jane Love and Jan Boxshall
Designers: Kathryn Briggs, Flixx Wedgwood-Walker, Sterling Creative
Photography: Graeme Simpson, Neil Lancashire, Matt Lowe,
Keystone Pictures USA/ZUMAPRESS, various others
Proofreading: Jane Love, Rebecca Robinson, Natalie Ahmed

Front cover photograph:
Graeme Simpson 2019
Text and design ©Slimming World – 2019

DEDICATION

To my long-suffering family, for all your love, understanding and patience over the years.

To all our treasured Consultants, managers and staff who work so tirelessly, so single-mindedly and with such unstinting belief to deliver the absolute best to every Slimming World member.

With all my love,

I hope that my 71-year-old memory has served me well in the writing of this autobiography. And I hope that if I've made any omissions or errors, if I've mis-remembered any details or failed to mention someone I really should have mentioned (I'm not a drinker, so I can only blame the years of believing I didn't need sleep to function), then you'll forgive me.

And a note about the title: Wild Women do© is the name of a song that means a lot to me, performed by Natalie Cole (songwriters: Gregory Prestopino, Matthew Wilder, John Samuel Lorber)

PROLOGUE

Joy, the nurse, the dedicated nurse, had accepted that she was never going to be wooed by any of the handsome hospital doctors she worked with during those intense war years. Joy saw herself as a plain Jane and had long since abandoned thoughts of ever finding true love. Unlike her fellow nurses – the pretty but often less dedicated ones, who wanted someone to cover their shifts so they could meet up with those dashingly seductive doctors – Joy had built up a nice little nest egg thanks to all those extra hours she willingly took on.

Joy, the 'other woman', the lover of Harry – a sophisticated and handsome man-about-town – could hardly believe this fairytale was happening to her. And all as a result of that nest egg, which had allowed her to shop at Rosa Gold's Dress Emporium in London, not far from where she worked and lived.

Harry, Rosa's younger brother, had quite literally swept her off her feet. One day, in the shop, he grabbed her, picked her up and swung her around, both of them laughing at her shock and delight.

Harry, the first person ever to have cuddled her (including, as far as she recalled, her parents). Harry, her knight in shining armour, rescuing her from a loveless life. Romance, for Joy, seemed nothing short of a dream that she'd never dared to dream.

There was just one tiny fly in this blissful ointment. Harry was a married man – separated from his wife, but still firmly married.

Their relationship was eventually consummated and at the age of 24, with next to no experience of sex or even physical affection, to her shock and dismay Joy found herself 'with child'.

Of course, there were paths open to Joy when it came to dealing with this unwanted pregnancy. She was, after all, a nurse. But she was a dedicated nurse, dedicated to caring for the sick and, more than anything, dedicated to saving life, preserving life. An abortion, illegal in 1947 and for the next 20 years, was simply out of the question.

Harry, the hero, rapidly proved to have feet of clay. Harry wanted nothing to do with the baby and was fast losing interest in the girl he had seduced. However, he (gallantly) stayed around until the birth and was the one who (bravely) drove the car to the hospital that April night in 1948, when Joy's waters broke and the labour progressed at breakneck speed.

By the time Joy was hurriedly wheeled into the delivery suite, the baby's head was already showing and, in the early hours of 20th April 1948, at around one o'clock, I came hurtling loudly into the world.

“ Don't judge me.
I was born to be awesome, not perfect. ”

CHAPTER ONE

mum's the word

My biological mother, Joy, was a 24-year-old unmarried nurse who became pregnant with her first and only boyfriend, Harry, a world-ly-wise businessman in his early 40s. Joy lived away from home, in the nurses' quarters of a London hospital, and so she was able to hide her guilty secret from her family.

Keeping me was out of the question. Despite her sadness at having to give me away, bringing up a child born out of wedlock in those days would have destroyed Joy's reputation, ruined her family relationships and ended her career. Harry was married (albeit separated) and certainly didn't want to be burdened with a child.

So, after breastfeeding me for 10 days and in spite of the closeness and bonding she felt, on 30th April 1948, Joy handed me over to Harry's sister Rosa, who in turn handed me to Emma Selina and Samuel Birch from the small mining village of South Normanton, in Derbyshire.

On the very same day, Harry (sensitive, responsible and loyal as ever) visited the hospital, not with a bunch of flowers but with a new woman ('floozy' would probably have been the word of the day) on his arm and announced that their affair was over. I can't imagine Joy's shock, grief and anger at losing her baby *and* the only man in her life, the man she loved wholeheartedly, all in the space of 24 hours.

At 42 and 45 years old respectively, Emma Selina (she didn't like her name and was known to her family and friends as Pem) and Samuel – Mum and Dad to me – had waited years and years for a pregnancy that never came. Our local Methodist minister, the

Rev. Harry Hazelhurst, a kind and lovely man with a wonderful family of five, lived next door to Emma Selina and Samuel on Hilcote Street. His wife, Mary, had a sister who worked in the same London hospital as Joy. And so the arrangement was made – the South Normanton couple would adopt Joy's baby and – perhaps because it was an unofficial arrangement – everything would be kept very hush-hush.

Mum was one of six children and Dad was one of seven, and many members of the family lived on our street and the ones around it – it was a tight-knit community.

We lived just across the road from Frank Sutton the farmer, his wife Edith and son Michael (my age). Next door to them were Mr and Mrs Bowmer and their two grown-up sons, who lived in a terraced house, attached to the house of my Aunty Nan, an extremely talented tailoress. She was married to Dad's gentle, kindly brother Tom, a coal miner. Virtually all the men in the village were miners or retired miners.

Tom and Nan had four children – Roger and Janet, already grown-up, and Edwin and Alma, only a few years older than me. I spent a lot of time with these cousins, and felt very much a part of the family. My grandma and granddad (Dad's parents) lived at the bottom of our road, in a bungalow with a tiny smallholding attached, where they kept chickens and grew vegetables. My Aunt Olive lived with them, with her two daughters Esme and Edwina.

Dad was also a hard-working miner who walked to the local colliery each day with my granddad, who worked well into his 70s. I remember watching them amble down the street together to the pit – a memory I'm still touched by today.

Mum was hard-working too, a housewife obsessed with housework. With Mum, every cushion was plumped to perfection, every drawer was organised to death, every inch of linoleum shone with its weekly polish and to this day, its smell reminds me of my childhood home. The sitting room was of the age, a typical arrangement with an armchair on either side of the fireplace, which always had a cosy, crackling fire burning (one of the advantages of being a mining family). There was a sofa on the back wall facing the fireplace, and in one corner was a radiogram, which Dad loved to fiddle with to find the clearest station. The radiogram was his pride and joy, second only to the immense pride he had in his car. Under the window was a drop-leaf dining table, which was assembled daily for our evening meal. In the other corner was a space that would eventually, in 1953, house the TV specially installed to view Queen Elizabeth II's Coronation.

I was never allowed to 'spoil' the immaculate settee by sitting on it, but I didn't mind at all because my favourite place to sit was on the floor, in between the two armchairs, being fascinated and hypnotised by the flames flickering in the hearth.

To make a little extra money, Mum would take in lodgers and she welcomed many different people into our home over the years. As far as I was concerned, this was absolutely brilliant. It saved me from the loneliness of being an only child in a spick-and-span house, where friends weren't encouraged to visit. Our lodgers were often working men who didn't live locally. I particularly remember a group of Scots, regular lodgers – especially the oldest, a man called Jim, who taught me how to play draughts and versions of the same – helping me hone my forward-planning skills. I would have been around 7 or 8 at the time.

These house guests came and went, and during the early 1960s we hosted our final lodger. He was a Hungarian refugee named Laszlo Novak (Laci), who claimed to have escaped his home country in the most dramatic fashion, through underground tunnels and across fields, often wriggling with his friends on their stomachs to avoid capture. At the age of 11, I greedily drank in all the stories of his daring adventures. I learned a little Hungarian (I do mean a little) and he became like my older brother.

Laci stayed with my mum and dad long after I'd left home, and didn't leave until he married Maureen. Their marriage lasted a lifetime until 2018 when she sadly passed away, leaving him and her grown-up family bereft.

Chapel was a big part of my life from the age of two-and-a-half. Sunday school gave way to regular concerts and Methodist chapel anniversaries, where from the age of six I used to sing on stage with my cousin Edwina, *'I'm a bow-legged chicken, I'm a knock-kneed hen'*, with all the actions of course. We went down a storm! That was followed by a few acts and a costume change, after which we sang that great hit of 1954, *'Gilly Gilly Ossenfeffer Katzenellen Bogen by the Sea'*. I remember the thunderous applause even now!

When I was very young, before we started taking in lodgers, I sometimes got a bit lonely and I often longed for friends to play with. So it wasn't unheard of for me to slip out of the house, escape the monotony and run a few yards up the street to where the magic was happening – a *school*, with *children*! I'd press my nose up to the glass of the big windows at New Street Infant School, desperate to go inside and play.

When I eventually started school (a bit earlier than was usual at that time) at the age of four-and-a-bit, my world lit up. Miss Greasley was our teacher and she was wonderful. I just adored her. Sometimes, at parent-teacher meetings, she would tell my mum how much I loved writing and arithmetic, how many pages I'd done, how clever I was – then I'd overhear Mum boasting to friends and relatives.

Nothing was said directly to me, but these messages stuck with me throughout my childhood. No matter how chubby I felt, no matter how thick or unruly my hair got, no matter how much my round rosy-red cheeks almost glowed in the dark, no matter how unattractive I felt compared to the lithe, lean, pale-skinned teens at the chapel youth club, I always wanted to live up to the Margaret that Miss Greasley proudly described to my mum.

When I was about eight years old, I discovered that I was adopted – it's a miracle really that in such a tight-knit community I didn't find out sooner. There we were, a group of schoolfriends, playing happily in the fields behind Hilcote Street, when a silly squabble erupted and one of the girls told me, with that touch of cruelty children so commonly use to score a point (oblivious to the consequences), *'At least my mummy's my mummy. Yours isn't!'*

Holding back the tears, I ran away from the fields and my taunting friends, straight home to seek comfort and reassurance from my mum. Dad was at work, of course. Avoiding my question, she replied, *'God gave you me,'* adding that I mustn't speak about this to my dad. Why? Surely he must have known? Confused? I certainly was.

Throughout my childhood, Mum, Dad and I would occasionally take the train down to London to visit a rather glamorous couple (or so they seemed to me) who owned a dress shop, and would dress me up in all sorts of fine clothes, which I thought was lovely! Mum told me that this couple had been refugees who she'd taken in as children during the war – a plausible story to me as a child, because it was something she'd done for others.

But of course they weren't refugees – they were Harry and Joy, my biological parents – who had given me away all those years before. Although Harry did a disappearing act just after my birth, he did reunite with Joy about six months later. (They lived together, unmarried, until Harry's death from motor neurone disease in his 80s. Even at his most poorly, he was a cheerful character who always enjoyed life. Despite the gradual onset of paralysis from his condition, he never lost his wandering eye – which, as a final blow to poor Joy, wandered right over to a young neighbour who came in to support her as she cared for him in those latter months. Joy died many years later, also in her 80s.)

The fact that, as a young girl, I'd been left to piece together the story of my existence – and the fact that no one was ever entirely open about the whole thing – led me to believe there was something awkward, embarrassing and possibly shameful about me.

Margaret Greasley, my beloved first teacher, had, indirectly via my parents, given me a different label – a positive message about myself. I always feel it was largely down to her that I had the confidence to do what I was to do later in life. Equally, I believe the feeling that I was some sort of misfit, something to be ashamed of, someone who'd been given away, drove me to prove that I was a worthwhile human being after all.

So that was me. Margaret the goody-two-shoes, the eager-to-please pupil who always got straight 'A's at junior school, before passing the Eleven Plus to get into Swanwick Hall Grammar. I loved school. In my mind, the plan was simple. I'd complete my O-Levels, then A-Levels, go on to university and become a doctor. No question.

Another part of me, though, wanted desperately to be part of the 'in-crowd'. I decided at an early age that my looks were never going to get me accepted. I was never going to look cool like the people I so admired, so I'd better develop a personality and become a fun person to be around. With that mindset and an early adolescence, my rebellious streak started to emerge at around the age of 10.

At about this time, I was in the penultimate class at the junior school, which was 3A, taught by one Miss Marsh – a fierce little woman with her gun-metal grey hair tightly permed and her dresses with their plunge necklines ruined by a modesty panel across her ample bosom. *Send for the fashion police!* Miss Marsh's passions were, in equal parts, perfectly formed handwriting and perfect needlework. Neither of these subjects were particularly close to my heart, but hey ho, we don't look for excitement at school and certainly not with Miss Marsh, so we just get on with it, don't we?

When it came to neat and precise needlework, I didn't exactly excel. Maybe that was why I got the distinct impression that I was NOT her favourite pupil. Nonetheless, I used these classes as a chance to let my mind wander free, while piercing the material with my needle (but more often my finger). Off in my own world, I didn't realise that I'd taken to whistling. I simply wasn't aware I was doing it. That was, until Miss Marsh boomed out, *'Who's whistling?'*

I gulped. It was indeed me. I stopped immediately, of course, but before long, adrift in my daydreams again, my unconscious whistling resumed. The next thing I knew was Miss Marsh's curled index finger viciously stabbing my arm, as she yelled in my ear: *'A whistling woman and a crowing hen are neither fit for God nor men!'* Well! That would never do, would it, friends? She yanked me out of my seat and made me stand on a chair in the corner with my back to the rest of the room. I was guilty as charged and had no choice other than to take my punishment.

I ended up in trouble with Miss Marsh again when, to my dismay, I managed to spill ink all over the empty and otherwise pristine back page of my exercise book. Talk about blotting my copybook! Of course, the eagle-eyed, Margaret-hating teacher really gave me what-for over that crime.

The following year, we all went up to the fourth form, taught by Miss Marsh's bosom buddy, Miss Stinson. Naturally, I stood no chance in the popularity stakes with her either, as Miss Marsh had made sure she was well aware what sort of ne'er-do-well I was. I remember on one occasion, Miss Stinson threatened to send me to the Headmaster (a nice man whose unfortunate role it was to punish wayward pupils) to be caned because I had made an inkblot in the back of an exercise book – yes, the same blot I'd already been punished for by Miss Marsh!

Of course, I protested! Miss Stinson didn't believe me and Miss Marsh swore it wasn't true (what a fibber!). Boy, was I furious. Charles Dickens had it spot-on in *Great Expectations*: *'In the little world in which children have their existence... there is nothing so finely perceived and so finely felt, as injustice.'* Falsely accused – injustice indeed!

Enraged, I locked myself in the toilet and refused to come out. For the first time in my life, I didn't care about the consequences. Then something unbelievable happened – absolutely nothing! No one kicked the door down, no one dragged me to the Headmaster's office to be caned. I'd stood up against authority and the world hadn't come to an end. This was my first experience of breaking through a limiting, false ceiling in my mind – a dangerous discovery at the age of 10, with adolescence poised to burst into life.

To be fair to Miss Stinson, she did teach us all to play the descant recorder. Some people did so well they were elevated to the treble recorder and just one to the bass recorder – *moi*! You would think that would have given me lots of Brownie points with this friend of Miss Marsh – but no such luck. It did lead me to learn to play the flute in the school orchestra, though, once I was at grammar school, and it did earn me the winning score in the local musical festival, where I was crowned 'victor ludorum'. How cool is that!

———————————

At grammar school, unfortunately for me, I also discovered something far more exciting than playing the flute. Boys and rock 'n' roll! And despite my strong work ethic and academic achievements, my rebellious streak continued to come to the fore. If *Queen* had been around then, I'd have been singing, *'I want to break free!'*

By the time I was 14 years old, I was being collected at the school gates by my first real boyfriend, Roy Miles. He was 19, with a motorbike – an Ariel Arrow. These days he'd probably be described as a 'bad boy'. He was a charming, charismatic and good-looking Jack the Lad. From some angles, as I gazed at him one moonlit night at the bus stop, he looked a lot like John Lennon. And he wanted me – *me*! Make room on cloud nine!

My rebellious behaviour wouldn't be so unusual or shocking today maybe, but looking back, I must have been a nightmare for my mum. She was very, very strait-laced – born in 1906 and raised in the wake of the (superficially) moralistic Victorian era. I was now a strong-willed rebel, determined to free myself from these overbearing shackles of unreasonable rules and outrageous restrictions. I just wanted to break free. Sing it, Freddie!

Roy and I went to the local youth club (he was great at jiving) and sometimes we'd go to the local cinema (back row of course), but mostly life centred around motorbikes and motorbike racing – Donington Park in Derbyshire and Mallory Park in Leicestershire were our local favourites. Being a few years older than me, Roy quite naturally wanted to do other things too, although as the product of a strict Methodist upbringing, I'd been well-rehearsed in the art of fighting boys off. And for a whole year, I resolutely resisted.

In the end, I stopped resisting. In October 1963, I missed my period. The next month rolled around and still no period. I asked for help from the only person I could confide in, my beloved, all-knowing boyfriend, Roy. He had friends. They had contacts – 'pharmaceutical' contacts.

The pills were black and looked a bit like Smarties. Taking two or three each day would supposedly bring on my period but be warned, it was dangerous to overdose. Strange, but I never saw it as getting rid of a living thing. I just wanted my period to start again and then I could get on with my life.

To be on the safe side, I swallowed the week's supply in one go. I say 'safe' in the sense that I *had* to get my period to return. I was well aware I was taking a risk. But it was 1963, I was 15 years old and well, I've told you what Mum was like. Death by overdose seemed preferable to having her know what I'd been doing, and preferable to an underage, illegitimate pregnancy.

Roy's mates clearly weren't pharmaceutical high-flyers (thank God), because absolutely nothing happened. Well, nothing except my urine turned black! And so we tried the age-old remedy of a bottle of gin in a very hot bath, at Roy's house of course, while no one else was in. Equally ineffective!

There was nothing else for it. I'd have to go to the doctor. Heart in my dry mouth, I confessed to the GP. He said he would need to perform an examination, but couldn't do so unless I brought along a chaperone. Even that idea sounded horrific. That meant I had to tell someone. The follow-up appointment – in the surgery after-hours (to spare my shame) – was a week away.

Seven days of emotional turmoil passed. I simply couldn't muster the courage to confide in anyone, not even my 18-year-old married friend Mary, so great was my sense of shame. Throwing caution to the wind and ignoring the doctor's instructions, I returned to the surgery alone – even more nervous than before.

I stepped on the scales, which (kindly) showed me weighing 10 stones. That was a pleasant surprise! I was barely aware that I had been losing weight. I hadn't been able to eat much at all for several weeks, sick with worry (make that sheer terror) that I might be pregnant at 15 and in big trouble (*and I was both*).

Without a chaperone, but left with little choice, the doctor reluctantly performed the examination and confirmed that I was indeed, as suspected, four months' pregnant. Because I was underage and had, in the eyes of the law, been raped, he said that both Roy and I had to report this to the police – or he would. He gave us 24 hours. He also insisted that I tell Mum.

Showing a flash of kindness, he volunteered to be the one to tell her and gave me a plausible reason to explain why the doctor needed to see her. I remember walking woodenly down the street and into our kitchen. I could hear my own heartbeat and thought that this was what it must be like to walk into death row. I found enough strength to speak the words that would get my mum one step closer to learning the truth. *'My period has stopped. The doctor needs to see you.'* Mum was already very annoyed that I had dared to go and see the doctor without informing her first. Little did she know that this was nothing compared to the news he was about to deliver.

I trudged the few yards alongside her, to the surgery, wishing the ground would swallow us both up. The doctor began by saying that he was sure she'd guessed the real reason he needed to speak to her. She sat very still and said no, she had no idea. So he told her. Her A-stream, university-bound, Sunday-schooled Margaret was pregnant at the age of 15. Mum's reaction was so violent it left me numb. I watched as, first of all, she appeared to collapse dramatically across the doctor's desk.

Time seemed to stand still and it felt as if my world had shrunk into a very small space. I think I stopped breathing. To accompany her collapse, which the doctor refused to accept as anything other than dramatics, Mum screamed and then started yelling all sorts of abuse, calling me a 'whore', and including barbs such as *'Like mother, like daughter'*. That phrase cut the deepest, deeper than the 'whore' insults. It was as if she had never really accepted me as her own daughter. I felt rejected all over again. My shame was immense.

The doctor's surgery was across the street from my first school, on the brow of Hilcote Street's hill, just at the top of our road. It was a short walk back home from the surgery, but somehow everything looked and felt different – no longer comfortingly familiar. As we walked side by side, down the hill, past the homes of our neighbours and family, past the home of the new Methodist minister, past Frank Sutton's field, which divided their house from ours, Mum planned my options.

We stood at our gate before we went inside to break the news to Dad. Mum insisted that I should have an abortion (abortion wasn't to become legal in Britain until 1967, another three years) and when I said no, she said then I had to have the baby adopted. When I refused to do that too, she made her mind up that I had to leave the neighbourhood – immediately.

My fear and shame was replaced with hurt, disappointment and anger. I think it was a big part of growing up fast. When we walked into the house, Dad was waiting in the kitchen. Mum told him the news and that she wasn't prepared to have me living there. I don't know to this day if Dad was sobbing, tears running down his face, because he was so disappointed in me or because he didn't want me to go. Probably a little of both. My lovely dad's sadness was much worse to bear than my mum's fury. My sense of shame was off the scale. I wanted to die.

There's something that's not necessarily logical about how it feels to be adopted and know your very existence was someone's guilty secret. To me, it meant that I wasn't wanted. I wasn't worth the trouble. I was a reject. Now, being thrown out of home by parents who supposedly *did* want me – but just didn't want me quite enough to stand by me when I desperately needed all their love and support – simply reinforced that feeling of worthlessness. I never wanted my child to feel like that and I think this intensified my determination to go ahead with the pregnancy.

In spite of everything – in spite of all my academic aspirations coming to an abrupt halt, in spite of being far too young to marry, in spite of being abandoned once again (this time by my adoptive parents), in spite of my self-disgust (I had brought all this life-changing bad news down on my own head after all) and knowing that I was a huge disappointment to everyone including myself – I refused to give up my baby. It's a decision I have never regretted.

Having been strong-armed by the doctor into reporting our misdemeanour, my next humiliation was visiting the police station to confess all. Roy had to do the same. He simply popped into South Normanton Police Station, to explain to the desk sergeant what had happened and was met with the response: *'Now what have you done, you silly bugger?'.*

I, on the other hand, had to report to Alfreton, the main local police station, accompanied by my mother. To my sheer horror, she was present as I was grilled by two *male* officers on every last detail of my physical relationship with Roy – how many times, where exactly, when exactly… the lot. I wanted the ground to open up and swallow me whole. What a difference between Roy's police experience and mine. Talk about double standards. And not a shred of care or compassion for a young and frightened girl.

Because everything was, of course, completely consensual, not much came of the ordeal and Roy faced no charges. The authorities left us alone to deal with the consequences of our actions.

After Mum threw me out, I never went back to school. Instead, I moved in with Roy's sister Mary and her family.

Roy was the baby of his family, with five siblings. Madge was the eldest and lived in Yorkshire, so we saw less of her. Neville was the second eldest – he was an easygoing, tall and lanky man, married to June, with five children. Then there was Betty, married to John, who was a really kind man. They had a young son, Philip. Next came Mary, who was kind enough to take me in when I had nowhere else to go. She was married to Wally – again a very decent man – with two daughters, Sandra and Janet.

There was also Jack, another older brother and the most academic, quiet and thoughtful of the Miles men. I found myself a little bit in awe of Jack – I think because of the way Roy deferred to him and spoke about him. Roy obviously respected him a lot. When we visited them in their neat and cosy little house in South Normanton, we always minded our Ps and Qs. That nervousness on my part led to one of my more famous boo-boos. Jack was a painter and decorator, hence the pristine condition of their house. Asking his advice when it came to buying the right paint, I meant to ask if Dulux was the best one. I wished I hadn't asked for his opinion of Durex! Boy, did my rosy cheeks glow bright that day!

Jack married Jean, a wonderful woman who I was privileged to have in my life, not only as my sister-in-law but as a colleague and friend, as she became one of our first staff members once we had an actual office for Slimming World (I'll tell you more about Jack and Jean later).

All five of his siblings spoiled the 'baby' Roy and loved him to bits. As a toddler, he was always a 'cheeky chappy', always their delightful baby brother and always got away with blue murder. I have very fond memories of Betty and Mary, in particular. My nieces Sandra and Janet and nephew Phil can feel proud and lucky to have had such kind, loving parents.

I stayed very healthy throughout my pregnancy and was quite happy in many ways living with Mary and Wally, but I wasn't looking forward to the birth, having heard many horror stories by now. I'd loved biology classes at school and had actually been fascinated by dissecting insects and cows' eyes, so I rather prided myself on not being squeamish. When the leader at our antenatal group explained that they were going to show us some visual aids, black-and-white pictures and coloured slides, to help us understand what giving birth had in store for us, I thought the other mums-to-be were being a bit over-dramatic in their concerns about seeing such graphic images. Imagine my deep embarrassment when *I* was the only one who had to go outside before I fainted! One of my redeeming qualities is having the good grace to know when I've been a complete idiot. Having a grand ego has never played well in my life!

For three months, Roy and I planned the most frugal of weddings. It took place four days after my 16th birthday in April 1964, by which time I was seven months' pregnant. I vividly remember how I felt when we visited the minister at Watchorn Methodist Church in Alfreton, to talk through what we wanted and what we could afford on the day.

As we were offered our options, we had to go through the humiliating process of turning down virtually every 'nice to have' or 'extra' because it would cost money. There would be no organist and there would be no wedding bells – particularly sad, as only a few months before, as a Girl Guide, I had loved being a trainee campanologist.

I was 'showing' only slightly. I'd lost weight up to this point – a result of the emotional turmoil, originally caused by shame, stress and the feelings of rejection, and now supplemented by my fear of the impending birth.

Somehow (and my memory fails me as to how), something we *did* have at the wedding, unexpectedly, was Mum and Dad. It was probably because Mum had made arrangements for her favourite seamstress to make my little white knee-length dress. Roy had a very nice friend, Michael Bush, who kindly agreed to be his best man. My wonderful, mild-mannered, loving dad gave me away – the man who, throughout the happy times of my childhood, had patiently and lovingly read to me, let me put Mum's rollers in his thin and balding hair and had conspiratorially, in direct defiance of Mum, bought me lollipops with his spare change. He walked me tearfully down the aisle and continued to sob through the whole service.

In fact, both Roy and I ended up with tears streaming down our faces, too. As the ceremony ended and we turned to leave the church, the warm-hearted, kindly minister tugged my arm and said: *'Can you hear? They're ringing the bells for you.'* Kindness like that changes lives.

66 *A woman is like a tea bag – you can't tell how strong she is until you put her in hot water.* 99

Eleanor Roosevelt

CHAPTER TWO

new beginnings

On Sunday 28th June 1964, I woke at 4am with stomach ache. I didn't put two and two together immediately, but after a while I realised my labour had probably started. Fun fact for anyone else born that year, the next time you can reuse your old 1964 calendar will be in 2020. Both calendars will be exactly the same (except for Easter and related holidays)!

The labour pains were quite light initially, and I'd promised to wash and set Mrs Bush's hair (mother of our best man at the wedding). I felt OK and decided to honour my commitment to Mrs B but, without a hairdryer, the time dragged on before I could remove the rollers and dress her hair. The second that was done, Roy and I went immediately to the Queen Mary Maternity Home in Derby. By now, it was 2.30 in the afternoon and the labour pains were stronger and coming more quickly. I was starting to feel very nervous.

The nurses weren't too friendly, quite hostile actually, and Roy wasn't allowed to stay with me – something that was common at the time, I think. Being stuck in a tiny room, alone, with hardly a visit from any of the nurses, did nothing to calm my nerves. I'd taken my radio with me – why I'll never know – and my book explaining labour and the practicalities of giving birth. Lying in bed, I kept reading while I listened to the 'Top 20' and as the pains became really strong, something very weird happened with my hands. Involuntarily, with an apparent mind of their own, they would become rigid and raise themselves to my eye level. When the pain subsided, so did my hands. How very strange, I thought, but with no one to ask I simply accepted it as normal, although my trusty book didn't mention anything about the phenomenon.

I'd just reached the point in the book where it described 'transition' – a point in labour when there's no space between pains and, apparently, you move from labour to pushing, because the baby is coming soon. It was five o'clock and Roy Orbison was hitting his high note, as No. 1 in the 'Top 20' that week was *It's Over*. How apt. I heartily wished it *were*! I started yelling for help and was immediately attended, thank goodness, and rolled into the delivery room. At sometime around 6pm, I was convinced I was going to die and then something wonderful happened. The baby's head was out and suddenly the rest became easy.

We called our baby Claire. She was absolutely beautiful. Born with a dusting of dark hair, she was the double of Roy. I was instantly overwhelmed with love for her. I was on such a high I couldn't sleep that first night, even though I'd been up since four o'clock in the morning with those early labour pains and it had taken 14 hours to bring her into our world.

I couldn't stop looking at her, marvelling at her, this 7lb 6oz miracle, those tiny fingers and toes, that cuter-than-cute nose and prettier-than-pretty lips. I was so excited, so mesmerised and so in awe of this beautiful creature we had made together. I wanted to be there, awake, to give her my milk when she wanted it. I was poised to learn everything I could about my baby, this new reality that, until now, I'd only read about. Just being able to hold her in my arms and gaze in wonder at every detail of my daughter was enough to keep me wide awake.

The next night, whether they had put something in my Horlicks or whether it was sheer exhaustion, they told me they couldn't wake me to feed her. So they had propped me up in bed and held her to my

Me and Mum,
Emma Selina (Pem) Birch.

Me at around 18 months of age (I can't
have learned how to say 'cheeese' yet!).

Mum, Dad and me (oblivious to the camera!).

My parents kept greyhounds, which became household pets. Here's me with my cousin Edwina (in front) – hopefully stroking them gently!

JUNE 2ⁿᵈ 1953
CORONATION
SOUVENIR
ELIZABETH·II·

My school photo in 1953 – the year of Queen Elizabeth II's Coronation.

Aged eight – with my hair in the ringlets that Mum loved so much.

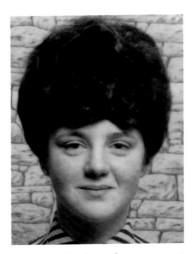

11 years old – just after my secret trip to Nottingham to have those ringlets cut off! I figured... sometimes it's better to be forgiven than to ask for permission!

Me and Joy, my birth mother – a rare snapshot.

Harry – my birth father – in his more senior years.

Roy and me on our wedding day (the bouquet covering my little baby bump!),
with his parents (left) and mine (right).

Roy and me looking very pleased with our newlywed selves!

My beautiful daughter, Claire, in a garden in Mablethorpe on our first family holiday.

Roy and me at home with a group of friends. Michael, known as Fred (far left), was the best man at our wedding – and later my intrepid amateur driving instructor!

The slimming fad of the 1960s. Limmits slimming biscuits – my first diet! Starving didn't bother me that first time!

The Scout hut in Mansfield where I held my very first slimming group in 1969.

Betty Oldknow, then and now. Betty was one of my first members, then became a 'teacher,' taking over my groups when I needed to spend more time growing the business. Fifty years later, she's still a Consultant (and every bit as gorgeous!).

Our new members now receive not one but four fabulous, colourful books as part of their joining fee.

How our publications for members have changed! From our very amateurish attempts in the '70s through to the stunning, glossy read that is today's *Slimming World Magazine.*

I loved this advert – and I still do. The logo bottom right (which replaced the 'fork' logo above top right) was designed by Linney's Michael Fisher, inspired by my visit to the Kennedy Space Centre.

breasts as she fed. I felt cheated that I had slept through all of this. To me, breastfeeding was the most heavenly experience.

I ended up expressing milk during my 10 days in hospital (new mums stayed in hospital much longer in those days), for a very good cause, the 'prem' babies. Knowing nothing about breastfeeding, I had no idea of the problems I was storing up for myself when I went home. No one at the hospital had enlightened me. My body thought my baby required all that milk and so, as nature intended, my hormones worked efficiently and continued to produce it. This caused immense pain, and much to my despair I had to abandon breastfeeding altogether after barely a month at home. It was one of the most physically and emotionally painful times I can ever remember.

Life as a young, newlywed mum in 1964 wasn't quite the one I'd pictured for myself. In fact, it was about as far from my dreams of the lecture theatres and science laboratories of medical school as you could get. Roy was earning around £12 a week and bringing home even less after tax, working as a travelling salesman for Kenning Motor Group in Alfreton. He earned a little more by working shifts on the petrol pumps at weekends, but it wasn't a lot. By now we'd moved out from Mary's and were living with Roy's parents.

The Animals were still a year from releasing *'We gotta get out of this place'*, but we could have written that song! It would have been the anthem to our early married life. We were desperate for money. We wanted, needed, to save up for a deposit on a house and move out. I was keen for us to be able to get our own place and put a foot on the first rung of the property ladder. I always saw rented accommodation as money down the drain and a restriction on our ability to make our home our own.

When Claire was three months old, Roy announced, *'Mag, you're going to have to get a job or we'll be stuck here forever.'* Not only was this another dream shattered – I wasn't going to be able to look after my new little angel (and she *was* an angel – you couldn't wish for a more easygoing child) – but I didn't see how it was possible. Who would take care of Claire?

With the wedding having plastered over (if not actually having healed) the cracks in the relationship between me and my mum, I went to her and asked for help. To my relief, she agreed to look after Claire while I went out to work six days a week. I realised Mum loved babies.

I thought it through and decided that although I would no longer be with my beautiful baby girl for the whole day, if Mum could get her into a good pattern of sleeping during the day, then I could enjoy being with her in the evenings and keep her up a bit later than was usual. I'd read dozens of books (of course) on bringing up babies, but I found none on maintaining the invaluable and wonderful bond between *working* mums and their babies.

So I had to make it up as I went along. I'm quite sure that as a 16-year-old mother (even a 36-year-old mother some years later), I got lots of things wrong, but I do still believe that in this impossible situation I made some good decisions.

My only experience of earning money up to now had been helping out as a weekend girl in our local hairdressing salon when I was 14-15 years old. Mum didn't believe in giving me pocket money as a teenager, so this was a way to earn five shillings a week (25p in new money) doing something I actually enjoyed.

As a child, my very long, very thick, very curly hair had been such a pain in the backside. My mum had broken brushes trying to get though the knots (no comb stood a chance). When I was about 11, I'd taken myself off in secret to Nottingham, to a shop called Griffin & Spalding that was, to me, the equivalent of Harrods. Griffin & Spalding had a hair salon and I asked them to cut off my hated ringlets, which I kept and took home to the one person who loved them, my mum (who was surprisingly calm at this further demonstration of my growing rebellious streak!). I had never got over the excitement of having short hair and working at our local salon gave me the chance to learn all about shampooing, setting, perming and cutting hair – plus it got me out of the house and meeting people, which I loved.

This time, my interest and enjoyment didn't come into the equation. I needed a job – any job – to help us save some money and raise our house deposit. I was well educated, but as I'd never had the chance to sit my O-Levels, I didn't have pieces of paper to prove it. This meant the only employment available to me was fairly basic work. Roy came home one day to tell me that he had seen a job advertised at Pinxton Co-op and I had to go and get it. I was shattered that this was to be my new life – not looking after my beautiful baby but spending my days working in a hardware store. It felt like more punishment for my appalling, disastrous behaviour in 1963. I deserved everything I was getting, including being forced apart from Claire every day. I went for the interview, flew through the very simple (to me) English language and arithmetic tests, impressed the hell out of the very nice general manager and got the job.

At first I hated it. No one spoke to me. No one would give me the time of day! I remember finding quiet places to get on with my job, picking up ornaments and dusting the shelves and, where no one could see me, sobbing into my duster. I was so depressed and so unhappy. At school, I'd had wonderful friends. At school, we had loads of fun. At school, every day seemed to be filled with laughter and friendship and lessons I adored. What a contrast!

Within a couple of weeks (it seemed much longer at the time), I'd passed muster, it would seem, and people started talking to me. After that, I was right as rain. It was an experience that taught me something about looking after newcomers, especially when joining an established group. A life lesson learned!

Six months later, that same lovely general manager put me in charge of a furniture store 100 yards up the road. I was all on my own running a shop and earning £4 for my five-and-a-half-day week. It wasn't particularly busy, but I noticed one or two people would call in, on some pretext or other. It was really to enjoy a chat and pass the time of day. Mostly these were men coming home from work, passing by the shop and just dropping in to say hello.

I was 16, going on 17 – not quite as innocent as a rose, as the song goes, but still naïve beyond belief! Remember readers, I saw myself as an unattractive girl, so I honestly never gave it a thought that these men, much older men, were interested in me in the way they were. A couple of very dicey 'attacks', one from a childhood friend's father, came as a hell of a shock. I'm smiling as I write this, because it was a hell of a shock for him too. I pushed him away so forcefully that he fell backwards onto a sofa whose price ticket had fallen from the backrest onto the seat. The big pin that had secured it to the backrest was now facing upwards – and I've never seen ardour cool so fast in my life! I realised in that moment that I'd have to be wary around men. Another life lesson learned.

As I mentioned before, I'd asked Mum to let Claire sleep as much as possible during the day while I was out at work so that I could make up for lost time, which suited Mum very well (she'd got all that cleaning to do, remember). When we weren't at work, we took Claire everywhere with us. We never used babysitters. I'd cleaned the library out of books about child psychology and parenting. I wanted to be the influencer in Claire's life. I wanted to prove to the world – to all those people who'd blanked me as I walked down the street, when I had become 'untouchable' – that this 16-year-old could be a good mother.

With Mum providing all the childcare, Roy and I moved out of his parents' house and back in with mine on Hilcote Street. It made sense, but it was by no means a comfortable situation. Mum was quite hostile towards Roy and because we were saving every penny we earned for a house of our own, we never went out in the evenings.

It was a precarious existence but we managed to avoid any outright hostilities and Roy and I were happy. Our days or evenings out were always visiting friends and family. After 18 months of extreme frugality, we'd got enough money together for a deposit on a house.

Maurice Harold Macmillan, the First Earl of Stockton, had been the Prime Minister and leader of the government from 1957 to 1963. Dubbed 'Supermac', he was known for his pragmatism, wit and unflappability. His party, the Conservatives, had launched a scheme where married couples could buy a new house with a £50 deposit. There was a method to their madness, as it's well-known that homeowners tend to vote Conservative. Whatever their reasons, that gave us the hard-fought-for opportunity to put our foot on the first rung of the property ladder. Mum decided to give us the £50 as a belated wedding present. I think she wanted us in our own home about as much as we wanted to be there! And so we bought our first home in Alfreton, on Beech Avenue – a corner house in a cul-de-sac with a large garden.

We ploughed our savings into furniture, much of it second-hand, buying the rest from the shop where I worked. Among our haul was a bright yellow Formica-topped kitchen table and four matching yellow plastic-covered chairs, for the princely sum of £5 19s 6d. The yellow peril featured prominently in the birth of Slimming World because this little kitchen table later doubled as my office desk when I started to plan the structure and eating plan of my new business (which, later of course, became Slimming World) in 1969.

Beech Avenue was our first proper home and the first time I was in charge of my own kitchen cupboards and the preparation of our meals. Remember Mum's obsession with housework? Well, one of the things that I'd missed out on was learning how to cook. I wasn't allowed into the kitchen for fear of the mess. The belief that I was useless when it came to cooking has stayed with me to this day, apart from simple British dishes like the Sunday roast and suchlike. So at the age of 71, dear readers, I'm still practising!

I can remember Roy inviting one of his fellow salesmen home for dinner. Aargh! What on earth was I going to cook on a very low budget and not let Roy down? Thank goodness I had a can of Campbell's vegetable soup and double-thank-goodness it had a meal suggestion printed on the back. I remember it as if it were yesterday. I covered an oblong dish with mashed potato, lined up a row of sausages along the centre (there was a photograph attached – triple-thank-goodness!), then all I had to do was to pour the undiluted soup across the top and pop it in the oven. Yay, success!

What wasn't such a success was the conversation between these two 'macho' men, who seemed to like talking about women in the most offensive way. When Roy started telling his new 'mate' stories about me, full of put-downs, my temper finally snapped. He kept ignoring my protestations – and me – and I just had to shut him up. Much to my subsequent shame but at the time without a second thought, I picked up my table knife and aimed it at his head. I was a bad shot and it whizzed past his ear and hit the wall behind his head, but he got the message and finally shut up!

Perhaps unsurprisingly after that, we didn't do much entertaining. Things were coming together, but we were still desperately hard-up. So in September 1966, I got a new job – as an office junior at a much bigger enterprise, an engineering company with an office in Sutton-in-Ashfield, just a few miles away. The days were long, starting and ending with two buses and a mile-and-a-half walk – but for £6 a week, it was worth it. Actually, I loved it. The boss, Brian Hall, was really nice (I'll tell you more about him later).

Before long, the opportunity came up to earn £9 a week by applying for the position of secretary to the manager. Mary, the girl who was leaving, encouraged me to go for it. I wasn't sure. I was only one term into my shorthand and typing course at night school and managing 100 words a minute shorthand and about 40 typing. Not bad at all in the few weeks I'd been learning, but not great in the grand scheme of brilliant secretaries who could note-take and touch-type like the wind.

I remember my interview for the promotion well. My future boss, Tom, did the interview and asked me how I was at short-hand. I explained my training so far and I told him that if he spoke '*s l o w l y*' I could probably keep up. To my complete amazement, I got the job! In fact, it was easy. There were hardly any letters to type and most of the time I was in my separate office, in the entrance, facing Tom's office. Apart from greeting visitors, my days were pretty boring. It was a shame there was so little work. As an office junior, I'd had all sorts of little jobs to get on with but as a secretary, I found myself twiddling my thumbs. No wonder Mary left – she must have been bored out of her brain!

Of the three bosses I'd had in my working life, none had been anything but decent and respectful. It therefore came as a bit of a shock when this boss showed a completely different kind of interest in me. I was still naïve, clearly!

Added to this awkwardness, the money wasn't *that* great and the difficult journey to and from work made it hard to spend time with Claire, so in 1967, at the age of 19, I decided to take another job. It was part-time and very different, in the Alfreton branch of Ladbrokes. It paid around £11 a week and I could be home by six o'clock. It was far more convenient and it paid some of the bills (just).

With very little money, I mean really very, very little, came my first independent mode of transport – a second-hand (or third -or fourth-hand) bubble car costing £50 – about £40 more than it was worth! Roy bought it for me because it only held one person, the driver, and didn't require a driving licence. I was barely an adult when I drove 'The Bubble' for the very first time – travelling up Carnfield Hill, the old road from Alfreton to South Normanton. The journey (and the car) lasted about half an hour. Poisonous blue smoke filled the cockpit. Coughing and eyes streaming, I had to abandon ship on the roadside, halfway up the hill, before it (and I) expired forever.

My next car was an old green Austin A35 van, which cost £75 and was at least roadworthy (not a death-trap) and in which I passed my driving test. Fond memories. It didn't have flasher indicators as we have today, but little orange sticks that flicked out from its mid-section. Hand-signals were also legally required.

Hard up as usual, I couldn't afford professional driving lessons, meaning I relied completely on friends. So I could learn and pass my test, I would nag and cajole any licensed passenger to sit with me on my van journeys, so I could build my driving skills. My husband was far too critical of my driving, but anyone else was a great help, including my under-manager from Pinxton Co-op, Alan Groom who, for his sins, just happened to live on the same road as we did in Alfreton.

Each time he submitted to my pleas (daily), he would kneel on the road in mock prayer before boarding my super-duper mode of transport, supposedly risking life and limb by putting himself in my hands. During our four-and-a-half-mile route to work, with every parked car I was obliged to overtake, he would brace himself, foot pressed hard on a non-existent foot brake and body wedged taut into the seat with his arm gripping the dashboard. All a bit over-dramatic, I thought.

I also owed a lot to my 'driving instructor', one Michael Bush, who as I mentioned earlier was Roy's best man at our wedding. Michael, who was known to his friends as 'Fred' (because that was his dad's name and sounded hilariously silly when applied to a young lad), had passed his own test just a few months before. He'd been professionally taught, so we reckoned his knowledge was fresh and would get me through.

There were a couple of things he told me that weren't correct though, for example, that I had to do a manual slowing-down signal, then a manual right-hand-turn signal and then I could turn right after all the standard checks back, front and all around. I questioned him on the logic of this. Why on earth would you need to make a slowing-down signal, when you were obviously going to be slowing down to turn right? He just shrugged and explained that you had to do a lot of daft things to get through your test that you would never do afterwards. I did as I was told.

At the end of the driving test, the examiner questioned me on this very point. *'Do you think it's necessary to do a slowing-down signal before a right-hand-turn signal?'* I sat silently for what seemed like ages before I replied that actually, I couldn't see the point of it. *'So, why are you doing it?'* Now this was tricky. I could hardly say that I'd been told you have to do a lot of daft things to get through your test that you would never do afterwards, could I? So I said, keeping it simple and not wanting to complicate things by introducing Fred Bush into the picture, that my husband told me to do it. The instructor replied: *'Well please tell your husband that he doesn't know what he's talking about.'*

I suppose I wasn't your typical learner driver. I wasn't nervous – in fact, quite the opposite – indeed I think Alan, my kindly daily passenger, wished I were less intrepid. My driving test was eventful, but not wishing to bore you with the details, dear readers, the short version is that I somehow passed first time. I was ecstatic, proud and relieved – my husband even more so – and of course, so too were my reluctant 'driving instructors', to whom I'll be eternally grateful.

My marriage to Roy was also turning out to be eventful, and not in a good way. Roy was always at his reliable best in a crisis, I discovered, as he was when Claire developed a frightening bout of pneumonia in 1967, when she was just three years old. She recovered quite quickly, but it left her with a weakness in her chest which was to return in terrifying circumstances a couple of years later. He came home at reasonable times and was a good support. I discovered that he wasn't at his best, however, when it came to money.

I'd left the home finances to him, which was a mistake. I'd assumed he'd be good at it, because he was the adult – the one who'd been employed for several years while I was still at school. But you know what they say about assume – it makes an *ass* of *u* and *me* – and so it did. He was a hard worker and never shied away from putting in the hours, like those extra shifts manning the pumps at the local petrol station, but unfortunately he saw himself as something of an entrepreneur. If we ever managed to start building a little safety net (we had once saved £60), Roy could always think of a business opportunity that would put this money to better use.

To be fair, I thought his logic was sound when he convinced me to use the money to buy a rotavator (well, he was a very good salesman!). With another £60 borrowed on hire purchase, we could afford one he'd seen in the garden centre for £120 and he could work weekends – charging £5 per weekend to rotavate people's gardens, as well as our own rather large plot, pay off the debt and start to make some good money. Impressive!

What neither of us knew at the time was that his ability to estimate the size of a job, and therefore the price, was non-existent. It took him a whole summer of weekends, and evenings too, to create a garden for someone – with the finished article to include a lawn, shrubs, a fish pond and a small patio, all for £5. I didn't know at the time that this was what he'd promised, nor did I know that he wasn't keeping up with the hire purchase payments for the rotavator.

The first I knew was when the debt-collector came a-calling! I felt the sting of that humiliating visit keenly and ever since, I've been ferociously against any type of unnecessary debt and, consequently, strongly against credit cards.

I've always hammered it home to my offspring that the innocent-sounding credit card is much better thought of as what it actually is – a debt card – and never to apply for one. Personally, I decided that I would never get into debt for want of some superficial bauble or frivolous item that I couldn't afford. Nothing would be worth it. So it never bothered me to severely tighten my belt when the need arose. It was a good lesson and one that was to help me get through some very tight times in future.

I went on my first diet at the age of 17, weighing a modestly overweight 12st 7lbs. As I've explained, living in our own home at last, I had a sense of freedom to run my own life. I had escaped Mum's control and this meant I could eat more of my favourite comfort foods. However, as my life experience expanded, so did my waistline!

Back in the early 1960s, there weren't many options available if you wanted some help with your weight. Doctors then, as now, weren't geared up to deal effectively with overweight and obese patients. Obesity was still a fledgling problem, affecting only one or two per cent of the population (as opposed to 26 per cent today) – so it was by no means the killer and quality-of-life-destroyer it is in 2019 (though the seeds for our obesity crisis were already being sown).

In the absence of any good, solid help, charlatans and false promises of no-effort weight loss abounded. I went to see one doctor who prescribed amphetamines. Although they removed all desire for food (and I do mean completely), I soon found that the side effects were so horrible that even zero hunger on a starvation regime and a consequent fast weight loss weren't worth it. My heartbeat became erratic and it felt as if my brain was vibrating in my skull. I seemed to be thinking faster than anyone else, too, so would quickly become irritated because they couldn't seem to keep up. So I stopped taking them.

So there I was, at 17, looking for help to lose weight. Are you old enough to remember Limmits slimming biscuits? They were meal-replacement biscuits, either sweet or savoury. The sweet ones, my chosen ones, looked a little like round bourbon creams, like today's Oreos. You were instructed to replace two meals a day with two biscuits, taken with a glass of milk.

Because I was in a desperate hurry to shed the weight (sound familiar?), I ignored the rules (no change there, then) and ate just one biscuit with a black coffee for breakfast, one for lunch then a tea-plate holding a boiled egg, a tomato and a bit of lettuce for dinner. For two months. No deviation. Feeling good as the weight came off! Feeling very pleased with myself. Yes, feeling great and looking great too!

Sure enough, the next time I faced the scales, I'd lost two stones. I was thrilled to bits!

'I've cracked it!' I thought. Believing that now I could go back to 'normal food' and, breathing a sigh of relief that it was all over and done with, I did what any intelligent, strong-willed, capable person does after they've fixed their weight problem. I retraced my steps and went back to a more comfortable way of eating – to my old way of eating – and regained every single pound!

I compounded that mistake with another one. Deciding (incorrectly) that 12st 7lbs was my 'natural' weight, with a shrug I thought, *'Well, not so bad. Size 16 – I'll stay here then.'* Another few months down the road, I stood on a pair of scales to discover, horror of horrors, that I was now 14st 7lbs – a new record! And even that wasn't the peak of my weight gain. I continued to break new records. Here, in the latter part of the '60s, began my fascination with slimming – with the science of nutrition, and more importantly, with the fascinating psychological and emotional aspects of losing weight.

By 1968, I was beginning to realise that I needed more in life – and not just financially. I needed a job that interested and challenged me. I knew that without at least four O-Levels – hard evidence that I was sufficiently intelligent and academic to be able to punch holes in a key card at a factory (yes, you needed four O-Levels for that) – I didn't stand a chance of getting an interview for anything that would capture my imagination. I'd need to create that position myself. I'd need to become self-employed.

By now I was 20 years old and I'd had an issue with my size for as long as I could remember. My blind faith in one wacko, unsustainable weight loss fad after another had led me from failure to failure, my confidence disintegrating a little more with each one.

At around 16 stones and still determined to lose this dastardly weight, I tried both major slimming clubs that were around at the time. One was a glorified coffee morning – completely unstructured and no use to anyone trying to lose weight. The other – rigidly structured – reminded me of being back in Miss Marsh's class at the junior school. In that one, you were left feeling lectured to, judged and humiliated. Even as a girl skipping about the schoolyard, I'd never been able to stand back if I saw another person being picked on and I'd get into fights, I mean real fisticuffs, to defend them. By my late teens and early 20s, I felt just as defensive of overweight people – myself being one.

Surely there was a better way to help people like me – surely? I believed every overweight person deserved to be treated as an adult, with respect, kindness and compassion – a conviction that's just as strong today. The more I thought about it, the more energised I became. I'd dabbled in hairdressing and jewellery parties in the evenings and at weekends to earn a bit more money but I just knew that this wasn't 'it'. I remember thinking to myself: *'If I'm going to be self-employed, I need to find something I know about. What do I know about?'* One thing was for sure. I was becoming quite the expert in failed diet attempts!

I had this feeling, though. Maybe it wasn't *me* that was failing – maybe the diets were failing *me*! Maybe the help I so desperately needed didn't yet exist. So I started to widen my reading. I pored over Richard Mackarness's *'Eat Fat and Grow Slim'* (better known as the Eskimo diet), John Yudkin's pioneering theories on sugar (the precursor to his 1972 book, *'Pure, White and Deadly'*) and Dr Atkins' emerging work on protein-rich diets.

Trial and (plenty of) error showed me two things – one was that restricting a particular food group was much easier to live with than restricting portion sizes or eating weird diet foods. I also noticed that diets which included a lot of meat and fish made me feel more full after eating (thank goodness!) – and therefore I was less likely to cave in to temptation between meals.

It would be some 30 years before Professor James Stubbs published his important scientific paper on the influence of dietary macronutrients and energy density on appetite and satiety – research that Slimming World sponsored together with the Scottish Office. Turns out my early hunch was right – protein-rich foods (closely followed by complex carbohydrates) *are* the most filling – and eating them helps us to stay feeling full for longer, too.

Maybe, just maybe, I was on to something. Could I start my own slimming club? Could I? There was only one way to find out.

66 *– Inside me there's a thin person screaming to get out!*

– Just the one, dear? **99**

Edina Monsoon and her mother:
Absolutely Fabulous

CHAPTER THREE

get up and go

As I sat at my little yellow Formica table, reading about nutrition late into the night and furiously scribbling down ideas, I had no idea I was sowing a seed that would grow beyond my wildest dreams. But starting a slimming club, it turned out, was a bit like slimming itself – obstacles everywhere! The first was in my marriage.

I discovered that for some time, Roy had been having an affair with a much older woman and home life had started to get pretty horrible. Since we'd tied the knot, Roy had become more and more of a flirt (or maybe I'd become more aware of it) – teetering on the edge of infidelity, sometimes before my very eyes.

At about the same time, he was becoming increasingly critical of me. We'd be driving along the street and he'd comment on women in their mid-30s – how they looked and acted, asking me why I didn't dress more like them, like a 'proper woman'? Why didn't I bake cakes, like a 'proper woman'? Then one night, he went out and didn't return until the early hours of the morning. As I lay alone in the darkness, I became more convinced with each passing minute that he'd been in an accident and had been killed. I thought I would lose my mind. By the time he walked through the door at 4am, I was already a grieving widow. He told me he'd lost track of time playing cards with colleagues – and that he was so very sorry. I was in a terrible state. He promised he would never ever do it again. I believed him.

Two weeks later, the same thing happened – this time with the additional pain of humiliation, because we had friends over for dinner and Roy failed to show up. We waited and waited but eventually we gave up and ate the food I'd prepared (which was probably that Campbell's soup recipe again!). The friends left at around midnight and I spent the next two hours in emotional agony, once again imagining the worst. At 2am, he came home. I couldn't believe he would do it again after all the apparently sincere promises he'd made such a short time ago.

Over the next few months his attitude towards me grew worse and worse, with never a kind word – in fact quite the opposite – it seemed I could do nothing right, and I was more unhappy than ever before in our marriage. One Friday, when I asked him what time he'd be coming home that night, he replied with a torrent of abuse about clocking in and clocking out. When he left the house in high dudgeon, I held on to my hair and banged my head against the kitchen wall.

No one was there to see that act of self-harm, but I knew something had to change. I called the local surgery and made an appointment for the Monday morning, hoping the doctor would prescribe some tranquilisers to help me. Then I realised something. I didn't need drugs, I needed answers. So the next night, as we lay side by side in bed, in the dark, I confronted Roy. I begged him to be honest and please, please, tell me if there was someone else. I had to understand what was happening, because it was making me ill. I wouldn't leave him, I promised, no matter what – I had nowhere to go after all. I couldn't go to my parents' home because I knew Mum would say *'I told you so!'* and *'You made your bed, now you have to lie in it,'* and other such comforting words. I had a daughter, no money and no viable escape route, so my assurances were genuine.

To my surprise and horror, Roy owned up. It was one thing to know my husband had been having an affair; but when he told me he loved this 'other woman' and that they were looking for a house together, I was so consumed with hurt and anger, I felt numb. And knowing the detail, some of it painfully intimate, changed everything. *'There's no way on God's earth I can stay with this man,'* I thought, *'I've **got** to go.'*

I packed our bags there and then, and the next morning, I bundled Claire up and drove to my parents' house. I sobbed as I admitted everything to them. As I tried to unpack and settle in, I found to my dismay that I'd forgotten to pick up the contents of the washing basket, and there were some things I needed for Claire. Oh Lord, I'd have to go back.

Returning to the scene of my miserable enlightenment, I noticed that the curtains were drawn. Now what? What was happening behind those closed curtains? As I walked up the path to the house, my imagination painted a picture of what I'd find inside. Instead, the door opened and there was Roy. He fell to his knees, in the doorway, in floods of tears, begging me to come back, saying how stupid he'd been, telling me how sorry he was and how it had hit him just what he was losing. I was unimpressed. My heart had turned to stone. It would take a lot more than these self-pitying words to convince me.

He swore he was going to finish the affair. As if I would buy that! He begged, he cried and he promised, but seriously, would anyone in their right mind believe it? Not after what he'd told me the night before. But I also thought about Claire, about the family we'd created, and what I'd be walking away from. And I thought there might be one way I could believe that the affair was over. *'OK,'* I said. *'I'll give you another chance – but only if you pick up that phone and end the relationship here and now.'* I stood by his side as he did it. I heard both sides of the conversation. What he told her then meant he had definitely burned his bridges with this 'other woman', who, it turned out, was called Joan and was in her mid-30s, some 16 years my senior.

He'd had the shock of his life. I told him that I'd never trust him again and that if I ever found anyone who genuinely loved me, I would be off like a shot. After that, Roy behaved… well, for a couple of years at least.

Then came the next trauma. Just before my 21st birthday, our bubbly Claire became very ill. It started with her growing listless, not like her energetic self at all. We took her to the doctor and told him that she hadn't been as bad as this since she'd had pneumonia two years earlier. He said he was sure she was coming down with measles and to look for spots appearing behind her ears the next morning.

He told us, in no uncertain terms, that measles was *'not a visiting complaint',* that she would be very poorly for a few days and that there was no point in calling for a doctor.

By the next day, Claire was delirious and her breathing was badly affected. The following day, Friday, I called the surgery, and the next. I begged and pleaded. I told them that she was exactly the way she had been with pneumonia. I was snapped at every day when I called the surgery, which I simply had to do no matter what they said, as I watched my little girl slip into what seemed to be exactly the same dangerous condition she'd been in two years earlier.

Claire deteriorated so rapidly it was beyond frightening. I was beside myself with worry and no one would listen. She was delirious, struggling to breathe and unable to eat or sleep, day or night. Of course, neither could I, as I sat by her side in pure fear.

The doctor finally agreed to call and see her on the Monday. He strode in, seemingly irritated, especially as we had the curtains drawn. He tore open the curtains talking about old wives' tales and then went to attend to Claire. He wouldn't look at me as he told me she had pneumonia. He said he would call for an ambulance but refused to use our phone. After he'd been gone about 10 minutes, he rang me and told me it would take too long for the ambulance to reach us and we had to take her ourselves.

Roy had shot off in our car to let his mum know what was happening and was now out of contact. No mobile phones in those days! The next few minutes felt like a lifetime as I waited for him to return, and I held Claire in my arms in the back seat as we sped off to Nottingham City Hospital, where, obviously forewarned, a team of doctors and nurses was waiting for us to arrive.

Someone ripped open the car door, took her out of my arms and ran. We hurried after them but we were stopped from following and told, not in a kind way, to stay in the waiting room. We were out of our minds with worry, but that didn't seem to have registered with the hospital staff – it felt as if they were blaming us for Claire's condition. After what seemed like an age, we were interviewed by a hospital doctor and when he heard our story, their attitude changed completely. The hostility disappeared as word spread. Eventually a nurse came to speak with us. She told us that Claire was the second child they'd admitted in a week – from the same surgery – who was on the brink of dying.

Claire was in intensive care for a week, and remained in hospital for another three weeks. It was a very dark time in my life. Thankfully, Claire doesn't remember much about it.

Somehow, in between hospital visits, I found solace in getting on with things, burying myself in a determination to press ahead with my plans – absolutely driven to get my business off the ground and escape the poverty trap we were in. Work has proved to be the saviour of my soul and sanity at many times throughout my life.

The turning point came – as with so many of life's pivotal moments – over a cup of tea. This one was with my neighbour, Josie, a lovely woman and a really kind friend. We helped each other in different ways. Because I had a bit of a talent for hairdressing and applying make-up, I'd save her the time and expense of the beauty salon – and because she was at home all day and I was out at work, she'd let herself into the house and I would arrive home to find my carpet vacuumed!

Josie became a very special person to me, and it was easy to trust her. I shared with her my vision for a new kind of slimming club, and told her all about my 'Sin-a-Day' diet.

Based on all the reading I'd done about restricting certain food groups, and harnessing the filling power of protein, my Sin-a-Day diet would be designed to free slimmers from the unbearable feelings of hunger and deprivation I'd experienced on every diet I had ever tried. It would allow people to eat unlimited quantities of protein, fats (yes – fats – more on that later) and vegetables, with limited amounts of starchy carbohydrates like fruit, potatoes, rice and bread. Some of the fundamental principles of our eating plan today, Food Optimising, were included – others needed a bit of fine-tuning along the way.

Back in the '60s and early '70s, the words 'diet' and 'dieting' hadn't taken on the negative connotations they have today. As for the idea of 'sins' – the word appealed to my sense of mischief and fun. I wanted, even then, to lighten the heavy emotional burden that comes with being overweight – to inject a sense of fun into slimming. I thought describing those 'treat' foods – that we love to eat but that unfortunately make us put on weight – as 'sins' would appeal to everyone's sense of humour and sense of the ridiculous.

My vision from the start was for a company that offered freedom and empowerment – a company that put the needs of its members first. I knew that if people were happy with the service they got in our groups, they'd keep coming, they'd tell their friends and the business would grow. This hadn't been my experience in any of the clubs I'd gone to. I'd felt judged and humiliated – and for those reasons, I most certainly didn't want to go back! Not one member of *my* groups would *ever* be treated like a second-class citizen, or made to feel lazy, greedy or guilty about their weight. Not one!

To that same end, there was one very special rule in my mind when I was writing the book explaining the Sin-a-Day diet. There would be no negative words – not a *'restrict'* or a *'do not'* or an *'exclude'*, *'cut out'* or anything like it – in the whole book. Instead I preferred, *'eat unlimited amounts of'* or *'freely eat'* or *'in addition, eat'* or *'choose from'* or *'enjoy'* – language that was about freedom and empowerment, about loving food, not about deprivation, hunger and restriction. And so our language remains to this day.

I later (in 2000) renamed our eating plan 'Food Optimising', because it is just that – about optimising the food choices you make every day. As Slimming World became better known, dieticians started taking pot-shots at us, suggesting that we were attributing moral values like 'good' or 'bad' to food by using the words Sins and Sin-free. At first, I thought it was ridiculous – but when I found out that it was causing our nutritionists so much trouble, I renamed them 'Syns'. For me, it maintained the original sense of humour but we could explain that it was the whole of the system, each part working with the other, that **syn**ergistically (see what I did there?) made this such a powerful tool for weight loss. 'Syns' kept that touch of humour and our members were free to enjoy 'synergy' in their eating. We do believe, always have, that a little bit of what you fancy really does do you good!

I felt strongly that as well as tackling their eating habits, people would find it easier to lose weight and make changes if they felt better and more confident about themselves from the off. This was the foundation of our unique IMAGE Therapy (more on that later) – but in those early days, I planned to show members how hair and make-up could transform their appearance. So, I had paid for training at the Peggy Slight School of Beauty in Nottingham some months before.

The money for this had come from savings I'd worked hard to build up, and it felt painful, but hey – this was an investment in our future! I'd been using my training to give treatments at home and make a small charge for them, which was at least some compensation for the outlay. I'd set up a cosy salon in a bedroom and made it look pretty, adding a wall heater, a treatment couch, chair and a Slendertone machine.

So, back to that cup of tea with Josie. As I explained the principles of my Sin-a-Day diet to her, I saw her eyes light up. Having also struggled with her weight, Josie was just as excited by the idea of starting a brand new slimming club as I was.

Josie's husband Pat was a very nice man and well-heeled, certainly by our standards. He had an extremely well-paid job laying the new North Sea gas pipeline, and he had a good pension from his 20-plus years in the Royal Navy. In addition, his adopted mother had died and left him her rather splendid house in nearby Swanwick.

Josie wanted to get involved, and asked Pat to lend us £200 – the equivalent of over £3,000 today – as start-up capital for my big idea. We decided to become business partners, though I use that term loosely. I was 21, Josie was closer to 40, and neither of us had the faintest clue about business.

I had come up with a great name for our new company – I thought! *United Slimmers' Society.* I could just see the headline on the newspaper ad – saying *'Come and join USS'* – so I was disappointed when the powers-that-be rejected my super name. Their reasoning was that it sounded like an already established organisation and as such was misleading. What a blow. And we hadn't even got off the ground!

The safest way to go and the fastest to be approved was to use our initials – although it was so much less catchy. Our name became, for this reason, the much less impactful 'J&M Slimming Club'. I wasn't happy with it, but the clock was ticking. Needless to say, I renamed the business *Slimming World* when we became a limited company in 1977. Sounds a bit more like something that might take off some day, don't you think?

The start-up money from Josie and Pat allowed me to give up my job at Ladbrokes, pay the rent for venues and place adverts in the local paper inviting people to join our fantastic new slimming clubs in Alfreton, Heanor, Sutton-in-Ashfield and Mansfield. I was grateful beyond words.

My very first group, *our* very first group, was held in a church hall in Alfreton in 1969. The membership fee was £1 and the weekly fee was two shillings and sixpence (12½p in new money).

We were only a few weeks into it when I realised my Sin-a-Day diet needed more work. The idea of allowing unlimited protein *and* fats worked beautifully in theory (and for me personally) but I quickly learned that there was a huge variation in the amounts of fat-rich food members could, and would, eat. Plenty of people took full advantage of the free rein over butter, cream and cheese (why wouldn't you?!) – and the weight losses weren't what I wanted them to be.

I wasted no time in tweaking the plan, limiting both carbohydrates *and* fats. The other thing I needed to drop was the beauty lessons. No one was interested, and besides, it was obvious that focusing on food and weight loss was not only what was needed by all the members, but what they wanted too. So far, so good.

The biggest challenge I faced in those early weeks and months was the inequality in mine and Josie's partnership. I couldn't understand it. It was clear that although she liked the idea of being involved in the business, she didn't like being front and centre in training others. She enjoyed running the Sutton-in-Ashfield and Heanor groups, but they never got off the ground, with just a handful of members in each. And in the meantime, much to my surprise, she'd taken another job, with a company which made cleaning products.

I wasn't sure why Josie's groups weren't succeeding or why she didn't want to help me develop the business. She was financially invested, but *I* was the one who was *really* invested – head, heart and soul – and I think that was obvious to Josie herself.

I began to take a small salary from my group takings, and gave the same to Josie – around £8 a week. It wasn't a fortune by any means, but it was enough to make a desperately needed contribution to my household while still ploughing as much as I could back into the business. In those days, it was all about opening as many new groups as possible – and to do that, I paid for a lot of newspaper advertisements. My dream, from the beginning, was to take J&M Slimming Club nationwide.

By the end of our first year in business, we'd opened around 25 groups in Nottinghamshire and Derbyshire and I'd handed my groups over to another leader, so I could focus more on building the business. That remarkable woman, by the way, is still with Slimming World as I write – almost 50 years after taking her first group in the Alfreton Methodist Church Hall and taking over the Mansfield group I'd opened in a Scout hut. Betty Oldknow (now in your 80s but as youthful and full of fun as ever), please take a bow!

Although by now I owed nothing to Josie financially (I'd repaid the £200 start-up loan within a few months), I felt indebted to her for helping me get started – so much so that I'd regularly paint over the cracks in our business relationship. Eventually I bought Josie out of the business for £2,000, the equivalent of £25,000 today – more than was warranted – partly due to youthful naivety but mainly down to enduring gratitude. Without her and Pat's loan to me, Slimming World might never have come to exist.

Looking back, I realise I could *possibly* have been seen as completely OTT (who, me?). I was ferociously protective of the fledgling company I'd created. Compromise was not in my vocabulary – I'd rather die than give one inch on my vision of a business centred totally on its service to members. That was nothing new for me. Now a sole business owner, I was finally able to be true to myself and my beliefs, not have them diluted by anyone else.

I suppose the earliest example I can recall of this ferocity concerned someone who ran a group in Kirkby-in-Ashfield – a wonderful woman who had lost 7 or 8 stones before J&M Slimming Club had even started. She was very slim and a real convert to healthy eating – an evangelical, 'Billy Graham'-type character who couldn't stop raving about how wonderful life was once you'd lost weight. She was terrific – a great communicator, a great personality and I loved her.

Her passion was simply infectious and when she opened her group, she had members flocking to join – 60 on her opening night. Within three weeks that figure had increased to 90-something – and that was pretty WOW! Did I see this at the time? Yes, of course, but it also rang some major alarm bells. What alarmed me was the inevitably enormous queue in her group. What alarmed me was potentially dissatisfied members spending up to an hour waiting to pay for a service they weren't going to get.

However, there was an easy solution, as I explained. I told her she would need to make hers a two-session group, one of which would run at 5.30pm, with the other following it at 7.30pm. That way, our members would receive the service they were paying for – with much less time queuing and more time to focus on them individually in the group. Unfortunately, she didn't like the sound of this. It was too inconvenient, and would take too long. With total conviction that my suggestion was the right course of action for the members, I didn't hesitate in saying: *'OK, then I'll need to find someone else to do it.'*

Getting the service right for members, giving value for money, was ingrained so firmly, so completely in my vision, that even though I knew I might lose one of my best, most motivated (and motivating) people, it was still a no-brainer. *Members first!* Thankfully, and miraculously, what had previously been impossible for her became possible. She made arrangements so she could cover the two sessions after all.

The lesson for me was to stick to my principles, not to compromise the needs of the many for the preference of the few – one in this case – and the risk proved not to be a risk at all. The lesson was to not be brow-beaten into surrender when it was clear what the right path was. And as happens so often, the right path is sometimes the hardest and the one that requires the most courage. I wished I'd seen it so clearly when I was 15 years old.

So by 1971, I found myself in the exhilarating (and equally exhausting) position of running our chain of slimming clubs, with around 40 groups by then, effectively alone.

Then everything changed. Roy had been working as a salesman for a hairdressing company (which was how he'd met Joan, she of the affair) and the way his pay was structured left us poorer than I could ever have imagined. So when he was offered a new role in Barnsley, Yorkshire, he jumped at it. There was a catch, though. We'd have to move. With my business in its infancy, this was a risk – but I also saw an opportunity to take my clubs to a whole new county.

We put in an offer on a four-bedroomed detached house in Darton, just outside Barnsley. It had Georgian French windows which led out on to a lawned garden and we could barely hear the M1 motorway just over our fence. I loved it! But when does the purchase of a house ever run smoothly? Having sold our home in Alfreton, there was a huge delay before we were able to move – so we were forced to move back in with my mum and dad. I'm sure you can imagine how that went down, on both sides!

One night, a small family squabble escalated out of control, and Mum – always on the edge of a potential eruption – burst into our bedroom that night, screaming the same sort of abuse I'd first heard in the doctor's surgery a few years before. At midnight, we gathered our belongings, packed them into the car and, with a sleeping Claire bundled up, we left the house. Roy rolled down the car window to say something to Mum, an apology of sorts, but didn't get the chance as she lashed out, literally, and punched him in the face.

We went to the only place we could think of where we might find shelter so late at night – to Roy's sister Betty and her so-kind husband, John. Sure enough, they put their rude awakening to one side and got us settled on the floor of their living room. The next day, I found us a flat to rent, and we moved in. It was cold and damp and I was worried about having Claire there, as she was so susceptible to bronchial problems after her bouts of pneumonia. I hoped that all the portable heaters we bought would help.

Mad as it might seem, in the next few weeks while we were living in the flat, we rescued a beautiful Old English Sheepdog, called Toby, which Roy had been told was going to be put down in a few days. When we went to see Toby at the kennels, he treated us as if we were his long-lost owners and I lost my heart to him.

The other amazing thing that happened was that my lovely dad, so gentle and hating confrontation as he did, had stood up to Mum at long last and told her she had to come and apologise or they would lose me forever. He was right. I'd had enough and decided that was the last time I would ever have anything to do with her. So imagine my shock and surprise when they knocked on the door of our flat and my mum apologised and asked me to forgive her. I guess there's a first time for everything.

At last, we exchanged contracts on the house in Barnsley – thank goodness! Moving week came. I remember thinking, 'Finally – *finally*!' We were back in control of our lives and a brand new chapter was ahead of us. Everything was looking rosy. Or at least it was until the end of that first week in our new home, when Roy's new employers – the very reason we'd moved to Barnsley in the first place – went bust.

66 *Don't worry if Plan A fails.*
There are 25 more letters in the alphabet. **99**

CHAPTER FOUR

the Barnsley experience

It's become something of an urban myth that I started Slimming World in a phone box. Not strictly correct (as you've already read) – but in the early days in Barnsley, I did spend a lot of time *running* Slimming World (or, rather J&M Slimming Club) from one.

We'd first asked to be connected to the phone line at Easter in 1971 and nothing had happened by the time we moved in, in November! This should give you a pretty good idea of the state of the country at the time. It was a disastrous period, when it felt as if the unions were running the country. It got so bad that some years later, my loyal, Labour-voting Dad was so disgusted with Arthur Scargill, the Yorkshire miners' leader, he announced that he was never going to vote Labour again. Wow! This was an earth-shattering announcement in our family.

At the end of '71 and the first few months of '72 there was snow on the ground, buses couldn't run, the miners and others were striking left, right and centre – and as a result, the country, certainly where we were, was on its knees. There were plenty of nights when we had no light or heat in any of the rooms where our groups were being held, which made our situation seem all the more desperate.

Roy suddenly had no job and, of course, until I could open groups and establish a presence in our new town, I wasn't bringing in any money at all. I'd never taken anything out of the business that I hadn't earned from my groups, so we were well and truly in a mess.

There was only one way out of the mire – and that was to work every hour God sent. Each day, I'd trudge through the rain and even snow to that big, red, cast-iron phone box and stand inside for hours (wishing the blasted thing had central heating!) making calls until my feet were numb and I could barely hold a pen.

At night, once Claire was tucked up in bed, you'd find me up until three in the morning, frantically hammering away at the typewriter, tweaking and refining my Sin-a-Day diet sheets and training documents (much as I'm doing right now, dear readers, with each draft of this book) and using the Gestetner machine to reproduce enough copies to give out in the groups I was desperately working to open. Unless you're a post-war baby of the '40s like me, you probably won't remember the Gestetner. It was a great, cumbersome machine with rollers and a handle, which you had to turn and turn and turn to print duplicate copies of a typewritten document. If you had a little money, you had an electric one, and if you were very well off you used a professional printing house.

Do you know, I didn't mind a bit that I was the printer and our spare bedroom was the printing house. It felt quite creative. So my enduring memory of this time is of winding sheet after sheet on to the rollers, then whirring away for hours and hours, night after night – but I was producing!

Bearing in mind it was the '70s and women's lib hadn't quite filtered through to Barnsley (or many other places for that matter), the school run, the washing, the cleaning, cooking, shopping and general nurturing fell to me too. I suspect that generations later, the attitude still lingers on in some homes. Parents – you know the balancing act well!

It seems inconceivable when I look at our company today – with all the beautifully designed Member Packs, recipe books and magazines for our groups – that back in the early '70s, it took my midnight escapades to produce just a few sheets of paper for each member to explain the Sin-a-Day diet, together with our Open Diet Sheets (which we now call 'food diaries'). It's just as mind-blowing that my selection process and training – which is today our biggest invest-ment, our pride and our joy – took place for just a few hours in my living room, with a small group of 'teachers' (as we called the Con-sultants who ran our groups back then), a week or so before they opened their groups.

When I first started the business, I never considered that people would need training on how to care for people, how to help them think through their next moves or how to find the right, appropri-ate, genuine questions and encouraging words to keep motivation high and help members plan the changes they were going to make. I thought our 'teachers' would share my instinctive sense of how to speak to people as adults, not children, how to ask questions and steer discussion, and how to set each member up for success.

I wanted each and every member to be spoken to as an intelli-gent, independent-minded person with freedom and control over their own decisions. I wasn't interested in creating a confessional or in going into the minute detail of why a member might not have lost weight. Everyone's life is different and everyone has their own personal challenges to overcome.

The bottom line is that 99 per cent of the time, the reason that someone doesn't lose weight, or gains weight, is that they haven't truly followed the eating plan. So our time needed to be spent being actively helpful, in a positive way. It's far more useful to talk about how to make the changes more easily, how to plan ahead, how what we put in the shopping basket can send us badly wrong – plus hundreds of other useful tips to get our members through a week with maximum ease and maximum effect. I wanted to raise people up and give them their hope back, and give them the support, motivation and advice they needed to go away and have a great week.

This was, and still is, my style, my approach, my vision. I explained it all to my South Yorkshire trainees. I explained how inadequate things were in our competitors' groups and what was so tedious for our members to have to sit through. I explained how to avoid falling into those traps that allowed the group to become boring or subtly humiliating to a member.

It was a while before I realised that all of this didn't come naturally to everyone. And it came as a shock! After all, everyone I'd chosen had *said* they wanted to help our members, and that they cared very much about their success! If you want to help someone, then you have to take the time to get to know them, to think and plan what will help them and the group as a whole.

It was longer still before I realised that all the training in the world was no use if the personal qualities of the group leader weren't right in the first place. *Or maybe my training wasn't very good!* One way or the other, things started badly in South Yorkshire. Either teachers ran their groups like a coffee evening or they went the other way and believed they had to be an all-singing, all-dancing leader, lecturer and entertainer – up on stage, performing to their audience.

At the time I used words like 'teacher' and 'class', not to suggest a school-like environment but because the group leader needed to *teach* people about the eating plan and how it worked. I realised fairly quickly, though, that 'teacher' gave the wrong impression and we started talking about groups, not classes, and called the people running our groups 'Consultants' – far more collaborative and supportive. But in those days, teachers they were.

So whether it was down to my lack of recruitment skills, the quality of my training, or both, South Yorkshire was the stuff of an HR manager's nightmare (or 'personnel' manager, as they'd have been known back then!). I'd managed to recruit a team of around eight 'teachers' and as I went around visiting their groups once they were up and running, I realised to my horror that no one was paying much attention to what I'd explained and trained.

One Monday night in March, I walked into a three-month-old Barnsley group, held at a leisure centre. I hesitate to call it a group. Four members! That's not a group in my book – it's a coffee evening – and this one without the coffee! The teacher looked at me with such relief, mouthed a silent *'thank you'* and I realised immediately she was looking for some help (I've always been quick like that!). So I stayed and I chatted.

None of these four Barnsley members were losing weight. Of course, there's only one way that can happen – they weren't following the plan. The initial purpose of my questions was to discover how that was happening. It soon became clear that none of the four understood the Sin-a-Day plan – at all. A bit of a stumbling block, which needed dealing with urgently, I realised.

Once I'd explained the whole thing, presumably for the second time (assuming, praying, that the teacher had already covered it at least once), I asked them to complete an Open Diet sheet, or food diary, for the next four weeks. I let them know that we'd check these the following week, to make sure they really understood everything this time around.

I explained why it was so important to write down every bite and sip as soon as it was taken – and not to leave it to our notoriously faulty memories – because full, open, accurate and honest recording was the only way we could help identify any problems. Importantly, I stressed, we didn't need impressing with how angelically perfect they were. We didn't expect perfection – just a trust and openness that would lead directly to their success. We needed the pure, unvarnished truth.

All this should have been covered on night one and I never suspected that this would be the first time these members had been asked to do it. I found out the truth the next day, when the (very angry) teacher knocked on my door.

Apparently, she was no longer grateful that I had done a class visit (see how quick I am?). She was incensed. She told me in no uncertain terms that she couldn't believe how I had spoken to her members, that I'd treated them like children. *'How did I do that?'* I asked. I'd simply asked them to write things down – something she was already supposed to have done. It's a key part of helping new members fully understand the system and get off to a flying start. A pain in the backside it may be, for the member to complete and the Consultant to interpret, but members certainly appreciate the results, allowing us to spot any misunderstandings about the eating plan and get them clarified before they cause a problem, like not losing weight!

At this time, March 1971, I was working every waking hour – and sleep only got in the way for about four or five hours a night – so it's no exaggeration to say that my 'one-man-band' act left no room to add yet another job to my long days. I needed more work like a drowning man needs pockets full of horseshoes.

However, when emotions run high, thinking runs low, and in a surge of outrage over the lack of direction for our Barnsley members, I announced I would take over the group immediately. Our young teacher looked at me in disbelief, turned on her heel and stormed off. She left me with the message that if I ever went back to the Barnsley group, her members had sworn they wouldn't return. Well, I've always loved a challenge!

I must tell you that what this situation did for me, and for my business, was a gift. It turned out to be one of the best learning experiences of my life. In fact, in the days, weeks and months that followed, my expectations and my approach to running groups changed forever. So, from my heart, I have a genuine reason to thank that lady from Barnsley most sincerely.

The first thing it taught me was that employing kind and caring people wasn't enough. To be truly effective, we needed people who could be kind, caring and empathetic but who were also prepared to do *whatever it took* to help their members lose weight. For me, it was simple – if members weren't losing weight, we were failing them and that wasn't right, no matter how attached those members felt to our lovely teachers.

Unpopular though it might be with members to lose a beloved teacher or Consultant, I couldn't allow them to be let down in this way – nor for the company's reputation to be damaged by such under-performance. My attitude has never changed in 50 years and never will. Every director of Slimming World feels exactly the same.

Right now, on this wintry Tuesday morning, I urgently needed a plan of action. Six days to the next group. An already packed work schedule. No time to get leaflets printed or distributed. No time to paint the town red with posters – and it seemed the advertising hadn't worked. First of all, I had to get to the bottom of the lack of members in Barnsley.

Yorkshire had been unfamiliar territory for me, so I'd allowed the new teachers to choose the best newspaper to advertise their group. The *South Yorkshire Times* was perfect for Rotherham but a big mistake for Barnsley. A quick chat with our local newsagent revealed that everyone in and around the town, and I do mean *everyone*, read the *Barnsley Chronicle*. Lightbulb moment! We'd been putting the ad in the wrong paper!

Back to the newsagent I went, with a poster displaying the Barnsley group's venue and times – which the shop owner kindly agreed to put in her window. Still pumped with determination, I pushed through my normal shyness (those of you who know me can stop laughing – I am really a shy person) and ended up engaging the owner and four more customers in a fact-finding foray of what we were up against in terms of competition.

All five of them were attending one of the two main weight loss groups around at the time, and each of them, according to my new friends, had upwards of 80 to 100 members attending every week. In addition, there were quite a few small, lesser-known clubs, as there were everywhere. Aha! So Barnsley *did* have women who wanted to lose weight! That was all I needed to know.

I had total confidence that what we had to offer slimmers was – and still is! – far superior to anything they'd so far experienced. We had the best eating plan ever invented – and still do. We had a philosophy, tactics and a motivational toolkit unmatched by anyone else – and still do. And if that wasn't enough, Barnsley ladies were about to get *me!* This wasn't my ego talking. This was fact. I would be the final piece in their weight loss jigsaw, their path to success – because I knew, totally knew, in my bones and in my soul, that on those weeks when they had stopped caring about themselves (which always happens), I would not stop, I would not forget what they were paying their weekly fee for, what they wanted to achieve.

I was a professional, in the true sense of the word, and I would still be there for them, working, thinking and planning how I was going to revive that all-important motivation that they'd temporarily lost. That was my job. That was my passion. And I am a very determined person (*'bloody stubborn'* and *'pain in the you-know-what'* have also been used!).

'Do you know,' I said to this small group of potential members, standing in the middle of the shop, *'we've got this slimming group – the diet is just incredible, you never, ever go hungry AND you lose weight. It's the best thing since sliced bread but no one seems to know about it? I'm taking over the group next Monday. Would you come?'* To my delight, they all said they'd be there. So that was five, and I'd only been out of the house 10 minutes!

The same week, I followed through on some advice I'd been given by Pauline Paley, an impressive Area Manager running our groups in Derbyshire – you'll meet her again soon. She'd had PR experience as the director of another company, and told me about something I'd never heard of before – editorials. These, she explained, were articles you could get printed in the newspaper *for free*, provided you went about it the right way. I couldn't believe it – free advertising! All I needed was a compelling story, ready-written to save the overworked reporters a job and something an editor would like to print to attract and excite their readers.

I could do that. But there was a slight problem. With just four members in the group – none of them losing weight – I had no success story to share (yet!) and I hadn't discovered the winning formula of including great photographs. I decided I may as well go for a controversial headline!

That very week, readers of the *Barnsley Chronicle* opened their papers to find: 'ARE BARNSLEY WOMEN AFRAID OF A CHAL-LENGE?' emblazoned in huge letters at the top of my editorial. In the article, I asked why, especially as I considered Barnsley women to be such smart cookies, everyone was ignoring the best slimming club in the area? A club that was flying high in Nottinghamshire and Derbyshire, helping members lose weight without ever going hungry.

I'd always enjoyed writing and I think the editor must have liked my approach (or they needed a story with a difference, or they were very short-staffed!) because they printed my original copy, *unedited*. I was amazed, delighted and proud as punch.

Monday night came. I arrived alone at the venue in Barnsley and set up the room. I guessed I'd need maybe 20 or so chairs – I already had my 'yes' from the five women at the newsagent, and who knows, maybe my swooping in and taking over from the previous teacher wouldn't completely annihilate the existing membership of four.

My optimism wasn't entirely unfounded. I retained 50 percent! Yes, half of the existing members returned – a grand total of two! So that was seven. Three more and I would be running out of fingers. But nothing could have prepared me for what happened next. Not 7, not 20, but 42 new members walked into my group that Monday night – 44 members altogether. If you're a Slimming World Consultant reading this, you can probably very well imagine the equal mix of elation and sheer panic I felt as I single-handedly enrolled and welcomed 44 new members (no computers to help in those days, remember). It was chaotic to say the least.

So, lessons two and three were really very simple (gosh, I'm starting to sound like Nanny McPhee!). Editorials worked. Boy, did they work! So too did getting out and about in the local community and speaking to people – it gave me access to local knowledge *and* helped spread the message about my group through word of mouth.

Lesson four – I needed to be better prepared. I was overwhelmed by new members on that first night and plenty of people in the queue were getting pretty mad. One woman in particular, a very smart-looking woman with elegantly French-plaited hair, perfect make-up and tightly pursed lips, stood out – the angriest in the queue. *'I've been pushed and pulled on that staircase waiting for ages to get in here!'* she said. *'It's disgusting!'*

'I'm so, so sorry', I apologised, *'I'm on my own, I had no idea I'd have this response tonight'*.

And then I had a little brainwave (it happens every so often). I got the impression this woman was a pretty switched-on sort of person, so I said: *'I don't suppose you'd like to help me, would you?'* As if by magic, those tight lips loosened and broadened into the widest smile you could imagine. *'Of course!'* she said. You could tell she felt so honoured to be singled out – and that night, she sat with me at the front of the group, helping me process the rest of the queueing members. That's when I learned yet another lesson – that people really love to be asked for their help and inclusion. They feel special and involved.

Over the next few weeks, I decided I was going to recruit as many people as I could sensibly find jobs for. I gathered a little army of members to help me with various jobs in the group – from collecting group fees and making sure everyone had signed in, to handing each member their weight record card to give to me when she reached the end of the line, so I could write the good news of yet another pound or so gone. I called these volunteers my 'social committee'.

50 years later, our 'social teams' in Slimming World groups all over the UK and Ireland all do very similar things (albeit with some more high-tech gear!) and every one of our many thousands of Consultants continues to be as grateful for their special, community-spirited help as I was on that historic night in Barnsley, way back in March 1971.

To go from 4 to 44 members in one night was mind-blowing. I remember thinking, *'I've cracked it! Job done!'* My brain was already calculating the hours I needed to get back to working in the background to improve and build the business. But almost as quickly as I thought my 'teacher' job was over and I could hand over this group to someone else, I realised something.

This wasn't the end – it was just the beginning.

By thinking like this, I was destroying my own vision by putting an artificial ceiling on what was possible. If I could welcome all these new members on one night, on the back of my very first editorial and with no serious effort at promotion and no results yet of magnificent weight losses, how phenomenal could this group become?

As I stood there in that leisure centre in Barnsley, I felt both overwhelmed and thrilled. I welcomed everyone, thanked them for coming and told them about our club, about the eating plan (which is what they were all dying to know about), about our way of supporting everyone as an individual and how they, as a group, would in turn become supporters.

I told them how we wanted to hear from them, sharing their successes, sharing the way they found a route through, sharing and sharing – and that the more involved they became, the more they'd help themselves too. With my fast-beating heart, with total conviction and with such a rush of excitement and emotion, I said: *'This group*

is going to form the core – the nucleus – of the biggest, the best, the most amazing and successful group ever. When you leave here tonight, if you've got any friends who need our help, who are wasting their money elsewhere or who are struggling alone, then be a really good friend, the best friend, and bring them here next week.'
AND THEY DID!

Within four weeks, the group had grown from 44 to 112 members. I added another session on the Monday night because I hated them having to queue. Instead of reducing the first session, we simply grew the second session. So I added another session on a Tuesday night and that grew too. So I added *another* session on the same night and when that grew too much, I added a Wednesday morning session as well.

No matter how many extra sessions I added, I couldn't get that original 5.30pm session on a Monday below 90 people – and the combined groups ran at around 250 members every week.

The buzz was incredible and I loved running the groups. Oh, how we giggled! The members – all women back then – would make outrageous confessions about their changing bodies, their husbands' reactions, about how their sex lives had changed. We'd laugh and we'd cry, we'd share and we'd support. It felt like raising a family.

There was a problem, though. I was trying to develop a business and I was overstretched beyond belief. Despite it all, growing Barnsley beyond my expectations turned out to be one of the most valuable lessons possible. We limit our success most when we limit our thinking. As slimmers, we do this all the time.

These are just a sprinkling of the negative, exaggerated and false messages that somehow become recorded in our minds and played on a loop until we believe them to be the unshakeable truth.

'I could never be a size 12.'

'I don't have the sort of body that loses weight quickly.'

'I could never give up chocolate.'

Thankfully for me (and Slimming World), my artificial and limiting ceiling came off as quickly as it had gone on. Eventually, I handed five thriving groups to another teacher so I could get back to my desk, my typewriter, the Gestetner and the almighty task of growing the business, finding and training new teachers and producing and distributing enough materials for a business that was now very much on the up.

66 *Learn from the mistakes of others.*
You can't live long enough to make
them all yourself. 99

Eleanor Roosevelt

CHAPTER FIVE

the birth of a business

There's only so much one human being can do alone. So thank goodness that around this time, I was approached by Pauline Paley, the Area Manager I mentioned in the last chapter – an impressive, lively, larger-than-life character, who asked to become a joint owner of the business (still called J&M Slimming Club at that time). As I was creaking under the weight of my workload and very impressed with Pauline's credentials, I agreed. Pauline bought her share for £145 – the equivalent of around £2,000 today.

Another silly figure, I suppose, with 40 groups already up and running, but I was feeling desperate. Pauline brought with her a mountain of confidence, a fearless approach to the media, be that radio or big regional newspapers, a lot of fun and wit and, to be absolutely fair, she lightened my life. I liked her a lot.

Pauline was on her own weight loss journey, with several stones to lose, and she seemed to know her stuff when it came to business development (evidenced by that invaluable advice on editorials). I felt at my weakest in this department. I wasn't afraid of hard work and long hours, I was fairly academic, reading lots about nutrition, able to analyse the rollercoaster of emotions when weight loss did or didn't happen, and I understood how these effects had consequences. And, I could communicate this effectively in written work or face-to-face. But when it came to understanding and feeling confident with the media, I was definitely in the second division.

So I looked up to Pauline. I was an instant fan. I was overjoyed that *someone* wanted to get involved, do some work, help me out and be on my side. Especially someone with Pauline's experience and charisma. She seemed like my knight in shining armour. I know they say, *'It's tough at the top',* which it is for sure, and without trusted managers, it can also be very lonely.

With an active partner on board, I couldn't keep running the business from a bedroom, so that's when we started to look for a proper office. By now, Roy had found himself another job travelling all over the place, so there was really nothing pinning us to Darton and Barnsley other than our house. The Nottinghamshire and Derbyshire groups were doing well and as both Pauline and I knew that area better than anywhere, it seemed logical to look for business premises back on home turf.

As luck would have it, the ideal building came up for sale, 34 High Street in South Normanton – a three-storey terraced house with a deli-type shop on the ground floor, which used to be filled with the delicious smells of cold meats and pies. I remembered it from my childhood. Immediately opposite was the car park for South Normanton's main shopping area.

We were able to get a loan from the National Westminster bank and so we bought it, and eventually, some years later in 1978, we bought a two-storey building across the road, adjacent to the car park. We were running a proper business!

The immediate challenge was my commute from South Yorkshire to South Normanton. I spent hours every day charging up and down the outside lane of the M1 (thank goodness they didn't have speed traps in the 1970s!). Although I enjoy driving, and for me it's always been a great time to turn things over in my head, I remember thinking *'I can't go on like this.'* With that in mind, it wasn't long before Roy and I sold up in Darton and moved back to Derbyshire and our next home in the small village of Riddings, just a few miles from the office.

This four-bedroom house was fairly uninspiring and I can't say I was thrilled with it – but, like many things in life, Riddings had hidden treasures. For me, the best of these treasures was meeting and befriending a wonderful woman – Jean Lalljee – and her lovely family, who lived across the road.

Jean Lalljee, born in Jamaica and educated in England, was my friend and mentor. She was older than me and very wise – loyal, dedicated and with an impeccable moral compass. She was a devout Christian. I still miss our conversations, which were always fascinating. It was like being on holiday, so different were those precious snatches of time spent with Jean – away from the daily routine of work.

Jean was a widow, with a delightful family of three. Jonathon (Jay) was the oldest, Sarah (the same age as my daughter Claire, now about nine years old) and Rachel (the youngest). Jean, as a single parent, was managing all of them brilliantly, even on a shoestring. She was like a second mother to Claire too, and was always willing to lend a helping hand when I was struggling with work commitments.

Over the years, I had the pleasure of being introduced to many of her family when they visited her from Jamaica and those were glorious times, with dull days livened up as her house filled with fun and laughter. I always felt they'd brought the Jamaican sunshine with them. Jean remained a friend over the years, until her death, tragically early, in 2011.

Work, even with Pauline alongside, became even more intense for me, and all those years of working 18-hour days were catching up with me. I became ill. At first I had no idea what was happening to me. A very strange sensation would take hold of me, a feeling that I was about to die – and then my breathing would change, and become more like panting. It only happened when I was alone, often when I was driving.

In the end, I had to consult a doctor, who told me that these were panic attacks. I needed to rest and take a break from the stresses of work, he said, so no visitors bringing problems to my door, or phone calls. The business would have to manage without me for a while. Impossible!

Although it was hard to tear myself away for even a day, and something I'd never done before, we took ourselves off to the Lake District, out of sight and out of contact. I had two full nights of scrumptious sleep and my symptoms disappeared, never to return. I know that solving panic attacks is very rarely that easy, but for me, that break was like pushing a 'reset' button and I was able to pick up where I'd left off.

———————

The next few years were a blur of hard work as I ploughed everything into making the business a success. Having worked under a few different managers (good, bad and indifferent) during my late teens, I'd formed a clear picture in my mind of how I wanted my company to run. Apart from the service we were delivering to members, of the highest importance then was building a positive company culture – although I'd never have called it that, or even been aware of such a concept. All I knew was that I wanted my employees to be happy. I wanted them to feel valued and enjoy coming to work, just as I did.

The office building itself had a long thin back garden, with a broken-down garage which became even more broken after my husband put his very leery thoroughbred horse Flair in there for the day, so the farrier could re-shoe her. (Roy had developed another of his passions, this time for horses – but that's another story.) Least said about that day the better, but suffice to say I was left to supervise Flair's stay and at one point, trapped inside the small space with the terrified mare, I was sure my end was nigh as her wild eyes became even wilder and she put her head down and charged at me! A nifty side-step left her missing me and ferociously hitting the wall of the wooden garage. Both I and the garage somehow survived.

In our main office, over three floors, our little team was quite scattered in small, closed-off rooms. I began to consider that back garden. It had a useful parking area alongside and bungalows behind. If we used the space to build a single-storey building, it would house us all and keep us together as a team. The three-storey building on the main road could be used for other purposes. We got the Council's OK and, before you could blink, or so it felt, we had a new, cosy, single-storey office.

The original building became a place to store stock and files and it also gave us the opportunity to create a staff restaurant and dining room, where delicious meals were prepared by our very own cook, Hillary. I wish I had photographs of that dining room, which had originally been the owner's bedroom. If I did, I'd proudly display them in our current restaurant, as a little piece of Slimming World's history. What a contrast from the one now installed in the Sparkly Castle, as Slimming World's Head Office has come to be affectionately known.

I still feel emotional and proud when I remember a little miracle that happened back in the winter of 1974. You might not believe it either.

The unions were in charge of the country. They had grown more and more powerful for so many political reasons and political failures. Everyone seemed to be on strike or taking some kind of industrial action – it was disastrous. The government was forced to take drastic action too, in the form of the Three-Day Week.

Most of you are too young to remember this, so let me paint the picture. It was a bit like a hosepipe ban – but instead of preserving water, the government was desperately trying to preserve electricity. So unlike your lawn getting a bit crispy in a heatwave (no big deal), businesses (large and small) had to close down completely for four out of seven days. This went on for three months solid. It was like the whole country was shutting down. It brought hardship to many, and brought many businesses to their knees. I (sensibly, I feel) avoid discussing politics (and religion) but if you're interested in this part of UK history, it's definitely worth a Google. Then you can research the different reports and views and decide for yourself.

The Three-Day Week affected us as it did every other business. We had no way of knowing how long it would continue. I suppose there was still a trickle of money coming in from a few groups, but the long and short of it was I couldn't pay the half-a-dozen or so office staff I had at the time. The money wasn't there. I gathered everyone together in our little office and explained that until things blew over, I couldn't pay them, so they'd have to go home until we could pick things up at a later date. I could never have been prepared for what happened next.

Knowing that they would be unpaid; knowing the state of the country, they stayed with me. Every single member of my little family continued to show up to work as usual. Thanks to them – to their dedication, their loyalty, their hard work and their team spirit – J&M Slimming Club survived one of the toughest periods in British economic history.

I thought that was pretty bloody marvellous – and I still do to this day. Further down the line, when we could afford it, I had the pleasure of repaying the loyalty of those special staff members who remained with us until retirement by awarding them a generous pension when they left. It was just my way of saying, *'Thank you, with all my heart'*.

It always jars slightly when I hear myself referred to as a 'business-woman' – or even as an 'entrepreneur'. When I was starting Slimming World, I didn't see myself as either – nor do I now, really. I suppose it's because I was never focused on the business per se. My focus was much more on what the business was trying to achieve.

I wanted to help people – people like me – to shed the misery and the burden of excess weight, without having to suffer unnecessarily in the process.

Earning money was important too – of course it was. We needed to be financially sound so we could build and grow the business and of course, I wanted to put our family in a stable position, just like anyone else does. But what drove me – what kept me up at night and what still keeps me up at night – was the quest to create a slimming club that would help every member to take control of their weight problem, without lectures, without judgement, without deprivation and without shame. The service we would provide, the best service ever invented, would be the way we would create our income. Delighting our members, exceeding their expectations, and helping them to transform their lives was always my driving force.

These days, businesses have whole teams dedicated to 'corporate social responsibility' – but this wasn't a concept I was aware of (the term probably hadn't even been invented back then). It just made good business sense to me. In today's world, being socially responsible has gained more popularity and credence than it had when I was starting out. I quote here from the website *entrepreneur.com* in 2017:

'Of course, businesses need to make a profit in order to sustain themselves but it doesn't have to be the primary reason for being. In recent years, more corporations are seeing the value of putting social good before their balance sheets. This has done considerable good for the communities served, the environment and society, in general. It's led to a serious shift and created a movement that is going beyond individual companies taking up a purpose for social good.'

Did I write that?!

By the time we moved into our office in South Normanton, I'd learned a fair amount about business, management, leadership, motivation and organisation from books and from my own eye-opening experiences. I'd learned that finding good Consultants (we'd dropped the word 'teachers' by now!) was a tricky business. My selections were too hit and miss. I'd single-handedly recruited and trained around 40 Consultants by this point and they had groups scattered across Nottinghamshire, Derbyshire and Yorkshire.

We issued much of our stock directly to those Consultants who preferred to pop in to the office and collect it themselves. We also had a simple system in place for producing and distributing the materials needed to those who were further afield – by now we were stretching towards the West Midlands. I even developed my own system to trigger the re-ordering and reprinting of our stock. It was as simple as having a coloured sheet with instructions protruding from the visible pile of papers when they'd reached a minimum level (smart, eh?).

I was still only 24 years old. Every one of my staff was older than me – by some years. I was the office junior! So thank goodness for the older and wiser heads who joined Pauline and me in the office and who, as I found by working alongside them, were loyal, reliable and completely trustworthy.

A prime example was our accountant Malcolm Severn – who was vitally needed because I was clueless about the tax side of things and I knew we had to have someone to take care of the legalities of accounting, at the very least. Malcolm was honest as the day is long and I trusted him implicitly. He had a luxuriant head of dark, thick, floppy hair – and a stammer. That stammer was a life-long battle for Malcolm and it used to put me on tenterhooks for him. His worst words, the ones that gave him the most difficulty, were those that started with an M or an S. Which given his name, was a particular problem. I almost needed to be strapped down and gagged to prevent me trying to help him when someone at the other end of the phone asked him to identify himself.

At one point Malcolm went off to York for a week-long course to help him control his stammer. He seemed to have had a great time, met some other lovely people and fellow sufferers and the teaching method of singing the words to a rhythm worked – and tickled his great sense of humour.

Then came someone to answer the phones to help Consultants with their stock queries, one Eileen Yorston – honest, reliable and someone who both nurtured and reined me in. Occasionally I felt so indebted to someone who had done something well for the business, I wanted to give them an over-generous bonus. It was those times when Eileen, always unerringly sensible, said something like, *'That's a bit over-the-top generous, isn't it Mag?'* Eileen eventually didn't have just one job. She willingly took on other duties as and when required. I trusted her implicitly too.

Then came someone to sort and dispatch the stock. Muriel, already in her late 50s, was a steady, reliable worker. Much later in the decade, we needed someone to go out in a van and help with stock deliveries, back in the days when we only needed one van, one man and seven days to get all our stock out to all our Consultants each week! Dave Armstrong was that man, and he's still a treasured member of our Head Office team all these years later.

Our next addition was someone to work with Malcolm in accounts – my incredible and beloved sister-in-law Jean Miles. Part-time at first, Jean was the book-keeper who worked closely with Malcolm. Jean, another very dear Jean in my life (along with Jean Lalljee – they liked each other a lot), was an incredible character. Her dry wit and terrific sense of fun always had me in fits of laughter and, unaware of her charm, she had a great and positive influence on the rest of the team.

To demonstrate her sense of the ridiculous, I can recount one of her little gems, and there were many – and they were constant. One day, when they were both retired, Jean and Eileen came to spend a few days with me in Mallorca. Eileen (who was in her early 80s by then) was telling Jean that she'd taken up swimming lessons, after a lifetime of never daring to do so. She was talking about her swimming instructor, who she didn't much care for. *'Why not?'* asked Jean. Eileen explained that he was always pushing her to do more or go faster. Quick as a whip, Jean replied: *'Well, he probably thinks you've got potential!'* That still makes me burst out laughing today!

Like Eileen, Jean mopped up other bits and pieces of work as they came in, giving a helping hand anywhere it was needed. And needless to say, she had my complete trust too.

Then, in the mid-'70s, came the lovely Anne Kirk, Pauline's sister-in-law, who was to become our PR and Advertising Manager. A kind, gentle person, who got along with everybody but who could be strong when required (as it often was with advertising sales people), she proved to be another intrinsic part of a loyal and trustworthy team. As I write this, I'm delighted to say that Anne is very much alive and vigorously kicking and long may that continue! Her daughters and grandchildren are now carrying on her legacy, as equally loyal and trustworthy members of our office staff.

Later in the 1970s, we were blessed to be joined by Sheila Hall – and what a true treasure she turned out to be. (By the way, you may remember me talking about my job as an office junior and my lovely boss, Brian Hall? Well much to my amazement, Brian was Sheila's husband, something I didn't discover for about two years!)

I'm sure I was the most blinkered, selfish, manic person in the world in those early days of Slimming World (who said *'what's changed then?'*) and that's my excuse for the fact that I can't remember exactly when Sheila arrived in our little 'office in the garden'. I'm ashamed to say that I can't remember when she became a member, or a Consultant, or an Area Manager or Regional Manager, out there in the field – rising up through the company year after year. I can only remember when she was there, at her desk, next to Eileen Yorston.

Sheila always was a little powerhouse. She was born with a right arm that never fully developed in the womb and to this day, I'm full of wonder and awe at her mother and the incredibly wise ways she dealt with this catastrophe.

She didn't tie Sheila's shoelaces as she dressed for school. She didn't rescue her from her struggles and she refused to show Sheila any pity whatsoever. I can only say that Slimming World has a lot to thank Sheila's mother for, because Sheila was something else.

As an Area Manager, then a Regional Manager, Sheila's role involved visiting groups and team meetings all over the UK, to make sure that the quality standards we strove for were being achieved. Sheila – always incredibly focused on the company's needs – travelled the length and breadth of the country, churning up the miles and putting in unbelievably long days, often arriving home after midnight, after a very early start, an intense day and a long journey back. Never, never ever, did I hear one single word of complaint.

I'll always remember Sheila recounting a story, her eyes twinkling with amusement, about one midnight, when she came charging through the quiet village of Edwinstowe where she lived, ignoring the 30 mph speed limit. She'd spotted headlights behind her but was surprised when they followed her through her gates into the private parking area outside her house and she watched with fascination as a policeman stepped out of his car and knocked on her window.

She duly wound down her window. *'Do you know what speed you were doing through the village, madam?'* he enquired. Sheila told him she did not. He told her what it was and, as you may imagine, the excessive speed was what had attracted his attention. He asked to see her driving licence, which was spotless. Not a single offence in 20 years or more.

Now, as you know, as we drive on the left in this quaint little country of ours, the driver sits on the right of the car. Sheila's right arm (with no hand) was, therefore, the one nearest the window and the officer. When he saw her clean driver's licence, he said, *'Well, it's a shame to spoil this, isn't it? Please put your hand out of the window.'* Sheila turned in her seat, reached across and offered him her left hand. He removed his leather glove and slapped her hand with it. To which Sheila responded, *'Is that a challenge?'* Ahh, you can just picture it can't you?

I must have taken much of what Sheila did for granted because I was putting in such relentlessly long days myself (my weak excuse) but at least much of my work was done from the office and from home, and I only made long journeys to deliver training or interview new Consultants. With only a map, no GPS and no sat-nav, Sheila found her way from the top of the UK to the bottom, through distant towns and villages, to groups and meeting halls, as though they were as familiar to her as her own back yard.

Sheila lived and breathed Slimming World's management philosophy. With a twinkling eye and a smile, she struck that perfect balance of warm *and* firm in her management of people. She knew how to be friendly – but never befriend. Very much like a nurturing mum or dad, she was incredibly good at letting people know when they were doing a good job – or not such a good job – with just the right words and a lovely, light touch that helped put challenging situations into perspective. I recall one example with a manager who was exaggerating the work they felt was needed to help a struggling Consultant. Sheila told her: *'She's not on her way into intensive care, dear,'* (everyone was *'dear'*) *'she just needs a glass of water!'* And, *'Don't tell me it's dark, dear, bring me a candle!'* – another of my favourite Sheila-isms.

None of us, except Malcolm and Jean, had any specific business experience – we just pulled together, worked closely side by side, and when we encountered problems, we solved them, together. I can testify without hesitation that any business just starting out, any business that's growing, and indeed any business that is well-established, needs people like these. I count myself so very lucky to have been surrounded and protected by such wonderful, loyal, caring and trustworthy people. I most certainly couldn't have done it without them.

As I write these words, it's a pleasure to take a moment to relive some wonderful memories of exceptional people. Many of them have now passed away, but I hold them in my heart forever. I hope the memories stay clear and bright as long as I live.

Much of what I learned in those early days couldn't have been learned from an economics class or a book. I knew that growth would bring challenges, but none of us knew what those challenges would be. When one came up, we'd invent our own simple little systems to keep the cogs turning. These were always very straightforward and low-tech. If there was ever a time when I was rash or impulsive (plenty of those as a woman in my early twenties!), the wise Eileen would move into parental mode and keep me in check. It was a bit like an ecosystem – if anything grew out of balance, it was naturally restored.

And that's how the caring, human, common-sense-led culture of our company grew over time – something that's still very quickly recognised by anyone who comes to work for or with us (and, over the years too, by official bodies such as 'Investors in People' and *The Sunday Times* 'Best Companies To Work For'). I learned many powerful lessons back in my early days in employment, and the ones which drove me to make our company a nice, fair and fun place to be have never left me.

My confidence with the financial side of the business also blossomed organically. Growing up, I'd witnessed Mum squirrelling away money in old purses, tins and various containers that would fit into her special drawer. She kept these amounts separate so that she was never in debt to anyone. The insurance money had its own container, the mortgage payment had its own container, and the building society savings did too.

If she knew money would be needed for a repair or some unexpected item, she was always prepared. Debt was not to be contemplated. Her prudence rubbed off on me, because despite seeing myself as a bit useless with accounts, I never frittered away a penny. I've already talked about my dislike of credit cards and the horror of our first (and only) visit from a debt collector. The concept of borrowing money has never sat comfortably with me. I've had to do it over the years, of course, but bank loans are dangerous beasts. Property is a bit different. You're far more likely to come out unscathed if other things don't work out.

As I mentioned earlier, we bought 34 High Street with a mortgage and when we built that single-storey, open plan office in the back garden, we designed it so that we could put up a few stud walls and turn it into a separate saleable dwelling if the need arose. Maybe I was more 'businessy' than I gave myself credit for...

> **"** *Be who you are and say what you feel, because those who mind don't matter and those who matter don't mind.* **"**
>
> Bernard Baruch

CHAPTER SIX

heartbreak and joy

1976 was turning out to be a good year. Things were going well. We had our office space. Pauline and I had a small, dedicated team working alongside us. I knew what I wanted and where I was going and, although I was still incredibly busy, I was able to depend on others to help more and more.

Then came a phone call that shattered my world. Jean, my sister-in-law and highly valued colleague, had left the office at 5pm, arrived home and found Jack, her husband, my brother-in-law, dead on the bathroom floor. He'd had a massive heart attack at 53 years of age.

I hadn't been particularly close to Jack, although I respected and liked him a lot – but Jean, who I loved dearly, was my trusted and loyal colleague and friend. I knew how close they were as a family. I was there, by her side, as the police arrived. Jack still lay on the bathroom floor. Jean was just destroyed, and I was heartbroken for her. I spent a lot of time with Jean over the next few months, supporting her, empathising with her and sharing her feelings of devastation and despair.

Around that time – possibly linked to my emotional turmoil – my periods stopped. When I told Roy, suspecting of course that I might be pregnant, I thought he'd flip because he'd told me many years earlier that he didn't want any more children. I'd accepted this and put the thought of more children out of my head. To my astonishment, he didn't flip and he wasn't even angry. All those years! Who knew?

Time gradually healed the pain of Jack's death for Jean, and my periods restarted. But it had put the idea of another baby into my head, and in the November of 1976 our first son, Dominic, was conceived.

I discovered I was pregnant shortly after our Woman of the Year ceremony – an event which today takes place annually at the International Convention Centre in Birmingham (and even with our 2,000-person plus capacity, we're bursting at the seams). If you've ever been, you'll know that it's hosted by a different celebrity guest each year, from Peter Howett in 1988 to Peter Andre in 2017 and, of course, beyond (take a peek at the photo pages to see a few of our famous hosts from years gone by).

In 1972, for our very first Woman of the Year ceremony, the setting was much more humble – the Sherwood Rooms in Nottingham. There was no celebrity to take the microphone back then (we didn't have enough money for such things), and it was just me hosting the event – alone! I was a nervous wreck. The worst nerves and stage fright you can ever imagine. My speech was handwritten on a small postcard-size scrap of paper, just a (very) short welcome, a thank you and list of our finalists. Even so, most of my saliva disappeared and what was there refused to moisten my mouth. Six hundred strangers – aargh!

I'm not sure whether it was my nerves or the four large G&Ts I'd consumed 20 minutes before my appearance on stage but something almost frighteningly weird happened. I turned into the Queen (certainly in my enunciation) for the duration of my address! Maybe starting the speech with, *'My husband and I'* was the trigger that set me off, but I can remember thinking STOP, stop, stop. I couldn't. The Queen was in the building and I couldn't control my own voice. Thankfully, I learned a valuable lesson that night. Over 100 speeches and 47 years later, even with audiences of up to 2,000, I thankfully no longer require an alcohol binge – or a regal alter ego! One tradition I do uphold, though, is entering the stage to that belter of a song *Wild Women Do*, by Natalie Cole (which explains the title of this book in case you weren't already up on your '90s chart-toppers). It's truly one of the most special nights of the year, taking the opportunity to pour my (always bursting) heart out to our members, Consultants and staff when so many of them are all together in one place.

Our winner that first night was a lovely lady called Joan, who had lost 7 stones by losing 1lb a week, every week! I thought that level of consistency was pretty special and I still do. Joan, if you're reading this, we lost all our records in the arson attack of '89 and I can't recall your surname. I hope you'll forgive me.

A few years later, with a London PR agency in charge, we welcomed our very first celebrity – Dennis Weaver – who played the title role in the hit TV series *McCloud;* and a year or so after that, the very handsome Frazer Hines who played Joe Sugden in *Emmerdale Farm* (as it was called back then). There was no awards ceremony but we welcomed the photographs, the publicity and the chance to honour our tremendous slimmers, all of whom enjoyed their year as a special ambassador for J&M Slimming Club.

Anyway, I digress. Back to late '76 and that joyous moment when I discovered I was to be a mother for the second time. Having gone through all the emotions of a suspected pregnancy after Jack's death, I'd been longing to add to our family. So receiving this news from our family doctor was nothing short of pure joy.

Another baby! A baby I wouldn't have to fight to keep, as I'd had to fight for Claire. A pregnancy without any of the shame and judgement that had tarnished the pleasure of my first. I couldn't wait to tell Claire the news!

As an only child, I'd always longed for a brother or sister, so I assumed that my daughter, also a lonely, only child for over 12 years, would feel exactly the same way. How wrong could a mother be? I'd never dreamed that Claire's reaction would be so very much the opposite.

I think her response must have been driven by the fear that there wouldn't be enough love to go around and that somehow she wouldn't have as much of me. Nothing could have been further from the truth, as every parent can testify. Parental love is unconditional and limitless – as I'm sure Claire would now agree, having made me a proud grandmother to twins in my 49th year.

July 1977, eight months pregnant, with a month to 'b-day', I was still working late into the night – deep in discussion by phone with one of our key field managers at the time, Ann. It was almost midnight. A little earlier I'd noticed some spotting and had ignored it. It was such a small amount of blood. Obviously insignificant. I was a very healthy, happily expectant 29-year-old.

I'd gained a lot of weight, but again, that seemed quite normal and no one had said otherwise. So, as Ann and I were winding up a long working day, I mentioned the bleeding. Now, Ann was a gentle woman – quiet, hard-working and, it transpired, wiser than her boss. She told me, unexpectedly forcibly for this mild-mannered mum-of-two, to contact the doctor – immediately! I started to protest and she wouldn't hear any of it. *'Call the doctor NOW!'*

OK, OK! I got the message.

To my surprise, the night changed from peaceful to hectic. The doctor must have been woken from his slumbers, but he was instantly alert and organising a quick-response ambulance to deal with a haemorrhage risk. I was told to go and lie down. Do nothing! Walk nowhere! Don't move! So off I went upstairs to pack a case for a possible hospital stay. I also had to wake Roy and explain what was happening.

By the time the ambulance arrived, I was obeying the order to lie down. Roy was waiting with the door open and for the first time I realised how small our living room was, as it filled up with white coats, medical bags and a stretcher. The kind doctor never stopped apologising as he came towards me with a rather large needle and

The very handsome *Emmerdale Farm* heart-throb Fraser Hines – one of our early '80s Slimming World celebs – posing with my sons Dom and Ben in the Design Studio. It was all rather low-key in those days!

McCloud star Dennis Weaver – the first celebrity we welcomed to help us gain publicity – posing with our 1977 Slimmer of the Year Valerie Smith. Just look at those flares!

Star of the hit TV show *Bread*, Peter Howitt was our charming, intelligent and incredibly handsome celebrity host in 1988.

How cute was our 1992 host, actor and singer Michael Ball?

Me with the wonderfully warm and hyper-intelligent entertainer and comedian Bob Monkhouse, in 1994. I just loved him!

How can you not love Shane Richie? Here we are together before the 2002 Slimming World Awards, long before he made his mark in *Eastenders* as Alfie Moon.

Our 2004 host, TV chef Ainsley Harriott, couldn't have been more perfect for the job. His natural friendliness put everyone completely at ease.

Singer Peter Andre was the first host to bring his band along to the Awards and perform for us in 2014 and again in 2017. What a true gentleman he was! And so talented and gorgeous!

With my dear neighbour and wonderful, caring friend Jean Lalljee and her
daughter, Sarah.

My beloved cottage, which Roy and I bought in 1977. This photo shows it some
years later – after we'd had time to spruce it up a bit!

Dominic, my second-born, was the most delightful, happy toddler. Those little cheeks!

Happy days – me, Roy and Dominic (and Claire behind the camera).

Ben, my youngest, as a boy – always buzzing with energy and determination. He was our little real-life Action Man, and still is today.

Fast-forward some years and this was Ben after completing his 6,000km charity cycling challenge in 2012.

Big smiles from our fabulous Head Office marketing and PR teams during the UK leg of Ben's epic journey. Graeme (right), for the record, took the photo on the cover of this book. At Slimming World, we like to keep it in the family as much as we can!

Claire as a teenager, with her dad Roy, on holiday in the South of France.

My beautiful children together in the late '80s.

A fresh-faced Danny, one of our family since he moved in with us as a teenager.

My husband Tony, as a dashing young navigator.

A picture of Tony and me, taken a decade ago in 2009 (how is it a decade?!).

The wonderful Jean Miles, my
sister-in-law and dear colleague,
with the wise and nurturing
Eileen Yorston.

Our rather suave and handsome
Finance Director David Rathbone
in 1986.

At Slimming World, we've always loved an excuse to get dressed up and have
a bit of fun! Dave (left) and Liz (second from the right) are still with the
company today, after many years of loyal and dedicated service.

prepared me for a blood transfusion. I was safely transported, accompanied by blue lights and sirens, to Derby City Hospital where the next day I was taken to the operating theatre (men in green, including their wellies and masks – quite alarming really, especially the wellies – I mean, how much blood was there likely to be?).

The threatened haemorrhage never occurred, but it was decided that the situation was too risky to allow me to go home and I would need to be carefully monitored. The fear was that my placenta could come away completely and leave the baby stranded, a condition called placenta praevia, I was told.

In the event, they decided, after a couple of weeks, that the safest course of action was to bring 'b-day' forward. Our son, Dominic James Miles, was born at 11.30pm on 5th August 1977. That was one very long day! I was absolutely exhausted. Another 14-hour labour was no fun. In fact just before his birth, I remember praying (begging) to God to let me die. I must have lost consciousness for a few seconds and I remember jerking back into consciousness and saying in a panic, *'I didn't mean it!'*

Roy was there and had been for much of the labour. As soon as Dom was born, the nurses wrapped him up and handed him to Roy while they attended to me, which was when they found that I had two placentas, the cause of the bleeding. Apparently, my pregnancy had started as twins and one didn't make it (I was pleased that I went through the nine months unaware of that, though of course very sad at the same time for what might have been).

I was busy with the nurses, so I only realised something was wrong when someone shouted, *'Grab him!'* It had been a long day for Roy too, and holding our newborn baby was a step too far. He had started to faint – with Dom in his arms – adding a final touch of drama and excitement to the day, as if we needed any more!

There were a couple of reasons why I'd been looking for a new home for the Miles family. Our house in Riddings was on a narrow side-street, with no designated parking, and a neighbour who'd complain when we parked our car on the street, outside our own house, opposite his driveway, making it quite awkward for him to reverse out. And though I'd be sad to move away from our beloved Jean and her family, we were ready to move on.

The other reason was that I had secretly been squirrelling away money into a building society for the last three or four years, a habit learned from my mum. Secretly? Yes, because the second I'd told Roy, he'd have come up with a wonderful money-making scheme it could be used for (remember the rotavator fiasco?) which would leave us in a worse position than before.

Of course, eventually I had to tell him that I'd saved enough for a deposit on a better house. That very day, sure enough, he promised a local farmer that we'd become partners in his failing farm, using every penny I had saved. Thank goodness he needed my agreement to access the funds and I, of course, firmly rejected his latest and daftest idea. It was one of those times that took our marriage to breaking point. They seemed to come around every couple of years.

The savings were the result of sheer hard work, and were started from those early years when I took very little salary and reinvested to build and grow the business. We'd been living frugally, working long hours, and Roy's circumstances had improved. He'd won better sales positions and finally, in 1977, he landed a great new job as the PR person for the Midlands' Electrical Contractors Association. He had his own office, a car and a secretary – and no fear of his company going bust.

I'd already been looking for a house for two years by the time I fell pregnant with Dominic. I was after something quaint and cottagey, reasonably close to our office so there was no need for a time-con-suming commute. We both wanted privacy, too, with no next-door neighbours for us to bother (which felt like freedom to me) and lots of land, if possible, so that Roy could keep horses – a passion which had grown since he'd bought Claire a Welsh mountain pony when she was about 10 years old.

I have a vivid memory of collecting said pony from a field in Yorkshire. Roy hired a large delivery van (we couldn't afford a horsebox), and I was given the job of driving into the wilds of Huddersfield, on my own. I decided I'd get into my role of lorry driver, so I wore my over-sized, brown corduroy cap (trendy in the '70s) and a scarf, flicking the indicators on in thanks when another lorry flashed me to return to the inside lane after overtaking.

I'd learned the lorry-driver etiquette already! So that was the fun bit. Then I arrived at the appointed field. It was autumn, but on these cold and windy plains there was snow on the ground. I spent several frustrating hours trying to coax our 12-hands-high beast into the back. One of the most difficult jobs ever! Thankfully, both the pony and I returned home alive and Roy grazed her on the fields of the failing farm in Riddings, which is how he came to know the farmer.

After much fruitless searching, I found our ideal house in an unexpected place. It didn't appear in the local newspapers or any of the estate agents' windows. The cottage came up in Roy's *'Horse and Hound'* magazine – and I knew almost instantly that it was 'the one'. Roy was still sulking after I'd turned down his grand investment plans with the farmer, and he refused to even go inside the house when we arrived at our viewing appointment – but when he saw the stables, and realised he could indulge his love of horses here, it was game, set and match! (Roy ran a stud farm from the cottage shortly after we moved.)

The setting was the stuff of fairytales. The 400-year-old property sat in its own little valley on the edge of Sherwood Forest, surrounded by trees and fields and with a river running through the gardens. The house had originally been a lock-keeper's cottage and part of the Duke of Portland's estate.

The cottage was in pretty bad condition. The kitchen, if you could call it that, was a nightmare. It had a few broken-down cupboards, a sink and a standing cooker with hob atop. I thought the oven was black, until I started to clean it, only to discover it was cream! I used cardboard boxes to create extra and much-needed storage.

There was no central heating – just a few electric storage radiators which were neither use nor ornament. The utility room was about four inches deep in bird droppings, as the chickens had claimed that part of the house as their own. There were no curtains and no carpets. The garden needed attention, but was still very pretty with climbing roses adding to the charm, as did the river Maun, its flow dividing the garden from our fields opposite, one of which had a public right of way across it.

Initially we were turned down for a mortgage, because of worries from the bank about the cottage's foundations. It took a lot of work by our accountant Malcolm to find an endowment mortgage for us, but he did it, in June of that year. Goodness knows what it cost through the insurance company – but thankfully it was affordable enough that we could go ahead. The extra interest was worth it because this was going to be our 'forever home' (as they'd call it these days!).

We moved house on 6th November 1977 and found ourselves no longer Derbyshire residents, but living just over the border in north Nottinghamshire. Dom was three months old.

I'd sunk all my savings into the purchase, so once again we were pretty hard up, to the point where we used carpet from our old house in Riddings in the cottage, patched together on the stairs. We went without curtains for years. The floor in the living room was wood (its freshly polished smell reminded me of my childhood home) and I splashed out on a large but inexpensive flokati rug to give it a cosier feel. This was a matter of priorities – and keeping our three-month-old baby warm was top of the pile.

Until we could afford to have gas central heating installed, I was utterly reliant on the open fire. The trouble was, the authorities had recently banned coal fires and the smokeless fuel available at the time was next to useless – almost impossible to get going and keep going. All I cared about was keeping my family warm. And to do that in a run-down cottage in the middle of nowhere in 1977 was no mean feat.

After more than one admonishing knock at our door, the man from the Council told me they'd take me to court if he saw smoke coming from the chimney again. I couldn't see any option but to hold my hands in the air and say: *'You're going to have to take me to court then. I'll explain to the judge that I've tried burning coke but it's really difficult to even get a fire going and I can't get enough heat to get the place warm – and I think it's dangerous for my baby.'*

Who knows whether it was my stubborn (and, OK, somewhat confrontational) reaction or whether some angel from the health visiting team had a quiet word in the right person's ear… but the Council left me alone after that!

Winter soon turned into spring and onwards into summer – and as Dominic grew, so did the comfort and beauty of our cottage. It's still our much-loved home in the UK today – the driveway lined with a unique variety of rose called Margaret's World which was given to me by Slimming World to celebrate the company's 25th anniversary. That was a gift I'll always remember and one which lives on year after year. The cottage has been our home for over 40 years and I can never imagine leaving it and all those memories.

If you've lived in the same house for a long time, you'll know how the memories nestle among the furniture, the flower beds – within the very walls themselves. When Dom was a toddler, work was still, as always, a big deal – but it had become a bit easier to have some flexibility, to the point where I could take three afternoons off work each week to spend time with him.

It was like a kind of therapy for me. I can't begin to tell you what an adorable child he was – such a joy. He was a happy, smiling baby and people took to him straight away. When he was two or three, we'd spend hours pottering about in the garden, weeding and digging. I can still picture him crouching inquisitively over his little patch of soil, chirping: *'Mummy! It's Walter the worm!'* – a little phrase I'd introduced him to, for some reason in a Lancashire accent!

Just as I'd been years before with Claire, I was a conscientious parent to Dominic and read all the latest thinking on child development and early education. I was particularly interested in the work of physical therapist and early learning specialist Dr Glenn Doman. He brought out books and a series of flash cards designed to be used with babies and young toddlers – using bold words in red and black to encourage recognition. I decided to try them with Dom.

We'd sit on the rug by a roaring fire and I'd hold up a big white card with big red letters saying 'mummy' and catch his attention to show him the card. I'd say 'mummy!' and then remove the card, and hug and tickle him. Five minutes later, I would repeat the process.

After many repeats for short periods, within a week, Dom 'read' the word himself. Once one word was mastered, we could move on to the next card, the one saying 'daddy', until he'd mastered that one too. With a beaming smile on my face, I would hold the cards, prompt the word and switch the card. The big achievement was when Dom could differentiate between the two. Cue rapturous applause and giggles! It was a joyful way of learning, which we both loved. At the age of two, he could read all the words for parts of the body.

So rewarding was this time that when Dom turned three, the realisation he'd be off to school within a year or so left me yearning for another baby. I was still only 32 – but the clock was ticking and I had always wanted a large family – as in four or more! I came off the pill in February of 1979 and became pregnant immediately. I was over the moon – just as I'd been with Claire (once the tricky bits had been resolved) and with Dominic. I was in a great pattern with work, nannies and cleaners – my house was in order (literally and figuratively) and I looked forward to the birth with excitement.

I had a straightforward pregnancy this time, and work was something that I still loved and was able to do until full term. And just as well, because in 1978, Pauline and I had decided to open a very upmarket kitchen, bedroom and bathroom design studio across the road from the office in South Normanton, and a second studio in Sheffield. I was busier than ever.

People often ask what drove this decision to open another, very different business to Slimming World. And the simple answer is, *because I wanted to!* I'd always had an interest in interior design, and after having my own new kitchen fitted and being disappointed by many aspects of the service, I thought, *'We can do better than that!'* (and yes we could, but my goodness, it wasn't easy!). There was an emerging trend for German cabinetry at the time, so the Miles-Paley Design Studio, as we called ourselves, imported, designed and sold beautiful, ultra-modern, European kitchens to the public. You probably know by now that I love a new challenge!

Having had breastfeeding problems with Claire, I'd been determined that history wouldn't repeat itself with Dominic – but with him I experienced a different problem. Instead of too much milk, my supply dwindled and dried up, possibly because of the stress of our house move. Now, pregnant for the third time, I read all sorts of books on the topic so that this time (third time lucky) I could give my baby the best protection and the best start to life, by breastfeeding successfully for longer than three months.

One of these books was very compelling, the authors backing their claims with scientific evidence that giving anything other than breast milk broke the chain of protection from mother to baby. They recommended all sorts of ways to protect your baby from well-meaning nurses in hospital, as well as much advice for afterwards.

They recommended preparing posters to stick round your hospital bed, and the baby's cot, clearly stating 'DO NOT GIVE THIS BABY COWS' MILK!' and 'BREAST MILK ONLY'.

So after going a week overdue (surely one of the most infuriating waits of any woman's life) I finally went into induced labour. I dutifully pinned up my posters as I breathed through each contraction and waited for my baby to be delivered. On 6th December 1980, in the early evening, my third child, Benjamin Alexis Miles, was born at the Nottingham Women's Hospital.

This was the first time my labour and birth had been aided by epidural. God bless epidurals! Also, for the first time, I was in a half-sitting position and was able effectively to see the birth.

Roy was there, as he had been for Dom's birth. *'It's a boy!'* the midwife exclaimed. The baby let out a reassuring cry, so everything seemed to be OK – yet I knew something was wrong. Time slowed. My brain didn't function. I was looking, seeing and yet not comprehending. Then Roy said: *'Oh, poor little thing, he's got a harelip.'* A 'harelip', as it had been known for centuries (though of course no one would use that term today), was an understatement for what Ben had. The medical terminology was a severe unilateral cleft.

Ben's cleft was so bad, it had completely taken his palate and a large part of the right-hand side of his face from his top lip and through his nose, widening out beneath his eye. The other side was perfect. I often think of a baby's head being modelled in soft clay, perfectly formed, and then the sculptor putting two fingers inside the baby's mouth and wiping upwards to the right, changing forever what had been there. Somehow, most of the clay remained but the parts were no longer in the right place. On the left, he had a normal nostril and lips, but on the right, from the centre of his upper lip up to below the eye, there was a great hole.

I was paralysed by shock for some time, unable to process what I was seeing. I just kept staring at Ben, wondering what had happened.

We were whisked away from the room I had so carefully prepared with posters about breastfeeding and taken to what I believe is now called the HDU, the High Dependency Unit. The roof of Ben's mouth was non-existent but at that amazing hospital, they constructed a plastic palate for him within 24 hours.

The specially trained nurses told me that babies born with this condition aren't able to suckle – and that breastfeeding would be impossible. *'But... but we don't **know** that,'* I said, *'If I try hard enough, we don't know that **he** won't be able to.'* Nothing was going to stop me from trying. And what a disastrous day that was!

Mother and baby were both in the greatest distress – Ben screaming with frustration because he was hungry and me crying with remorse. Eventually, I agreed to squeeze some colostrum on to a teaspoon so Ben could be fed by a tube, which was gently guided down his throat and into his tiny tummy.

As you know, I'd already had two babies, so I was familiar with the usual drill in hospital wards. Nurses bustle in and out – pausing to goo goo and gaa gaa as they hover over the cot and tell you how beautiful your new baby is, as do nursing assistants, tea ladies and cleaners. With Ben, the staff had presumably been pre-warned and each time they came in, they simply avoided looking at him. Then one day, an older nurse came in, walked straight over to the cot, gazed at Ben and without hesitating, she said: *'What beautiful eyes! You know, when they've sorted him out, he's going to be absolutely gorgeous.'*

I hadn't cried over his little damaged face until then, but that kindness helped the dam to burst. It's a memory that still brings me to tears when I recall it, as it does right now. I'm delighted to tell you that the experienced nurse was absolutely right. Ben has braved multiple surgeries, never given up, still deals with dental problems to this day and through it all, he's become stronger and is most definitely gorgeous!

66 *Imagine someone who loves you so much,
they make you love yourself.* **99**

CHAPTER SEVEN

life goes on

It's just as well things were ticking over reasonably well at Slimming World, because Ben's condition became my priority. After he was born, I wrote a candid letter to the whole staff team, explaining what had happened and how it might affect the business in the short term. I soon found a simple solution, which was to have Ben with me, in a big, bouncy, old-fashioned, second-hand, chocolate-brown pram, purchased just for the office. It was so important to me that I could be on hand to comfort and feed him.

Things weren't easy. Roy and I were having yet more problems with our marriage by this point and the Miles-Paley Design Studio was in financial difficulties. This wasn't helped by one of our managers giving us inaccurate financial reports and working behind our backs to open his own business.

Dominic was still a preschooler and although Claire was by now a young teenager and more independent in some ways, she was very much a strong presence in terms of adolescence, rebellion and boys!

Meanwhile, the process of repairing Ben's face and palate was a terrible ordeal for him – and for me. Ben had his first operation at 12 weeks old, in which the surgeon pulled skin and flesh downwards and inwards to form a nostril and a complete top lip, effectively closing the hole in his face.

For the first 15 months of Ben's life, we had to go to hospital every two weeks to have a new artificial palate fitted to the roof of his mouth. This was a nightmare process, required (they believed at the time but since abandoned as a practice) to encourage the growth of his own palate. At each visit, a new mould had to be created, which involved filling our tiny baby's mouth with foam to the point where he'd turn from red to blue, almost choking. It was nothing short of torture and utterly agonising to watch. Thank God it's no longer done.

Knowing plenty about the theories of subconscious memory and how our earliest experiences can shape our brain development, I was convinced that my baby would grow up hating me and not knowing why. After all, it was *me* delivering him to this nightmare – time after time. Surely his baby brain wouldn't understand it for what it was, the best way to help him. Surely he'd be mentally scarred for life. Happily, that wasn't the case.

When Ben was 15 months old, his palate was judged to have grown sufficiently to be able to close the roof of his mouth. A brilliant plastic surgeon got Ben's soft palate into place perfectly on the first attempt – a procedure that could take up to five attempts, the hospital told us. This meant Ben would be able to speak normally and not nasally. Everything we'd been through up to this point was starting to be worth it. Slowly but surely, Ben's damaged face was being put right.

Then, when he was just three years old, we discovered that he was partially deaf, quite severely on one side, with glue ear – a condition that usually affects young children and corrects itself with age, but would most likely be a chronic condition for Ben.

There followed constant procedures throughout Ben's childhood. Procedures to help him hear properly, procedures to remove teeth growing in the roof of his mouth and procedures to transplant bone for his teeth to grow through properly. Sadly, all five attempts to transplant bone failed. There were many more operations to come but from the ages of 12 to 18, all that could be done for him was to fit braces to his teeth.

In the middle of all this, Ben was struck with another devastating problem. At the age of 13 he developed Perthes disease. Perthes disease is a rare childhood condition that affects the hip. His treatment, because of his age, was not to have surgery but to be put in a cast that stretched from his waist to his ankle, with stainless-steel hinges to enable him to move without putting any weight on the joint.

In Ben's case, the head of his femur had crumbled quite badly and separated from the hip socket, so the purpose of the cast was to allow it to recover and grow again and to guide the ball of the femur head back into the hip socket while it slowly regrew. It meant he needed crutches and a wheelchair for the next two years. We were shattered that this disease had been visited on the most active of our children, who'd been through so much already. Sometimes life certainly does give you lemons, and when the lemons have been given to a beloved child, who's had enough to deal with since birth, then it's pretty hard for his mum to feel inclined to make lemonade.

Although as active as any child, from a very early age Dominic enjoyed quieter moments, drawing cars and motorbikes and pushing his tiny matchbox-size cars up and over anything, including his mum, his imagination turning every bump and curve into the hills, valleys and forests of a rally course. I was extremely tickled by this, in more ways than one!

On the other hand, Ben (Benji we called him as a child) was always our little 'action man'. He was fiercely independent, and with cries of: *'No, no, no! Me do it!'*, he would insist on climbing up the kitchen cabinets to stand on the worktop, reach the top cupboards and take out a box of his favourite breakfast cereal rather than allow me to get it for him. When he started school, the teachers told me he was going to make a very talented gymnast.

I needn't have worried about the lemons – Ben made his own lemonade. Within hours he was finding ways to turn his wheelchair into a new action toy, doing tricks on two wheels, much to my horror. Within days, he had become equally adept at turning his crutches into an aid to creating some new acrobatic moves.

He used to 'walk' the mile and a half to the nearest gym, much faster than his friends could run alongside, covering several yards with each 'step' as he swung through on his crutches. After a year, the specialist thought he could manage without the cast, provided he kept to his crutches and chair. Tony, my new partner and quite the action man himself (I'll tell you more about him later), was so overjoyed with this news that he decided a special celebration was required. That very day, the bottom of our garden became a bonfire site and that night, with the bonfire ablaze and Ben by his side, he threw the expensive but loathed cast on top of the bonfire and watched it burn.

Three months and another X-ray later, we were told it had been a little premature to take off the cast, and Ben needed to wear it again. Yes, there was nothing else for it but to have a new one made. Oops!

When Ben was 15, the cast, crutches and his wheelchair could be finally thrown away for good. I was sad to see that his leg, the one covered by the cast, the one he hadn't been able to put any weight on, looked the same as when he was 13 years old and still a child. His 'good' leg was several millimetres longer, bigger, stronger and well-developed. Ben, being Ben, threw himself into every form of exercise under the sun to bring his leg back to full strength.

We were advised that there was a possibility that Perthes disease could reappear in Ben's later teens or early 20s. It did. This time, he had surgery and an artificial hip fitted, though even now, doctors disagree as to whether this was the right course of action.

Some of the Miles family have a history of early heart problems. Jack died at the age of 53 of a heart attack, as you know. Roy (from whom I was by then divorced – more on that later) died at the age of 60, also of a heart attack – so I've nagged all three of my children to have regular checks to make sure they stay safe. In 2008, when he was 28,

Ben's doctor warned that his cholesterol levels, mainly the genetically inherited ones, were high, putting him at serious risk of a heart attack in the next few years.

Ben decided to change his lifestyle and became firstly vegetarian and, later, vegan. Within six weeks, the doctor re-tested and was amazed that Ben had lost six kilos and his cholesterol levels, including the type that's genetically 'inherited', normally virtually unaffected by lifestyle change, had dropped dramatically.

Spurred on by this rapid improvement, Ben decided he wanted to get physically fitter. In 2009, he had an accident on a quad bike and broke a bone in his back. Although this had healed, he was still plagued by back pain, so it was with some trepidation that we bought him a road bike for Christmas. For the next year and a half, he started to train himself for a cycling challenge.

Ben's step-brother, Gary, suggested he do it for charity and between them they decided that Ben should cycle from the southernmost point in Europe, Gibraltar, to the northernmost point in Europe, North Cape, or Nordkapp, in Norway. This would be a journey of many thousands of kilometres, with a diversion to the UK built in to cycle around the country attending special fundraising 'parties in the park' with Slimming World Consultants and members.

Ben decided he wanted to raise money for SMILES (Slimming World's own charitable foundation), which was supporting the NSPCC at the time, and also for a small Mallorcan charity which helped orphaned teenagers make the transition from orphanage to adult life. The starting date was set as May/June 2012, which was the best time to deal with the climate changes he would experience along the way – from searing heat to biting cold.

Ben had moved to Mallorca when he was 19 years old and, during his training, he covered every road and track on the island, usually alone, usually at night after work, sometimes accompanied by his gym trainer Dave, until Dave could no longer keep up. On the trip itself, Dave accompanied Ben for a short time and Gary became the back-up driver, general supporter and searcher for nightly accommodation. I remember Gary saying that he felt a bit awkward admitting that driving for 14 hours a day was tiring, knowing that Ben was cycling hard for the same amount of time! The trip was a great success, with over £100,000 raised for the charities, and Ben ending it as lean and fit as it's humanly possible to be.

Being in and out of hospitals for much of his life has been an eye-opening experience. We were positively lucky in comparison to some, I've always reasoned – and in spite of my worst fears, as Ben has grown, we've been able to stay close. He's a tough customer mentally and physically – psychologically strong and extremely active. Nowadays he loves the gym and boxing. *'For goodness sake don't let them hit your face!'* I find myself saying on repeat! The things Ben has been through have made him stronger, and me too. If he believes in something, he won't be put off by anyone or anything.

As I write this in 2019 – Slimming World's golden anniversary – Ben is in his 39th year, and he's as stubbornly determined, independent and manically energetic as ever. After starting up his own gardening business in his early 20s, he now does a phenomenal job of managing our Mallorcan property, Son Amar, home of an incredible dinner show, a fabulous events venue for weddings, parties and conferences, and a spectacular fountain.

Ben has also created the Son Amar Green Foundation, an impressive example of recycling, upcycling and zero waste that would be unique in any industry and is mind-blowing in the hospitality industry. Ben has trained our staff and invested in equipment so we can recycle, upcycle, and reduce waste to such a degree that we now produce just one cubic metre of waste in three months, where before, we produced 36 cubic metres per day!

With a terrific amount of effort, he's transformed Son Amar into a zero-waste, carbon neutral business. In fact, we're so environmentally friendly that in 2019, we were recognised as one of only a small group of companies globally that meet the ecological gold standard 'SR10'. Ben has three gorgeous children and his brother and sister are just as proud of him and his remarkable achievements as I am.

In autobiographical terms, it's probably remiss of me to speed through more than 30 years in one go – but I couldn't have told the beginning of Ben's story without telling some of the rest. It's proof that even when life steers you into the longest, darkest tunnel, there can be a light at the end.

Back to 1981, a year after Ben's birth, my marriage to Roy was in trouble. Big time. Where had the love gone? If we were to try to get it back, we'd need to get things on a more even keel.

I made an appointment with the Marriage Guidance Council (later renamed *Relate*), a free counselling service available around the UK. I went alone because Roy refused, at first, to get involved. I wanted to save my marriage, desperately, but I was also angry that yet again, I was the one making all the effort. On my first appointment, I was in a very negative frame of mind. I had assumed, absolutely incorrectly of course, that I was going to be told how to adjust *my* attitude, how to change *my* ways, how *I* had to live with the situation and how *I* would have to learn to cope with it.

Rachel, the counsellor, was brilliant. She listened to my tightly polite but angry tirade about how unfair this was going to be, getting advice on all the effort *I'd* have to make. And then she calmly explained exactly what her role was and what it was not. Yes, my friends, I had it all wrong. Her job was to listen, she told me, to get a full picture and to eventually talk to both of us, if we could persuade Roy to come and join us. Her job was to help put the marriage back together if that was what we wanted and if that was realistic. If that wasn't going to be achievable, her role was to help us through the break-up.

For my part, as I realised complete openness was required, I answered her probing questions with total honesty, even if I thought it might show me in a bad light. I described what felt like a constant psychological battering from Roy and questioned my own reaction to these attacks, that left me emotionally bruised. Was I being over-sensitive? I told her the great things about Roy and the not-so great.

When she asked if Roy was involved in Slimming World and whether he supported me in my work, I could answer truthfully that he wasn't involved and that he didn't mind at all that I put in long hours, so in that sense he didn't obstruct me – and that was how he supported me. After a couple of sessions with me alone, she asked me to have another go at persuading Roy to come, either by himself or with me. This time he agreed and he chose to come with me.

What an enormous eye-opener! She actually got Roy to talk about his feelings – something I had singularly failed to do, no matter how many times I'd tried. He would either ridicule the idea, make a joke of it or get angry. In the *Relate* session, he responded honestly. She repeated my description of our regular evening rows, how he would pick a fight and go on the attack and, although I would stand my ground for a while, it would always end in tears.

She asked if that was an accurate description. He said it was. Then she asked him how he saw me... what sort of person was I, in his eyes. He said happy, confident, successful. Then she asked how he saw himself. He answered – all the opposite, a failure, unhappy.

She drew a see-saw, tipped so it touched the ground on one side, with the other side high up in the air. She asked him to say where he saw himself on the see-saw. He indicated that he was the one at the bottom and where he saw me was up in the air. Then she asked him, when he eventually had me in tears, where did he see us then? He said he was high in the air and I was at the bottom. She asked how long it felt like that and he said seconds. And that then we were both at the bottom.

I was fascinated and hooked by the whole counselling experience and it was the start of my deep interest in psychology.

―――――――――

Christmas 1982. It was the most surreal moment when finally it came. The man who'd been with me since 1962, when I was 14, was leaving. Leaving me and our children and leaving our home. Claire moved out the same year. For Roy and me, it was to be an official separation leading to divorce two years later. I was 34 years old and we'd been together for 20 years. Some of those years had been happy, very happy. Roy was, at heart, a salesman and as such, had a natural, easy, chatty charm. He was funny – he often made me laugh prior to these later years.

I remember him often having a joke at my expense, which I didn't mind at all, in fact it still makes me chuckle. He would say things like: '*My wife's like an oil painting – best seen from a distance!*'

Some of those 20 years, though, had been far from perfect. Our marriage had finally broken down beyond repair, and we were both deeply unhappy. We both knew that things had been severely broken for the previous three years but neither of us wanted to make the big break. Although we both knew we had come to the end, it's a hell of a decision – for anyone. When I took those vows at 16, I meant them. I believe they meant something to Roy then too.

I'd look back to our early days together, remembering things like our little honeymoon – nothing more than a walk hand-in-hand around Nottingham market. We were so happy. And I wondered again, where had the love gone? I suppose it was still there, a little bit, not yet completely dead, not yet finally buried, but too far gone to ever be resuscitated. I cried every day, quietly, secretly, for the next two years. Then came the decree nisi and the announcement that Roy was to remarry. I never cried a single day more.

―――――――――

I'd been divorced from Roy for two years when the next big shift in my family life came along. My father had been suffering from emphysema for years, the result of smoking and a lifetime down the coal mines. The authorities denied it was anything to do with the coal dust and so refused him compensation. Dad was also suffering from prostate cancer.

I used to pop in every day on my way to work to see him and Mum, who were still living in the same house on Hilcote Street, my childhood home. Everything seemed reasonably OK, but my daily 10 minutes wasn't enough time to notice that my mum was starting to suffer from Alzheimer's.

At Christmas time in 1985, they came to stay with me for their usual two-week 'holiday' and finally, my dad spoke up about how they were living. For a few years, I'd been asking Mum to sell their house and let me make them a granny flat at our house, so they could come and live with us. She refused even to bring up the subject with my dad, saying he would never want to leave Hilcote Street. This made sense, because I knew he had a deep attachment to the house. I'd often been told how, as a boy, he'd held a candle for its builder and swore to himself that one day, he would own it.

This Christmas he said he didn't want to go home. He told me my mum was forgetting to feed him and he wanted to live with me. I was stunned but relieved that he felt this way and of course shocked to find that he'd been going hungry – and that I'd missed the signs during my daily visits. Did I feel guilty? Is the Pope Catholic?

Unable to convert the adjoining stables fast enough to create the granny flat I'd imagined, I had to quickly create something for them – their own space, within the house, in a way that gave them privacy but enabled me to keep an eye on them. We had that place. It had been a large utility room and toilet on the ground floor, next to the kitchen. With a little redesign, I was able to shrink the utility to a small space housing a few cupboards and the boiler.

I made the new room, their room, really cosy, with a fire, a TV, two comfy armchairs and a spare chair for visitors, a bed with built-in hanging space for their few clothes, and in the toilet, I added a shower. With their door open while they were up and about, I could see them from the kitchen and keep a closer eye on them when I was back from work. During the day, so could our housekeeper, who also made sure they had cups of tea and regular meals.

Dad's health was getting worse and worse. He was getting weaker and could hardly walk to the garden due to shortness of breath. He was under the care of the local hospital and whenever I took him there, it was such an ordeal for him. Even in a wheelchair, waiting around for hours was difficult. I realised that the care he'd been receiving wasn't up to scratch. While the hospital Resident assured me that the Consultant was fully aware of Dad's case and supervised it, I discovered that in fact, he hadn't been seen by the Consultant for years. I was furious on his behalf.

Dad was a staunch socialist. He often recalled being at gatherings in his youth, when prominent Labour politicians had spoken passionately about the plight of the working classes. He was particularly impressed with Aneurin Bevan, often known as Nye Bevan, a Welsh Labour Party politician and the Minister for Health in the UK from 1945 to 1951, who spearheaded the foundation of the NHS. The son of a coal miner, Bevan was a lifelong champion of social justice, the rights of working people and democratic socialism. Dad was a firm believer in the NHS and refused to pay (or let me pay) to 'go private'. I understood absolutely. The gap between rich and poor had been shocking when he was a boy during those early years of the 20th century.

One of the funniest things Dad ever said to me (before the Scargill years) was: *'There's only one way you've ever disappointed me, Margaret. YOU WON'T VOTE LABOUR!'* I burst out laughing, but wow – my dad was disappointed in me! This was *my dad*, for whom

I could do no wrong! He loved me to bits. He never said so, but he didn't need to. It was obvious. I always felt his love, unmistakably. He really was the most caring, sincere and open man you could hope to meet. I was so lucky that he took me into his heart and made me his one and only daughter. His 'disappointment' that I didn't align myself with the Labour government of the day made me love him even more, if that were possible.

Eventually, the lengthy hospital visits were causing Dad so much discomfort that he agreed to let me fund a private consultation. I made the appointment immediately.

We parked directly outside the small private clinic. What a contrast. Dad was seated in a comfortable armchair in the cosy waiting room for no more than five minutes before we were called in. The very same Consultant who was reportedly supervising my dad's case changed his medication immediately. Apparently, the medication he was being given for his slow-growing prostate tumour was creating fluid in his blood and putting a massive strain on his heart, which was having to work extra hard to pump it all around. The Consultant said it would never be the cancer that killed him. I think he gave my dad several more months of life, as his health improved quite quickly then.

Dad died at 11am on 11th December 1986. His death nearly coincided with his birthday, but was a month out. Dad was born on 11th November 1903, a date itself almost coinciding with the date of Armistice Day, 1918 – the 11th hour of the 11th day of the 11th month. He went into heart failure on the night of 10th December, when all we could get was a locum doctor to come and see him.

The locum went away telling me that Dad was suffering acute heart failure and to contact our family doctor the next day. Dr Peter Bakaj was our family doctor – a wonderful man, who had become a family friend. He gently explained to me on that December morning what was happening and what would happen in the next few hours. My dad – my wonderful, long-suffering dad – was about to die.

Embarrassed, I confessed I was afraid. My only experience of death had been in a hospital, when my father-in-law was dying of lung cancer and the gurgling sounds of near death had been alarming. I wasn't there at the moment of his death – just an hour or so before. This time it was my beloved dad and I was to be alone with him and my mum, who was no longer living in the here and now.

Peter Bakaj talked me through it. He said there would be no drama. He gave me medicine to give Dad when the next painful attack hit him. Just one spoonful. He said it would make his death pain-free and very peaceful. He explained that his breathing would be even, sometimes with a little pause. The pauses would get longer. Then one of the pauses would be forever.

It happened in exactly that way.

66 *I know for certain that we never lose the people we love, even to death. They continue to participate in every act, thought and decision we make. Their love leaves an indelible imprint on our memories.* 99

CHAPTER EIGHT

the end of one era, and the start of another

The full reality of Mum's Alzheimer's became even more obvious once my dad was no longer by her side. There are so many tragic, funny, frightening and difficult times when you're caring for someone with this disease, I would have to write another book if I gave you all the details.

Suffice to say, you still have your loved one with you – but they aren't *really* there any more. I had to get a nurse to stay with Mum while I was at work, but night times and early mornings were down to me. With double incontinence combined with an inability to think through what was happening, my mum would get into quite a mess during the night. I didn't want anyone to have to deal with all of that, so it would be me who'd strip the bed, clean up the room, shower my mum (while she tried to fight me off), and finally have everything ship-shape by the time the nurse arrived at 10am every day. The 30-minute drive to work was much-needed time to relax and get ready to start on my daily work at Slimming World, in a job I still loved.

In spite of all the stresses and strains in my home life at this time, Slimming World was doing well. We had over 800 groups, with an average of around 30 to 35 members per group, overtaking our competitors *Slimming Magazine* and *Silhouette*. Some groups had many more members, of course, and some had far fewer, depending on the time of year. Although we weren't going at a rate of knots, we were doing OK and growing steadily.

What *wasn't* ticking along nicely was the relationship between Pauline and me, which had had its ups and downs since she came into the business as my partner in 1971. Pauline could be a superb people-person – a real hoot, witty, funny, fast-thinking, charismatic and quick to spot a PR opportunity. However, we strongly disagreed on some fundamental business decisions and those disagreements were growing more frequent and more hostile.

She believed that the way to grow Slimming World was to pour a lot of money into newspapers and national advertising – whereas I believed that the most important thing of all was getting the service to members right, and that advertising was more cost-effective when placed in *local* newspapers. The main responsibility for local promotion should be in the hands of our self-employed Consultants. National advertising was just not cost-effective at all. We had proved that. We had tested it out. The results were crystal clear.

Despite this, it remained a bone of contention – among other things. On top of these disagreements, Pauline told me that running two (very different) businesses side-by-side – Slimming World and the Miles-Paley Design Studio – was causing her a lot of stress. I'd heard prior to this that Pauline had contacted a bank to see if she could borrow money to buy me out but hadn't been able to secure a loan. So I knew that she, too, was unhappy with our relationship.

Eventually, in 1982, she suggested that one of us should manage the Miles-Paley Design Studio, while the other concentrated solely on Slimming World. We'd retain equal shares in both businesses. I asked Pauline to choose which business she wanted to run. She chose Slimming World.

Hard as it might be to comprehend, after 13 years of pouring blood, sweat and tears into a business I'd built from scratch, I relinquished executive control to Pauline. I believed in the design business and

I was more than up for the six-day week, the challenges and the long hours that came with it. I'm quite a visual person, I love beautiful design and I was quite happy to take on this newer challenge.

And I thought that because all was set up and running pretty smoothly, Slimming World would tick along whoever was in charge. My goodness, when I get it wrong, I really do get it wrong! All mistakes can become great learning points and this became one of the greatest learning points of my life.

Four years passed, during which time I had no involvement with the day-to-day running of Slimming World – at times very hard to bear. Pauline got on with things in her way and I got on with things in my way.

Carlines was our accountancy firm at the time. It was a visit from one of their accountants, Adrian van Daesdonk, that changed everything. Adrian wasn't like your typical accountant. He was more like a salesman – very outgoing and confident.

He came into the design studio to see me many times, directly after meetings with Pauline (the Slimming World offices were just across the road). One day, after a spell of almost daily visits to Pauline at the Slimming World offices, he told me that something had to be done. Matters were getting serious. He told me – quite candidly – that he was extremely worried and added: *'Pauline's desperate for you to come back to Slimming World.'*

Knowing, as I did, that we'd stopped co-managing the company for good reason, I explained to Adrian that I couldn't go back and work with Pauline, who had let me know over the years that she didn't really like Slimming World. She saw it as making money from other people's misery, which to me was a very back-to-front, upside-down way to see it. We made money by helping people find a way *out* of the misery, giving them the knowledge and support to live a much happier, healthier life. When I asked if she felt that way about doctors, physicians and surgeons making money out of sick people, she thought the analogy absurd. Yes, Pauline and I were miles apart in our thinking, possibly always had been, and maybe only now, after all these years, was it was becoming screamingly obvious.

A few days earlier, Pauline herself had called me to say that everything was coming to a head and that in two weeks, in February 1986, when the next VAT demand came in, we wouldn't be able to pay it. We would have to close down Slimming World.

Adrian was right, something had to be done. The number of groups had fallen from more than 800 in 1982 down to around 200 by February 1986 and the average group size was down to just 12 members. Drastic action was required – immediately – and Adrian was the one to catalyse me into taking it.

I knew I couldn't work with Pauline again. The only way I could come back to Slimming World was if I could buy her out – but after the expensive divorce from Roy (I'd hung on to the house by remortgaging it), I simply had no capital. Although Claire had by now left home, I still had two school-aged boys at home to feed and clothe (and the rest!) with no maintenance coming from their dad. For me, no big deal. I knew how to be very careful with money and I simply cut my coat according to my cloth.

But raising *more* to buy Pauline out? My goose, as I saw it, was cooked. Who would lend me that sort of money? I've never liked borrowing money, but I knew I had to save Slimming World, come hell or high water. There was no way I could sit back and watch it all slip away. It was my baby and I would save it at all costs. *'I think a bank manager would lend you the money to buy the business back – if Pauline would be willing to sell her share,'* Adrian told me. *'I think they'd be willing to back you, I really do.'*

Adrian offered to value the business to set a fair figure. The debts were greater than the assets and we were about to be declared insolvent. No need to waste more money doing a futile valuation, I told him.

Instead I settled on a figure in my head – £50,000 – an offer that Pauline would recognise as very, very generous. All along, I prayed that Adrian was right and I could raise the money. Carlines prepared a business plan for me to take along to the bank. Nick Murphin, our Barclays bank manager at the time in Chesterfield, glanced briefly at one page, before closing the business plan, leaning back in his chair and saying: *'Talk to me.'* So I did.

To my immense surprise, he said: *'I'm going to lend you £45,000.'* It was a huge leap of faith and I'll be forever indebted to him for his belief in me as a person, and in Slimming World as a business. If it hadn't been for Nick Murphin, we wouldn't have a Slimming World today.

It was the last time I ever saw Adrian, as he left Carlines shortly afterwards under difficult circumstances which I won't go into here.

Carlines sent us a new accountant in his place, in the shape of a young David Rathbone – who is, today, Slimming World's Director of Finance.

I think it was Jan Boxshall, now Slimming World's Joint Managing Director, who once described David as 'the least finance director-y finance director' she'd ever met – and if you've ever had the pleasure of seeing him play the dame in the local pantomime (which he does each year), or heard him performing energetically in Slimming World's own band (they perform every year at our Christmas party), you'll know exactly what she meant!

This certainly wasn't my first impression back in '84! After the laid-back Adrian, David came across as very stiff and formal. I'd become accustomed to Adrian's relaxed, open approach, so I was most put out when the firm sent David in his place. I think it's fair to say I was pretty horrible to David at first. I wasn't happy about Adrian's disappearance, and I wouldn't let it drop.

The more I challenged David, the more defensive he became – and the more defensive he became, the more I challenged him. Eventually, one day, he gave up the fight and stopped trying to defend the indefensible. From then on, we were able to build a relationship that I believe both of us will always treasure.

£45,000, then, was the amount that the bank was going to provide. If Pauline accepted my offer of £50,000, this left me with a shortfall to find – but from where? Out of thin air? I was up to my neck with the mortgage, the bank manager had lent me all he could and none of my friends or relatives had money. The only person I could think of who might lend me the money was Harry – my birth father.

Harry had been coming to stay with us for four days a year, every year, since Roy and I bought our first house, when I was just 17. As I've told you and I'm sure you can imagine, we were quite skint. He told me then that I didn't need to worry about money because he was going to leave me all his money in his will. At the time, this struck me as a pretty daft thing to say to someone who was living hand-to-mouth, day-to-day. As if I could defer getting a job and earning money on the promise of an inheritance that was likely to be years if not decades away! Even if it turned out to be true, what were we going to survive on for the next 40 years?

Fast-forward to 1986 and Harry's promise of a substantial inheritance suddenly held a different significance! I rang him and asked if he'd lend me £5,000. Deep down, I think I must have hoped he'd simply give me the money. He had never spent a penny on my upbringing yet on his visits for his annual 'holiday', he liked to tell people that I was his daughter, which, not surprisingly, offended me greatly.

He didn't give me the money but he did lend it to me. Every couple of weeks, he'd ring me and ask when he'd see his £5,000 again – so as soon as I was able to gather the money, I paid him back. I found it all quite humiliating. The bank manager had been more generous and put more faith in me than my biological father.

So on a Friday in February 1986, I made the offer in writing. I knew it was over-generous and I thought Pauline would know that too. To demonstrate that it was – and to allay any possible distrust in my 'valuation' – I said if she offered the same to me, I would take it. I hoped that would stop any delay and prevent the extra cost of having Slimming World officially valued. I put a time limit on the offer, giving her the weekend to mull it over with her husband, but I wanted an answer by Monday or the offer was gone.

Of course, it was ridiculously generous – so it was no surprise, but still a relief, when Pauline accepted. I also thought it would mitigate any ill will she might feel towards me for effectively divorcing her as my co-director, as I would have liked to continue our friendship now that our prickly business relationship was over. Unfortunately she refused to come to the phone, or acknowledge my letters, and we've had no contact since that Friday in February 1986. I remain sad about that to this day.

———————

If I thought I was energised back in 1969, the surge of adrenalin-fuelled electricity that coursed through me now beat it hands down. In February 1986, with new eyes, a load more experience, and learning and training under my belt, I proceeded to pick Slimming World up from rock bottom, dust it off and start all over again. My motivation was mighty powerful – after all, I'd gambled everything on my own ability to succeed. My home, my family – my life – depended on it.

Slimming World's culture – which had once burned so brightly – had effectively fizzled out. Managers, Consultants and office staff had come to believe that the era of the slimming club was over. That's when I realised, for the first time, that the life had been choked out of this once exciting company.

I was horrified. How had the passionate spirit been crushed to this degree? My heart sank at the realisation that *my* Slimming World had virtually disappeared. It was almost unrecognisable. Where had the vision gone? Where had the joy gone? Where had the life gone? Once again, I found myself asking, where had the love gone? Where was that get-up-and-go? Well, it had got up and gone!

A realistic and positive belief system has to come from the heart of the company. It hadn't been there for years, so our wonderful managers and therefore our Consultants and our office staff had been led into thinking that our demise was inevitable. The kinder ones among them felt sorry for me, that I had taken on an 'obviously' impossible task. The less kind and more forthright told me to my face that I was out of touch. Who, me?

'Oh dear, what a shame, slimming clubs have had their day.'

In spite of all this, embers of the brand I'd worked so hard to create still flickered at the heart of the company. The severely dampened fire just needed someone to inject some oxygen and it needed to be blown on well and urgently!

I mean, how could anyone believe that being overweight was not a major problem in desperate need of a solution? And a problem that was getting even bigger, if you'll excuse the pun. How could anyone doubt how desperately people needed our help – so many people, so many lives, so much illness, so much unhappiness and a major challenge for the country? The United Kingdom was fast becoming the most unhealthy country in Europe, with an increasing obesity epidemic. The cost to the health service was escalating at an alarming rate. How could anyone think the fight was over? It had barely started!

It's amazing how negativity takes root so fast, isn't it? Think about the gossips who just love to spread it, and exaggerate the issues to entertain and gain an attentive audience. Think about how some journalists seem to love putting down the positive attitudes that bring success – and jobs – to thousands. Anyone would think they'd rather enjoy seeing failure instead. Is it a British disease to despise those who build up rather than tear down?

Well, whatever the philosophy, whatever the psychology, I was angry! Anger, I find, produces energy. I wanted to shake everyone awake and snap them out of the fantasy. I wanted to scream at everyone! I didn't, of course. I'm much too well brought up to do that! And a wise person once said, you can catch more flies with honey than you can with vinegar.

With my (sometimes) strange sense of humour, I also rather like the alternative theory that you can achieve more with a kind word and a gun, than with a kind word alone. I used to think it was Al Capone who came up with that one, but I've since learned it was just a line of Robert de Niro's script when he played Al Capone in *The Untouchables*. No matter, I thought the concept was funny and it made me smile.

I used everything I could think of to cause the earthquake that would shake the foundations of this broken structure. Humour was definitely a big part of that. I knew that any training I'd ever had was made far more understandable, persuasive and memorable when it was lifted and strengthened with humour. And boy oh boy, what an amazing thrill it was for me to be able to reignite those flames. The thought makes my hair stand on end as I write about it. Even the memory gives me goose pimples.

There's no other way to put it – I was manic. My life, my ability to support my family and pay my mortgage were all resting on me being successful (no pressure there then!). It drove me beyond normal human behaviour. My vision – of what needed to happen and how – was so crystal clear that I became completely obsessive and oh, so very happy. I was driven. Can you feel it?

Reminds me of another *Queen* song, *'Don't Stop Me Now'*. You could have called me *Mrs* Farenheit!

I knew I had to distil all my learning, my passion and my experience into a trainable resource that would inspire and guide. It was all about helping Consultants give their members a service so full, so fantastic, that we would turn the weight loss world inside out and we could all *float around in ecstasy.* I wanted every Consultant to be that *shooting star leaping through the sky*, helping every member *defy the laws of gravity!*

Where to start? How to get every corner of the company feeling this new breath, this new wind of change that was blowing right now, through the office and out into the whole of the UK?

First off, I decided I'd write a training manual – a one-stop shop of Slimming World information and best practice. This manual would reinforce the face-to-face training I was giving. It would help our Consultants master the art of group therapy – Slimming World style – which I renamed and rebranded from 'individual attention' to IMAGE Therapy (an acronym for Individual Motivation And Group Experience). I called my manual *'Secrets of Success'.*

During my time away from Slimming World, I'd picked up an adage which really stuck with me – *'If it can't be written down then it can't be trained.'* So as part of the process of writing *Secrets of Success*, I thought long and hard about how real-world conversations with members tend to go in group. I identified traps that could skew the process and make it less effective. And I identified what would be needed by every member who was genuinely doing their level best to change those dangerous habits that were causing problems to their weight, health and self-esteem.

Secrets of Success, in a nutshell, was about creating a framework for great IMAGE Therapy. Because IMAGE Therapy is (and always has been) at the heart of successful, lifelong weight loss – helping members to feel better about themselves, to think about the reasons they personally struggle with their weight, and to make positive steps forward – even when the going gets tough.

If you've ever experienced the magic yourself, you'll know how powerful an hour in a Slimming World group can be. The time goes sooo fast – you're never bored! The Consultant listens – really listens

– to what each member tells them. They cleverly, warmly and subtly keep it pacy, giving every member just the right level of help they need. And they move the conversation on if one or two members get into a lengthy 'confessional' (details of every meal or a blow-by-blow account of a bad day) to avoid a dangerously negative use of precious IMAGE Therapy time.

You leave really believing in yourself (even if you walked in to the room with the weight of the world on your shoulders). Your Consultant, and the other members of the group, help you to make your own plan for your path to success – and you walk out of the group floating on a cloud of excitement for the week to come. With a plan – your own, tailored plan, made by you – you know exactly how you're going to avoid every pitfall and sneaky trapdoor that may come along to scupper your weight loss. You think deeply about your own personal trigger foods, danger zones and sabotage traps, raising them sky high in your awareness so you're better able to deal with them. This will be your best week ever!

The process of writing *Secrets of Success* allowed me to think through every aspect of IMAGE Therapy as a process, to make sure it was delivered in a truly inclusive, welcoming and supportive way – in every group, with every member, every week. It gave me the chance to show every Consultant how to ask penetrating open questions, give them tips on how to be great listeners, how to lift members to a lighter side with some gentle humour and how to encourage every member to make a plan – a foolproof plan – for the coming week.

IMAGE Therapy was, and still is, at the heart of *Secrets of Success*. It's not easy training to deliver – nor is it easy for trainees to grasp. But if it were easy, anyone could do it. It's a skill base that has taken years to develop and it was such a labour of love for me. Clarity in communication was everything. There could be no room for misunderstanding.

Of course, none of this great IMAGE Therapy knowledge was any use to our Consultants unless they had a vibrant, buzzing group of members to help. And to build such a group, they needed to become a bit of a whizz at something else – promotion in their local community. So *Secrets of Success* tackled this subject too, in great detail, alongside an array of other chapters covering everything from the nutrition thinking behind our eating plan to recruiting a great social team to help out in group, dealing with the 'business' side of things – stock control, banking, etc.

I wrote everything in a deliberately down-to-earth, relatable way that I hoped and prayed would motivate and inspire our Consultants. There was a light touch of humour here and there, there was compassion and understanding, and there was real, from-the-heart love for helping people lose weight. I still aim, always, to make my words real and resonant – particularly in my *From The Heart* letters and articles in *Slimming World Magazine* (and I've added some of our favourites at the end of this book, so you can be ze judge!). Hopefully my words within this book resonate too!

To complete *Secrets of Success* alongside my day-to-day work at the office, I'd get home early enough, as often as possible, to spend a couple of hours with Dom and Ben, who were 9 and 6 respectively (Claire was now 22 years old and living in her own place), then I'd hit my typewriter from 10pm and hammer away for two or three hours, well into the wee small hours. I never tired of this task. I loved creating something that I thought would be so worthwhile. But I couldn't resist tinkering. I'd get myself bogged down reworking the same few chapters over and over, never satisfied, always thinking I could do more, give more, do better, and after about a year of this, it hit me that the only person *Secrets of Success* was stimulating, inspiring and motivating was me!

Seeking perfection with something so close to your heart is always going to be not just elusive but impossible. Was it Mark Zuckerberg who said: *'Done is better than perfect'*? Seemed to work for Facebook. So, in all its 'imperfect' glory, I finally allowed myself to stop writing and to publish *Secrets of Success* – and be damned! What I'd started in 1986 was finally given to Slimming World 15 months later in 1987.

I wanted – needed – everyone in Slimming World to see what was in my head and feel what was in my heart. This manual was one way I could make that happen.

Today, *Secrets of Success* lives on – not as 100 typewritten sheets, but as full-to-bursting, ever-evolving, professionally designed and printed manuals. It's affectionately referred to by Consultants and Head Office staff as 'The Bible'.

And yes, it made a difference. Hallelujah!

Consumed by my intense, innate, intuitive feeling of how Slimming World should 'be', 1986 was also the year I learned about something called 'brand'. To create a brand, a successful brand, I soon discovered that I was the one, the only one, who could define what that brand should be. In 1986, there was no one else who had the clarity of vision, the purpose, the philosophy, and the belief. Indeed, in February 1986 I discovered, as I mentioned earlier, I was completely alone in that belief. Everyone else had lost theirs during the four-year period I hadn't been running Slimming World and some, as I've said, were quick to tell me I was out of touch.

I'd been thinking about giving Slimming World a new image for some time. I knew this would need to be far more than a new logo and new stationery (although they'd be needed as part of the package). The 'branding' process went deeper than that. It was about defining, officially, who we are – and weaving that through absolutely every part of our existence.

I began working with a young and trendy local designer called Michael Fisher, who ran a little design company on Newgate Lane in Mansfield, called the Design Works. It was owned by Linney

– then a printing house, now a world-class, multi-channel marketing services group.

Michael was fantastic. I loved him to bits, although I didn't like the first logos he came up with. They were uninspiring and, to me, didn't capture the spirit of Slimming World. I was passionate about design, about stylish, modern, elegant design and beautiful, aspirational images that work to enhance our visual brand. I wasn't so dusty in the creative department, although I say so myself. Once Michael 'got' that, we were away.

He presented me with idea after idea for Slimming World's new identity. I rejected all of them! It wasn't until a holiday to America and a trip to the Kennedy Space Centre that I finally found the inspiration I was looking for. I loved how ultra, ultra-modern the place was – the planets, the orbits, the pared-back design was so cutting edge and exciting. When I raved about it all to Michael, especially the image of the orbit, he got it, got me and got Slimming World. What he did with that idea, and how he used it in the design of our logo, was spectacular.

Michael had a rare understanding and a major creative talent for weaving feeling and emotion through his work. He ran the Design Works like it was his own little company and he'd generously share with me a lot of his vast knowledge about how companies build, develop and protect their brands. I loved our chats. He really broadened my knowledge of what companies with money could do – and I realised that we could do some of those things too, albeit on a smaller scale (no money in the pot just yet).

What Michael helped me to realise was that Slimming World's 'brand' could include far more than its visual identity. The 'brand', if used well, could demonstrate everything we stand for – all our values, our sense of fun, compassion and warmth; things that couldn't easily be written, quantified or trained, but that were (and still are) the DNA of our company culture, at both Head Office and 'out there' in the field. All this could be included in what was termed 'the brand' and could touch every part of every communication, even our internal memos! That bit was an eye-opener. I immediately let members of staff know that I wanted all internal letters and memos to contain warmth and humour, no matter what the subject.

I've lost count of the number of times people through the years have asked me: *'Why don't you just sell up and cash in?'* – and that's because the beating heart of Slimming World could so easily stop dead if we went public (I don't think my beating heart could survive that either!). The 'brand' and our precious culture would be held on to only in a superficial way and decisions would be made to appease profit-focused shareholders. That's not who we are – and our succession planning ensures it's never who we will be. (I reserve the right to haunt Head Office in 100 years' time if I see otherwise. And I think I'd be a tough one to exorcise!)

Our strapline may have changed a few times over the years – from 'the club that cares' to 'because you're amazing' through to our current 'touching hearts, changing lives'. The sentiment behind it and the 'brand' itself, however, never changes – Slimming World exists to help members achieve their dreams in a warm, supportive, positive way; in a way that helps them not just to lose weight, but to make permanent changes to their thoughts, feelings and actions around food and drink. That's why, today, you won't hear anyone at Slimming World utter the word 'diet'.

We are so much more than this.

> **“** *You cannot soar with the eagles as long as you hang out with the turkeys.* **”**
>
> Joel Osteen

CHAPTER NINE

rebuilding the cathedral

Generosity is at the heart of the Slimming World brand. Our eating plan is generous – in its design, its freedom and its flexibility. Our Consultants are generous to members – going above and beyond to run truly great groups and show genuine care to every member. Our members are, in turn, generous to each other – in the support and care they show to each other.

I've always wanted our employees and Consultants to be generously rewarded for what they do – sometimes to a fault on my part.

So it won't surprise you that, in spite of dire warnings from people about spending money I didn't have, 1986 was also the year that I took 10 Consultants to Florida as part of our very first annual performance-based competition, now known as the Grand Accumulator. I wanted to knock everyone's socks off – to show Consultants all over the country how much we valued them running their individual franchises *just as they'd been trained.*

There was (and still is) nothing complex about the Grand Accumulator. It was all about earning points and bonuses for things like welcoming lots of new members (demonstrating that you'd done a great community promotion), Consultant recruitment (so often simply the result of demonstrating your personal passion for the role) and gaining editorials in the local papers.

Again, it was about generating a wind of change. I wanted every person to be blown away by it, no matter who they were or how many groups they ran. I needed to breathe vitality, positivity and belief back into the company – and I wasn't afraid to use bold (outrageous, even) methods to achieve that end.

Having seen with my own eyes the consequences of diabolical negativity, a war on negativity became a hallmark of my management from then on.

'NEG SPRAY' was just one of my little inventions. At management meetings, on my desk, so that everyone could see it, I'd place a bucket and one of those supersized cans of hairspray – with a new label, 'NEG SPRAY', stuck over the brand name.

You've probably come across the kind of people who think they're being 'realistic' when in fact they're being negative. Their minds are closed and they shut down new ideas and suggestions before they've seen the light of day. Maybe you're aware that you do this yourself (even the best of us have fallen foul at one time or another!). My simple definition of negativity was that you could only criticise an idea if you had a better one to put in its place.

And coming back into Slimming World in 1986, I had to find ways to make an impactful but light-hearted stand against any sort of negativity and pessimism. So, if the conversation in meetings turned negative, a threatened blast of 'NEG SPRAY' did just the trick – everyone would laugh and after each putting a coin in the bucket for charity, we'd move on with fresh, constructive attitudes.

And attitude, I believe, does count for so much – almost everything.

Have you heard the story about the fleas and the Bunsen burner? I first came across it in the early '80s, as part of some sales training I went on in London during my time running the Miles-Paley Design Studio.

Put some fleas in a glass jar. Fleas, as you know, are amazing jumpers, so they quickly jump out of the jar. However, screw a lid on the jar and the fleas soon learn not to jump so high. They don't like bashing into the lid. After a while you can remove the lid and they have learned not to jump too high and they stay at this more limited level, within the jar, without a lid.

So how do you get the fleas jumping higher again? You put a Bunsen burner under the jar!

I'd retell this story to my teams and, with a glint in my eye, I would say, *'...And I am your Bunsen burner!'*

The story is really about artificial ceilings.

When Roger Bannister, the famous athlete, removed the artificial ceiling of the belief that it was impossible to run a mile in less than four minutes, many more people did it within the following year.

The flea and the Roger Bannister stories are both fascinating and relevant – but the short and sweet story of the stonemasons struck a much more powerful and emotional chord for me:

One day, a young man was walking along the road when he came across a stonemason carving a piece of stone.

'Good morning,' said the young man, 'what are you doing?'

'I'm carving this stone,' said the stonemason.

The young man continued on his way and shortly came across another stonemason working another piece of stone.

'Good morning,' said the young man, 'what are you doing?'

The stonemason looked up and, with shining eyes, said:

'I'm building a cathedral!'

Powerful stuff, isn't it?

Ever since those transformative days of the late 1980s, I've never questioned the importance of recruiting positive, ambitious people into Slimming World – people who soak up every ounce of our culture, take it into their hearts and minds and support their teams to do the same.

People like our treasured Sheila Hall. People like this don't come along every day. In fact, as anyone in any Human Resources department anywhere will testify, they're incredibly hard to find, and even harder to keep hold of.

Despite this, I've never been satisfied to settle for someone with less-than-ideal personal qualities – no matter how qualified or experienced they may be. As Slimming World forged ahead towards the 1990s, we needed the very best people – both at Head Office and working with Sheila in the field. Until we had them in place at every level, I felt that I was, once again, alone.

By the end of 1986 I knew, more than anything else, that we needed emotionally intelligent, talented people to form our management, the core of our company. People who would be committed to our culture, who would walk the walk, not just talk the talk, and who would be as unwilling as I was to give an inch on my dreams – or that powerful, beating heart of the Slimming World brand.

By 1987 – just a year after I'd taken back the reins – Slimming World was on the road to recovery. We were growing again, by around 40% in a year, and I was on a roll.

Back in the days when Pauline and I were co-running the company, I'd always wanted to drive our core messages across the whole field by hosting management meetings and special days for our Consultants. Pauline had objected strongly – she'd told me she felt embarrassed standing up in front of everyone. Nor did she want to be absent and let me host these sessions, in case people thought I was the only one running the company.

For me, because I knew that those core messages were being diluted and distorted between layers of managers out in the field, where it mattered so much, this was an urgent and necessary step.

Today, thanks to the digital revolution that's taken place during these last 50 years, we have so many ways we can get our messages out there to our teams – emails, videos, websites for members, websites for Consultants, social media, WhatsApp, SMS messages – plus we have a dedicated training team that's second to none.

In the '70s and '80s, some of these things were either in their infancy or simply not invented! So to communicate those vital training messages, I needed to be able to speak, face-to-face, to as many Consultants and managers as possible.

It was horrifying to find that our deliberately simple and minimal rules were being adjusted, added to and compromised, that our care and compassion was being ground to dust, and that the eating plan was being undermined. All over the country, I was finding a dangerous tendency for managers, Consultants (and members) to make up their own rules. So much so that I found groups were being run in a way that made them unrecognisable as Slimming World groups.

Our brand, that brand I'd worked so hard to create, was being eroded and effectively destroyed. It was amazing that Slimming World was still holding its own, and I was deeply upset by it.

I found so many things, from small distortions to huge ones – ranging from managers who loved exerting control in an aggressive way to Consultants who thought Free Food should be limited, weighed and measured (a complete contradiction to the concept of unlimited 'Free' Food). Left unchecked, this would have inevitably led to a distortion of our methods and undermined belief in the *real* Slimming World way, whether it was around the eating plan, our management philosophy, the way we ran our groups or, all too often, a car crash of all three and more.

Of course, this resulted in some disappointed, angry members and Consultants and I didn't blame them – because they weren't getting the treatment I so sincerely promised and they deserved. For me, this problem had to be addressed head-on and without delay – because our reputation, our service, our lives and livelihoods depended on the Slimming World brand being clear, strong and honest. It's why we work so hard to maintain our standards today. We are constantly vigilant. We are never out of the danger zone and I don't imagine, for one minute, that we ever will be.

In '87, I was free to do exactly what I felt and knew was right – no one to have to convince, no one to argue with! The sense of liberation was delicious; a bit like the thrill of driving a car for the first time after passing your driving test. Just you, the steering wheel and the road ahead. No one to tell you what to do or where to go. Foot on the pedal and off you go. Talk about exhilarating!

It wasn't long, however, before I met my first roadblock.

One of the many issues following years away from the day-to-day running of Slimming World was that I hadn't had any influence on the selection, recruitment and training of our regional managers. Many of the best people had left the company. Those who remained, like Sheila, had very often stepped bravely and nervously into the breach.

They had also been persuaded that they wouldn't, they couldn't, be effective – after all, the days of the slimming club were over, weren't they? Added to that, their skills lay elsewhere than management. Everyone did their best but they were completely inexperienced and untrained to deal with the challenges of that high-pressure and somewhat lonely position. Quite frankly, we were in a mess.

I'm a great believer in well-structured management. When there's belief, passion and a clear focus at the heart, it spreads through to everyone in a team, department or company. Back at the tender age of 23, as I signed the mortgage papers for our first office, I suppose I thought that 'management' would be about employing staff, divvying up the day-to-day jobs and (easily) finding like-minded individuals to help me with the task of training and supporting Consultants out in the field. Oh, how much I had to learn!

The learning curve grew steeply from day one. I'd need to motivate, to inspire, to hire, sometimes to fire. I'd need to become an expert at reading between the lines. I'd need to address people-problems – clashes of personality, lateness, absence, even deceit. Management, I realised very quickly, was as deadly difficult as it was incredibly important.

Once again, alongside plenty of on-the-job trial and error, so often the library was my educator. Favourite books were those that contained simple, instantly useful pieces of advice on things like delegation or goal-setting, for example, *The One Minute Manager* by Ken Blanchard. I also delved into the more heavyweight authors like Peter Drucker, with his concept of management by objectives, McKinsey with the Pyramid Principle and the importance of structured thinking and communication, and John Adair with his Action-Centred Leadership model. If you've never come across it, it's a simple and incredibly effective approach to management, characterised by three overlapping circles which represent the needs of the team, the individual and the task to be achieved – the idea being that in good management, these sets of needs are met equally.

I can't put names to all the authors I found personally motivating, but I know that many of the more inspirational books were by American business people, and I admired their ethical approaches to super-charging teams and individuals. I remember the feelings they stirred within me, as all great messages do. They gave me the confidence I needed to know that, despite those inevitable mistakes, I was getting a lot more right than I was getting wrong. As the leader of the company, I needed this feedback, because I could be my own harshest critic.

Then I found Eric Berne (not literally as the world sadly lost him in 1970) – at a monthly conference of the East Midlands Businesswomen's Association. One of the members, a professional trainer, was giving a fascinating talk on Berne's theory of Transactional Analysis (TA).

TA is a psychological theory and therapeutic technique that businesses can use to aid effective communication and forge positive working relationships. It does this by helping us to understand why we behave in the way we do – and why other people behave in the way *they* do. It helps us realise that we can change our behaviour to achieve a different response.

Put at its simplest, Transactional Analysis is founded on the premise that we all flit between three basic 'ego states' (based on the work of Sigmund Freud) when we interact with other people – parent-like, child-like or adult-like. The adult 'us' is calm, rational and unemotional (think Mr Spock from *Star Trek*!). The parental 'us' can be either critical or nurturing. The child-like 'us' is more complex, and can switch between compliant, rebellious and natural/carefree. Often there's crossover, and we exhibit a little bit of two or three ego states at the same time.

For me, one of the most powerful elements of TA is its visual nature. There are some extremely useful, simple illustrations you can draw to help people solve problems.

I loved all these diagrammatical tools, like the 'OK Corral' and the 'Drama Triangle' – I found them enlightening (just Google them if you'd like to know more – and there are some fantastic TA videos and TED talks on YouTube).

At every level, Slimming World is a company of 'feelers' – nurturing, caring, emotionally intelligent people. And rightly so. The downside of that comes when those qualities are knocked out of kilter by a difficult situation or conversation – emotion takes over, rational thinking goes out of the window and control is lost.

That's where these diagrams came into their own. Just sketching something like the 'Drama Triangle' or the 'OK Corral' and asking an emotionally fraught manager or Consultant to identify where they sit within that diagram would help them to dial down their emotional response and bring their 'computer brain' back up. I found it helped them and me take a step back when things got heated, and approach the situation with fascination rather than fury!

The concepts of TA resonated with me – as a business owner, a manager, a wife, a mother, a friend *and* a slimmer! I saw how powerful and relevant it could be within Slimming World in particular – a business that's heavily reliant on positive human relationships, on trust and on effective communication.

I could see it clear as day. Transactional Analysis would be the starting point and the framework we needed to rebuild a strong management structure and positive company culture. The more I learned about TA, it felt as if all those things I had seen, heard and experienced suddenly made so much more sense.

Our TA trainer at the conference was smart and engaging, and she had a way of explaining TA that was just so easy to understand. So shortly afterwards, I asked her to come and develop a training system for our managers at Slimming World. By now, at nearly 40 I had some experience under my belt and a clear picture of how I wanted Slimming World to run and to be run.

With this expert help, we wrapped a workable, measurable reporting process around my big vision – one that would help managers especially to develop their teams in a positive, constructive and forward-looking way. This reporting system survives to this day, such was the helpful clarity it brought to our management systems.

We initially called our weekly planning and reporting system 'Record of Achievement'. I soon discovered that this was unpopular, because it was very backwards-looking – investigating what had been done (or not done) in the previous period. Instead of being a supportive and inspiring exercise to lead each person to greater *future* success, it had become a time to go on the defensive and run for cover.

Wouldn't it be so much better to help our managers and Consultants make plans for the *following* week? So much better to assist them in looking ahead to their success, a success they would choose and could plan for, putting achievable steps in place, in the same way we helped our members plan their week ahead? Much later, born out of this realisation and inspired by a newly trained Regional Manager,

Doreen Seymour, our powerful personal development and management reporting tool, *'Plan for Success'* was created.

Our TA trainer was organised and methodical, with a superb eye for detail. As a therapist, she became very good at reading me – and if something was bothering me, she'd always pick up on it. We became quite close. Unfortunately, money (of all things) came between us. Without going into any more detail, it was a shock and a shame because, sadly, it ended our relationship for good.

––––––

Around the same time as I was breathing new life into Slimming World (which was all-consuming), I was still running our design studio, and juggling the two businesses wasn't easy. It wasn't long after the Miners' Strike (which ended in 1985), which had devastated the local mining communities and had a massive knock-on effect on the local retail industry. The miners' expenditure in local businesses went down – so the owners of *those* businesses also had to tighten their belts. Unfortunately, these very people formed the customer base of the Miles-Paley Design Studio – and it was drying up before our very eyes.

Add to that the problems we had with some over-generous discounting and errors made by our designers and sales people (one of whom had been Roy – a great salesman, but as you know no mathematician!) and it became abundantly clear that the Design Studio was no longer a viable business.

It would be better, I decided, rather than close shop entirely and put all our studio employees out of work, to focus on the manufacturing side of the business – so I opened a factory in the local town of Mansfield alongside the river Maun, the same river that flowed through our garden. I was never shy of a challenge! Our fitters would need to do their bit by adding new skills to their already super talents – new paint finishes such as faux marbling, dragging, frosting, rag-rolling and the like – but they weren't keen to learn.

Never one to be blocked by other people's negativity, I forged ahead and went on a training course myself, along with my then-partner Steven (more on him later). Together we learned the skills, came back and practised them, and Steven became a craftsman, excellent at coach-lining, sponging and spraying. Our new equipment included a special drying oven, so we were able, with Steven's help, to hand-make some beautiful doors.

The business did very well at first. The quality of our products was outstanding and we won some big contracts from building companies – but eventually, a crash in their industry led to the same knock-on effects that we'd seen with our retail business. Needless to say, after only four years and with a heavy heart, I closed down the factory in the late '80s and turned my attention wholly and completely to Slimming World.

It was just as well, because when you're making big changes in a company – working with people you didn't recruit yourself – feathers are inevitably ruffled and people fly the nest. When one of our Regional Managers resigned suddenly in the early 1990s, I found myself (not for the first time) massively overworked and caretaking a vital role I'd rather not have had. Twenty years on from my steep learning curve in Barnsley when I took over and transformed that failing group, this next experience turned out to be just as eye-opening. Looking back, I can identify many similarities with the TV show, *Undercover Boss*, although I wasn't undercover. People were quite open with their refusal to do what they were being paid to do and somehow thought it was OK.

The region consisted of three Area Managers (these days we would call them Team Developers) – all female and each managing a small team of Consultants, as well as running their own group. Stepping into these unwelcome Regional Manager shoes meant I was about to discover some equally unwelcome facts. Nothing could have better highlighted the reasons we were having some of our problems.

After all the work we'd put into creating a robust reporting system (so that we could ensure that our members benefitted in the long-term), our foolproof system with goal-setting paperwork and weekly phone calls between managers and Consultants – the reality was that the purpose, methodology and protocol of the system was being ignored completely. It was either misunderstood, deliberately ignored or both. People were NOT doing what they were meant to be doing. Not at all!

At every level throughout the company, individuals had (and still have) regular one-to-ones with their manager – designed to help them with their personal and career development. Within the field, they took the form of weekly phone calls between Consultants and Area Managers, and between Area Managers and Regional Managers.

The point of this was to find any areas where they struggled, so we could work on solutions together – all part of our ongoing training. Every system of training and reporting is always, *always* for maintaining standards and bringing the best service to members.

I soon discovered that two of these Area Managers – the people who should be doing their utmost to use *Plan for Success* to develop their teams, so our Consultants could flourish – simply weren't doing it. And they came up with some wildly inventive excuses for why they weren't. Sadly, we ended up parting ways. The third Area Manager, however, Chris Brankin, remained with us. She thanked me most sincerely for helping her to understand the *real* goal-setting and planning process and said she was amazed at how clever it was!

In the early 1990s, Chris became Regional Manager of a small team of Area Managers in Cambridgeshire, reporting in to Sheila Hall. We always reckoned that, just like a stick of Skegness rock, if you split Chris down the middle, she'd have '*Slimming World*' running right through her. She was a natural-born Consultant, running five groups to this day, in Lincolnshire. It's partly thanks to Chris that we discovered a very special person indeed – a woman who's *also* still with us, as our Chief Executive Officer. That someone was Caryl Richards.

Caryl joined Slimming World as a member in the Easter of 1991, and Chris recruited her into the role of Consultant in July 1992. I was introduced to her later in the same year at one of our annual general meetings, as Chris had asked Caryl to give a presentation on Consultant training (Caryl's passion). This was training which she'd very recently completed with great success, even though at that point she hadn't been promoted.

I watched and listened with fascination. Without denigrating anyone, I need to tell you that Caryl stood head and shoulders above every other Consultant or manager I had ever met. She just 'got' it – she got it all. She radiated energy, intelligence and honesty whenever she spoke. Later that year, I awarded her '*Up-and-Coming Consultant of the Year*'. She was, and still is, awesome.

However, as Caryl will tell you herself, her road to the top certainly wasn't paved with gold. In fact, she nearly quit the Consultant role after struggling to attract many more than 20 members in her first few months. After attending one of our Slimmer of the Year competitions and chatting to a high-flying Consultant with six sessions and almost 300 members, Caryl discovered that what she really needed to do to get her groups off the ground was a fantastic editorial, which basically amounted to free newspaper advertising – a really big deal in the pre-Internet age (which as you know I discovered for myself way back in the Barnsley days). For as long as we have newspapers in print, it still is a big deal in my book!

After placing an editorial the size of three small matchboxes and gaining nine new members as a result, Caryl pretty soon caught on to the power of the papers and was soon securing herself and her local colleagues full-page editorials, with success stories, recipes and tips which brought members flooding through her doors. She became known as our editorial guru. Within just a couple of months, her group grew from 20 to 145 members and she'd recruited several Consultants to join the team.

By March 1993, Caryl was working her magic as an Area Manager in Peterborough. And it won't surprise you to learn that in 1994, after growing the area from just 7 to 35 groups within a year, Sheila Hall – by now our National Manager running all of our field teams – wasted no time asking her to become a fully employed Regional Manager looking after five counties from Cambridgeshire and East Anglia to Essex. I remember Sheila asking for my help, as Caryl was reluctant to take on this extra work and extra responsibility. Her team was so important to her, she didn't want to neglect them in the process of taking on a bigger role.

The immense amount of work required to reach Caryl's standards in every one of those areas, was, to be fair, impossible. I just knew that with her intelligent touch and her sensible, safe hands on the tiller, 30 minutes of her time spent with Consultants would reap more rewards than a whole day of someone else's. She had yet to realise that herself. After a few phone calls back and forth, Caryl listened, she heard the logic and, in the end, she agreed and took the biggest step, for her, to become a Regional Manager – a foot on the ladder to a directorship.

A year after that, Caryl rose yet again to Field Manager – a move that was heavily influenced by myself and heartily endorsed by Sheila. From there, she became National Manager and a director, before working alongside me for two years as Assistant Managing Director from 1999. By 2001, a decade after walking through our doors as a young mum looking for help to lose weight, Caryl Richards finally became our (first ever) full-time Managing Director.

I've leapt ahead again because I want you to understand how very rare and special Caryl was – and still is. I'd never come across someone who was as obsessed as I was with the quality of Consultant training. Nor someone with her attention to detail, with her sharp mind and analytical brain.

Not that she felt this way about herself and, in my humble opinion (well, as humble as I ever manage to get when it comes to Slimming World), still doesn't fully recognise her own incredible gifts. Quite the opposite – in fact, on plenty of occasions when Sheila or I tried to promote her, she wasn't having any of it! Fear was foremost! That was because she couldn't see a way to fit in all the many, many roles she would have to cover (perfectly – in Caryl's demanding mind) in a typical region that required more Area Managers, a lot of TLC, a lot of training and a lot of supervision.

Isn't it fascinating how even the most talented and capable women have a tendency to underestimate themselves – whether it's their ability to lose weight and be slim, or to rise through the ranks of a business into senior roles? So it fills me with pride and joy to think back to the late '80s and early '90s – and the chain of events that led me to our fantastic future Chief Exec.

Because, after the year we had in '89, Slimming World was due some good luck…

" Management is doing things right; leadership is doing the right things. "

Peter Drucker

CHAPTER TEN

out of the ashes

With a thud and a hiss, the aeroplane door swung open and we stepped out into the tunnel that would take us back to the hustle and bustle of everyday life. It was September 1989 and the end of a great weekend away in Paris with some of our senior management team. It was the first time I'd left all three of my children for more than a day.

Around the point where the tunnel connected to the airport building, I spotted a sign that read: *'Would Richard Moss please call Slimming World'*. (Richard worked at the design studio and was married to Maggie, one of my team at Slimming World – another who is still working with us today, I should add!)

My mind went into overdrive. In less than 30 seconds, I'd concluded that something terrible must have happened – something *so* terrible that no one could tell me personally. The children were dead – I was almost certain of it. It was all my fault for leaving them and I'd need to live with this guilt for the rest of my life.

Frantic with worry, my heart beating, sick to my stomach, we made our way through the airport searching for the nearest phone booth. With a trembling hand, I picked up the receiver, pushed a 10 pence piece into the coin slot and dialled my daughter's phone number.

Oh the sweet, sweet relief when Claire told me that *all* that had happened was a robbery and arson attack on our offices at 34 High Street.

Computers and fittings had been stolen, archives of photos and press coverage had gone up in smoke, every scrap of our stock was destroyed – but no one had died! The joy! The administrative hub of my business – my whole professional world – was in ruins, but compared to the fate I'd imagined, this was a minor blip.

Buoyed by this huge sense of relief, I returned to Derbyshire, rallied our staff and within a day, we'd installed a phone line in our tiny two-up, two-down premises across the road (thank goodness we had it) and informed our network of Consultants what had happened. Offers of help began to flood in. From all over the country we received cuttings, pictures and photocopies so that we could put back together 20 years of Slimming World history. Our insurers were brilliant, meaning that by the end of the following week, we were fully operational again – even if we did go home every night covered in soot!

Our Slimmer of the Year Awards Ceremony – which was due to take place in less than a month – went ahead as planned, at a swish London hotel. Despite losing all the paperwork related to their appearance, we *still* welcomed celebrity hosts Jonathon Morris and Peter Howitt (if you're of a vintage to remember the comedy *Bread,* you'll remember them as Adrian and Joey Boswell – they caused quite the stir!) and we *still* crowned our 12th 'Ms Slimming World'.

I remember telling the local press: '*We won't let a bit of a fire beat us*' and I meant every word. In fact, those embers of Slimming World's team spirit and special culture – which I'd been fanning manically since 1986 – were set ablaze by the rallying spirit of our teams everywhere. So that out of the ashes came a fresh new start for our rapidly-growing company.

Before long, we'd found and bought a big new plot of land nearby, on Clover Nook Road in Alfreton. I commissioned plans for a stylish, art deco-inspired building with a pitched roof, car park and even a goldfish pond wrapping around the right-hand side of the building. The space we'd have would be a marvel compared to our previous hotch-potch of premises – designed especially for us, with a professional kitchen and restaurant, offices and meeting rooms across both floors, a swish reception area and a big space for the sorting and dispatch of stock.

Slimming World was on the up once again – and it felt amazing. At home, however, things weren't so rosy.

As you know, Roy and I had parted company some years earlier, in 1982 – and I spent the following few months in no small degree of anxiety over the children's futures without a father figure in their lives. No matter how bad a marriage becomes, the pain of separation runs deep.

Perhaps that's why I was drawn to Steven Bramwell – or 'Bram' as everyone called him. He had been one of the local schoolboys who was always drawn to the cottage in the late '70s, maybe because of its idyllic setting with fields and water and trees. Maybe it was because there were always plenty of jobs to do and fun to be had, maybe it was because a teenage girl lived there, maybe they enjoyed being around the horses and Roy was happy to have some help. Whatever the attraction of the cottage, they continued to be daily visitors for years, though as they left school and started work, the daily visits stopped – except for Bram.

He was like spun sugar for the soul – laid-back, happy and helpful. After he left school, Steven worked at Mansfield Brewery – sowing the seeds of issues that would emerge later in his life.

Bram was quite a few years younger than me, but something clicked – and there was a very natural sort of connection between us. As we became closer and he spent more time at the house, I saw how wonderful he was with the boys. Ben was still a toddler and needing a lot of help with his feeding and sleeping.

Unlike Claire and Dom (unlike most children, in fact), Ben never had the chance to have a regular feeding and sleeping routine. His non-existent palate left him unable to suckle and made feeding difficult. Despite having plastic bottles that allowed us to gently squeeze and drip milk into his mouth, he could never manage a full feed and would drop to sleep only to wake 30 minutes later, hungry and crying to be fed again. So we never developed that important routine and I could never achieve a pattern of natural night-time sleep phases.

Of course, I took advice from nurses and health visitors, but that meant holding him tight at night and ignoring his furious screams until, exhausted, he would finally drift off to sleep. I couldn't do it! I couldn't bear to have him so distressed. For two-and-a-half years I went without much sleep and unless you have experienced such an unnaturally extended period of broken nights, you may not appreciate that it's like a form of torture. In the end, unfazed, unflappable Bram would hold Ben tight and comfort him until he settled. He was a life-saver.

Sleep deprived and ploughing every last scrap of energy I had into Slimming World, I can't describe how grateful I was for his help and support. He never felt threatened by my career success and his fun, energetic nature made him a great companion for both me and the boys. After 'seeing' each other for a couple of years more, I decided we should cross the 't's and dot the 'i's and get married. Deep down, I think I knew our relationship probably wouldn't last forever but I reasoned that if anything happened to me, Bram would do right by Ben and Dom and I would make sure he was financially supported. If he decided he wanted his freedom and a family of his own, I would understand.

We were together for the best part of a decade, but by the late '80s we were starting to drift apart. As a couple, we'd developed an interest in canal boats and we'd regularly cruise the waterways with the boys in tow. Bram was interested in going to sea, but I was hesitant without proper tuition after a rather frightening episode in the tidal Trent and the Great Ouse. That's when we approached the

Royal Yachting Association and booked ourselves on to a course. I hoped (naively) that this might give our relationship a new focus.

Our first lesson took place in February 1991, with an instructor called Tony Whittaker.

Tony was an antidote to the chaos going on in my personal (and sometimes professional) life. He was strong, masculine and in control in a relaxed way. He wasn't funny or chatty like Roy (who always lived up to the salesman archetype); nor was he uncomplicated and laid-back as Steven had been. He was intelligent, straight-talking and, at 50 years old, seven years my senior – which felt very dependable and very mature. I found him 'self-contained', thoughtful, knowledgeable and enigmatic. The more I learned about him, the more fascinated I became.

Tony was born in 1941, in Flintham, near Newark, Nottinghamshire. His father was killed in the war when Tony was just three years old, so he'd grown up with his mother, and later, his stepfather George Whittaker – a blacksmith. His brother John, 15 years his senior, had been a father figure for much of Tony's childhood. Tony loved his brother and to this day, he still does.

As a very young child, Tony struggled at school. He was, in fact, dyslexic – but of course no one knew about such things in those days of the early 1940s. There was no understanding or support. Instead, children like Tony were labelled 'stupid' or 'slow'. Tony was most certainly neither – so knowing Tony as I now do, he would have spent a large part of his childhood desperately needing to prove that to the world, his stepfather included.

George, wanting to help Tony with what he saw as a serious problem, decided to send him to a boarding school in the south of England. You're probably imagining blazers, leather satchels and imposing cap-and-gowned schoolmasters. In fact, Tony's boarding school was run by Shaolin monks. They had decided to spread their peaceful religious and cultural life farther afield and had established schools throughout Europe.

This Chinese connection was important to Tony's stepfather. George had worked in the engine rooms of ships during the war alongside some Chinese crew. He'd heard stories about how stoically the Chinese had tolerated horrific tortures inflicted on them by their Japanese enemies. George was in awe of their philosophy – of their disciplined lifestyles and their respect for routine and peace. A school run by this elite order of Chinese Buddhists, he concluded, would be the ideal place to sort out Tony's reading and writing difficulties.

Sure enough, Tony's experiences at the Shaolin school shaped him forever. Each morning, they'd get up at the crack of dawn and exercise for about two hours – Tony unaware (until many years later) that he was learning martial arts skills. Then they would have breakfast and the school day would start.

The school had, by law, to teach the legal curriculum of the country but this school was nothing like the norm for a 1940s British school. When official lessons were over for the day, there would be all sorts of extra-curricular opportunities, led by enthusiastic masters who genuinely loved teaching.

The school sounded idyllic and I asked Tony if any of the pupils were ever naughty – surely a natural consequence of childhood and adolescence. Discipline was maintained in an impressive way. If a pupil ever stepped out of line, the punishment was always some kind of physical exercise – and instead of overseeing it, the master would carry it out *with* the pupil, whether it was laps of the schoolyard balancing something on their heads or holding a handstand for 10 minutes. If a student didn't keep their appointment for their punishment, the whole school was brought out to do it. You can imagine this was an extremely rare occurrence.

In the summer holidays, Tony would come home to Newark. His mum earned much-needed money by cleaning the 'posh' houses in the village of Flintham, where Tony was born. One day, nine-year-old Tony went along with his mum to the house of a Captain Maltby. Maltby was something of a naval celebrity, having commanded the famous *Windrush* ship, which brought thousands of soldiers back from far-flung lands after the war.

Having recently been taken to Skegness, the nearest seaside town to Newark, Tony had seen the sea for the first time. He was blown away with how vast it was and he had many questions. Meeting this famous Captain, he could now ask, very respectfully, some of those questions and discover how on earth you could steer a ship in the right direction. An inquisitive (and probably very bored) Tony asked the captain: *'The sea's so big and there are no signposts – how do you know where you're going?'*

This wide-eyed question began a two-year period during which Captain Maltby took great pleasure in teaching Tony another important skill – a skill that was to change the course of his life, not just the course of a ship. Navigation.

When Tony was 11, George discovered that the boarding school wasn't the least bit concerned by Tony's dyslexia. They didn't understand it, but they didn't need to. What mattered to them was how well you respected yourself and the world. *'When your brain's ready to learn to read, you'll read,'* they said. George was, to his mind, paying good money to get Tony 'sorted out'. He wasn't convinced by this aspect of Shaolin philosophy, so he stopped paying the fees and Tony came to live back home in Newark, where he began attending a regular state school (a shock to his system, to say the least).

When he was home from school, Tony did his best to support his mum with the family finances. He took jobs such as harvesting sugar beet in the local farmers' fields. His training and work-ethic were such that he could do the work of two people single-handedly, so he earned double wages. I think he was very proud of being as productive as he was.

At the age of 13, Tony was spotted at his local boxing gym by a professional wrestler and asked to join his wrestling 'stable' at the weekends. He started to earn money – a lot of money – a lot more than his step-father. Once a month on a Friday afternoon, the team would pick Tony up from school in a Jaguar (which he thought was heavenly) and drive down to Southend, where he'd be flown to Paris or Brussels to perform in big wrestling shows.

'Big Tone', as his team mates called him, towered above most boys of 13 – and his youthful features and show-off tricks (including walking the tightrope around the ring) won the attention and applause of the crowd. Many of these skills were, of course, acquired as a result of Tony's years of training at the Shaolin school.

At the age of 14, Tony was once again fatherless and his mum became a widow for the second time. Tony and his mum were with George when he suffered a fatal heart attack. They could do nothing for him and had to wait until the next morning for the doctor to arrive.

When Tony left school at the age of 15, he continued to pursue another of his favourite hobbies, mountain climbing. He kept this up as long as he could while working for a Nottingham steel company, where his brother John worked as a steel erector. Tony was installed into their drawing office and went to college in Sheffield to study engineering. Despite achieving qualifications, Tony didn't particularly enjoy this sedentary work. Instead, he worked with his brother John and learned how to become a steel erector, and the physical skills learned at his boarding school came in handy once more.

Around this time, when Tony was about 18 years old, he spotted a newspaper ad for a navigator to go to the Gobi Desert – a vast, arid region in northern China and southern Mongolia – to guide mature students through some testing terrain.

One of our Regional Managers, Elizabeth Reid, up from the New Forest, outside our first single-storey office in South Normanton in the early '80s.

Slimming World's office after the devastating arson attack of 1989. Had it not been for this, I would have much more memorabilia to share on these pages.

The sum of our Head Office staff in 1989. Thirty years later, we've grown just a little…to over 400 staff!

After the fire of 1989, we built this striking
pitched-roof building, complete with a
moat teeming with goldfish, just a couple
of miles from our original Head Office at
the other end of the village. Little did we
know how quickly we'd outgrow it…

Our now-Chief Executive Officer
Caryl Richards and me, sporting
classic early-'90s hairstyles.

Consultants who've visited Head Office for training might recognise our salon,
left (then our warehouse) and the beginnings of our current building on the right.
How we've grown since!

Our swish new Head Office, which was completed in 1997…

…and after almost a year's building works in 2018, I was invited to sign the steels of the brand new extension, to our 1997 building. It incorporates a multi-room training centre, a photography and film studio, underground car park, atrium, restaurant, meeting rooms and much-needed office space.

Our team of directors pose with the project manager from our building firm, shortly after our new building was completed. Doesn't it look futuristic?

I love this photograph of Caryl Richards and me – taken in Miami a couple of years ago.

Tony and I loving life on our boat, *Sole Mate*.

As published in the very first issue of *Slimming World* magazine – the original team! Three are still with us today – our Food and Publications Manager Allison Brentnall (bottom left), our Joint Managing Director Jan Boxshall (bottom right) and Creative Director Lynn Hayes (standing directly behind Jan).

The wonderful Anne Kirk – our first PR and Advertising manager.

Our first Field Director – the powerhouse that was Sheila Hall, pictured here with her husband Brian.

Our Journey 5000 tour bus – home to Tony and me for three months in 1996, when we raised £500,000 for Slimming World's charitable foundation SMILES.

Tony was a great companion and navigator en route – no sat navs back then!

One of the happiest days of my life – marrying Tony in 1996. We had just two guests – Sheila and Brian Hall. What a sunny, special day that was.

And we're still in love to this day.

Our first motor cruiser, named *Sinfree*.

The stunning beachfront bar we owned in Mallorca, Mood Beach.

We welcomed many famous faces over the years that we owned Mood –
Goldie Hawn was one of my favourites! I was starstruck!

It was his first job as a professional navigator and he enjoyed teaching the interested students. He was, however, completely in their hands when it came to speaking Chinese. The students had among them some exceptional linguists and Tony was dazzled (still is) by their ability to learn a strange new dialect and to be able to communicate with remote Chinese tribes.

I loved listening to Tony recalling his adventures – climbing mountains, wading through snow on skis and of them huddling together at times where joint body warmth kept them safe.

On his return, Tony went back to working with his brother John for a while, before taking other jobs in the same industry. Tony never set out to become a 'businessman', but when he broke away from John to go it alone, he became busier and busier, and found he needed to employ others. Before he knew it, he was an employer running a company.

In between busy times, Tony found the time to add to his navigation skills. He answered an ad for someone to go and work with Caterpillar (CAT) as a navigator in Pakistan. Having tragically lost a member of their team to Pakistan's unforgiving, disorientating desert landscape, CAT had a new policy – no one was to leave the camp without a navigator. At interview, Tony was asked one question: *'Can you change the wheel on a Land Rover?'* Tony's reply was that he could fit a new back axle if required!

Tony got the job. He spent far longer out in Pakistan than he'd ever intended – months as opposed to weeks – erecting steel out there as well as navigating. When he came home, his steel erection business grew and I've always been tickled by the name he gave his company – Whittaker Erections!

When he was in his late 20s, Tony joined a local aero club and took up flying. He was later persuaded to become an instructor, which he discovered he loved. It was far more interesting than flying alone. Some of his teaching was done locally but when he was erecting the steel for a cold store in Aberdeen, he ended up doing far more flying instructing than steel erecting! For Tony, nothing compared to the thrill of low-level aerobatics – one of his other 'relaxing' pastimes! What can you say? I guess he's one of life's adventurers.

By his late 30s, Tony's steel erection business had grown. By now he had accumulated 12 cranes and two access platforms, and the local marina in Newark began to use these for lifting boats in and out of the River Trent. Through this, he got to know a lot of boat owners – who would ask him to navigate for them from time to time. That's how Tony came to be involved with boats, both sailing and powerboats – and through that, eventually, became an instructor for the Royal Yachting Association (RYA).

I had my first lesson with Tony in February 1991 – and the more lessons I had, the more the mutual attraction grew. I'd met the love of my life – my soul mate. The rest, as they say, is history.

Bram and I brought our relationship to an official close in September 1991, and Tony and I became a couple in November. By January 1992 he was a part of the family, living with the boys and me at the cottage. It's hard to know, as a mother, how your own romantic relationships will affect your children throughout their lives. Of course, it did worry me knowing that the boys had to deal with a transition between two quite different father figures, as they grew through childhood into adolescence.

Skipping forward briefly to 2003 though, when Roy died, Ben reflectively said something that really touched me – something that helped ease all my anxiety: *'No matter what's happened in our lives, Mum, you always seem to have had the right person with you at the right time just when we needed them. Bram was just like a big brother who played with us all the time and then when we needed someone stronger, along came Tony.'*

How wonderfully mature and compassionate was that?

With Tony, a whole new branch of family came into my life – Tony's daughter Dawn, her husband Mark and their children, David and Samantha; and Tony's son Gary and his children, Sophie and Erik. Another addition to our clan arrived in around 1992, when Tony and I 'kidnapped' (Tony's word!) one of Dom's classmates, Danny Colbert. Dom and Danny had become firm friends at Heathfield Junior School and weekend sleepovers were a regular occurrence from around the age of 10.

We discovered that Danny – who was the most willing, eager-to-please boy you could ever hope to meet – had a pretty troubled family background. He suffered his circumstances with more grace than I ever could, although when it got too much (and it often did), he'd find sanctuary in our cottage and in his friendship with Dom.

When Danny was around 15 or 16, he told us that his mother was going to live in Lincoln with her new husband. His school and all his friends were in Mansfield Woodhouse and he didn't want to leave, so he asked if he could move in with us at the cottage. It wasn't a difficult decision. Danny had already been staying with us most weekends anyway. So he came to live with our family and continued to do so with his girlfriend, Samantha, until they got their own home and moved out.

Danny came to work at Slimming World's Head Office, where he is still a part of our Facilities department. He's become a much-valued member of the team. Listen carefully if ever you're at Head Office and you might hear a sunny tune being whistled – that's our Danny!

Around the same time as Danny moved in with us, Tony became interested in the day-to-day management of Slimming World. Quite unlike Roy and Bram, who'd always very much left me to it when it came to Slimming World, Tony had owned his own business, so he had plenty of opinions on how a company should operate. Opinions I didn't always agree with! We had plenty of heated debates about the right approach to take. After a while, Tony stepped back from day-to-day involvement, though he still accompanies me to the office today, has his own office with a TV and is well and truly pampered with cups of coffee as he patiently waits for me.

With the havoc of the arson attack behind us, in the 1990s – in spite of the recession that started in earnest in the late '80s and continued into the early part of the decade – we saw one of Slimming World's most rapid periods of growth ever. I don't think we could ever put that down to one thing alone – more to an emphasis on improving quality in several areas. My focus, as always, was on improving our service to members – and to do that, we needed to make sure we were recruiting the right people and training them to the very best of our ability.

We brought in 'open evenings' (which we now call Opportunity Events) so that interested members could find out more about the reality of becoming a Slimming World Consultant. Before that, people came into the role not realising that 90% of the work happens behind the scenes, not 'on stage' in group. The bit that always appeals to people is the bit they've enjoyed week after week – leading a group and helping lots of people achieve their dreams (and indeed, it is thoroughly rewarding and life-changing) – but before you can reap those rewards, there's a lot of hard graft!

To be successful as a Slimming World Consultant, you need to do plenty of homework – thinking about where each member is with their weight loss, and planning enabling questions to ask each one before you next see them in group (essential). Members don't see that bit – but boy, do they feel the benefits. You need to hone your IMAGE Therapy skills with plenty of reading and top-up training. Members don't see that either. Nor do they see the work that is regularly needed to promote groups locally, in the community.

We'd introduced national meetings by now, called Sharing in Action, where managers all over the field would come to share and learn best practice on a whole host of subjects from recruitment through to promotion and IMAGE Therapy. It was from these meetings that our famous '5 Prong Attack' of promotion was born in 1993. Developed by one of our Regional Managers (in Liverpool), this fast became the most effective promotional toolkit we'd ever had. If carried out as trained, over a 10-day timescale with no tweaks, it was guaranteed to bring a Consultant at least 25 new members the following week. Later added to and honed, this multi-pronged approach is still the way we promote Slimming World groups in 10,000 communities in the UK and Ireland today.

With social media constantly developing and platforms such as Facebook and Twitter, an incredible help, it's a whole new world today when it comes to deciding where best to spend time and money. And it all has to come together. We can't afford to leave out any promotional strand. Not one. However the landscape changes, we need to constantly keep up and yes, it's true, you get out what you put in. That's your reward. With Slimming World, that reward can be mega! Mindblowing! Life-changing!

Ever since we introduced Opportunity Events, our recruitment process has been refined and refined to ensure that the people we bring through to Consultant training are the sort of people who care deeply about helping others lose weight, as they themselves were helped – and are prepared to invest in themselves and in their business. They need to be great at 'aware-ing' (one of my neologisms) – on listening really carefully to what members are telling them, and being aware, too, of what members *aren't* telling them (by tuning into things like body language signals).

You may have noticed that Slimming World has hardly ever promoted its groups on national billboards or TV – and that's because our policy has always been to invest our profits back into exceptional training, *not* into expensive (extortionately so to my mind) national advertising methods.

My obsession with training dates right back to the very earliest days of the company (when it took place in my front room with two or three Consultants at a time). Having already dipped my toes into the vast waters of Transactional Analysis and the skills of building EI (Emotional Intelligence), I was keen to invite a fantastic TA trainer from the US, Abe Wagner, to Derbyshire to deliver special training sessions to our Consultants and managers.

Abe was just the most brilliant trainer you could ever hope to meet. Mr Personality Plus, he'd deliver fantastically entertaining, engaging sessions using his wicked sense of humour and his fast-paced, stand-up comedic style. It certainly made learning all the more pleasurable and more easily and lastingly absorbed.

Abe's teaching took you on a journey through yourself. No matter how many people he was delivering training to, he'd make it easy for you to relate to the learning on a profoundly personal level. It got me thinking about some of the deeper-seated reasons why I stopped myself from losing weight. Delving into my subconscious was a true revelation – fascinating, sometimes painful, always incredibly useful.

One such discovery dated all the way back to my childhood and two aunties, Laura and Elsie. Aunty Laura was Mum's sister. She was a fairly unglamorous, mumsy sort of person – always wearing a hairnet. Like a big, comfy sofa, you couldn't help but love her. Whenever we went to visit, the house she shared with Uncle Charlie was warm and filled with the smells of roasting meat and gravy. If she wasn't hovering around a stack of pots at the stove, she'd be buzzing around the dinner table feeding everyone until they were fit to burst. She was the most non-judgemental, happy soul you could ever hope to meet and I loved our visits.

Then there was Aunty Elsie, who was married to one of my mum's brothers, Bill. In complete contrast to the lovely Laura, Elsie was tall, thin, tight-lipped and critical. She was one of those people who made you feel constantly uncomfortable, and whenever we visited her, I'd spend most of the time in stony silence watching the brown carriage clock on the mantelpiece, waiting for it to be time to leave.

Looking closely at myself all those years later, and uncovering all the hidden reasons I had *not* to lose weight, I realised I was still associating buxom roundness with the lovable Aunty Laura, and slimness with the unlovable Aunty Elsie. I didn't want to turn out like her. I didn't want to give everyone grief – I wanted to be a warm, welcoming, non-judgemental type of person, just like Aunty Laura.

This process sowed the seed for one of several Motivational Tools used by Slimming World Consultants to this day – the *For & Against List*. It helps struggling members to dig deep, really deep, just as I did through Abe's brilliant training – to examine both the reasons why they *want* to lose weight (this is the easy, rational, conscious bit), as well as the reasons why they might *not* want to lose weight (some of which are hidden in our subconscious). The self-discoveries our members make when they take time to fill out a *For & Against List* can be quite dramatic.

The problem with a teacher like Abe Wagner was that he set the bar very high. Finding someone of his calibre to deliver training as a permanent member of our Slimming World staff was going to be unlikely – well, let's face it, impossible.

However…

Around the same time, I was having personal therapy sessions with Alan Channing – a therapist who I'd met through Transactional Analysis evening classes in Derby. His listening skills were superb. He had a way of asking all the right questions – and would occasionally say: '*I don't want to know the answer, Margaret. The only person who needs to know the answer is* **you**.' That was amazingly liberating.

We'd discuss things like my rebelliousness and how I was stopping myself from achieving the things I wanted to achieve (including my own weight loss). He'd ask me to think about my 'trapdoors'. Where were they? When did they open up and swallow all my best-laid plans? These therapy sessions were like a journey of self-discovery and the incisive questions Alan asked began to inspire me in all sorts of other ways.

I was inspired to write a training resource especially for Area Managers, called *The Voyage of Discovery*. 'Telling' or 'directing' managers as to what they needed to *tell* their teams can be useful sometimes, but only when people have very little knowledge, understanding or experience of the job in hand. Telling and directing people at the wrong stage in their development can be counterproductive. *The Voyage of Discovery* explained and guided, showing managers the benefits of using great questions and listening skills in their weekly phone calls with Consultants. The ultimate aim was to help Consultants identify their roadblocks and become self-motivated to develop their groups.

What I noticed, though, was the discomfort managers seemed to feel around actually doing it – asking questions. So I did some checking out, starting with myself. I asked myself a question. What did I feel about questioning someone? Wow! What an enabling question that turned out to be! I felt like the aggressor. Like I was trying to catch them out!

How come? Wow! Another enabling question! Because sub-consciously that's exactly what I was doing! More often than not, I had an answer in my mind as to what they ought to be saying. No wonder they felt threatened, no wonder I felt uncomfortable. And I discovered those were the feelings of many other people. Questioning = interrogating – with all those negative connotations.

Fortunately, I had experienced being asked non-threatening and very enabling questions by TA therapists like Alan and Ken (Ken Brown was our Human Resources manager and a super TA therapist). Their questions were very freeing. Their questions had a way of clearing away the fog. Their questions were like a light being switched on, illuminating the many options I had available when I'd been feeling stuck. So what was the difference between my threatening and disabling questions and these very useful, very enabling questions?

As I discovered, the key that unlocked the secret for me was to ask questions that I didn't know the answer to. Questions like: *'What might crop up to stop you from doing the promotion you've planned this week?'* or *'How does the conversation usually go in group with a member who's not losing weight?'* These sorts of questions are 'open' and enabling questions because they open up a conversation and help the other person to think these things through, possibly for the first time. They aren't 'leading' questions, trying to lead someone in the direction you want them to go in – manipulative and quite threatening. 'Closed' questions close down a conversation, resulting in a yes or no answer. Both kinds of question feel uncomfortable and I personally think they lead to a destruction of trust.

I soon discovered that asking questions that I couldn't possibly know the answer to was extremely powerful and extremely empowering. Sometimes, those questions would uncover things outside of the awareness of the person answering. Like what thoughts and opinions the other person had about things, what feelings they had about things. I was fascinated. I wanted to see the pictures they had in their heads.

When I asked questions that would help me to see that picture, then very often both of us discovered things that were really useful. It was indeed a *'Voyage of Discovery'* and we took it together.

Naturally, I was proud as punch of the way the company was growing. Who wouldn't be? But what I *really* cared about *wasn't* being the biggest. All I cared about was being the *best*. Quality, quality, quality. I wanted Slimming World to be the most caring, the most effective, and the most loved by our customers – our members. This is still what I care about most – and it always will be.

I believe our success is down to the fact that Slimming World has always put the needs of members first. They are the be-all and end-all of every single decision, incentive, change or development that comes from me and our management teams. Their extraordinary achievements are what light up our world; and their passion for our brand and our methods is a constant source of inspiration for us all.

Even in light of our success in the 1990s, I knew in my heart of hearts that to deliver the service our members *really* deserved, there was still work to do. This became more and more apparent within the first three months of 1996 – a rollercoaster of a year that was incredibly fulfilling, dramatic, memorable and life-changing – both for me personally, and for Slimming World.

66 Last night the Internet stopped working so I spent a few hours with my family. They seem like good people. 99

CHAPTER ELEVEN

thriving and surviving

In my 71 years on the planet, I've fallen in love with many pursuits – sculpting, wood-carving, playing the flute, interior design, boating… I could go on. One thing that's never stolen my heart though, is intense physical exercise. My dear sons Dominic and Ben, despite their busy lives, always make time for the gym, boxing, bike rides and power walking. I understand they both want to keep fit and strong, of course, but they are dedicated beyond belief. Even after a full-on day at work which leaves them exhausted, they wouldn't miss the gym. For them (and you'll understand this if you're the same), the process of pushing their bodies to the limit is intensely regenerating and calming. *'The buzz is addictive, Mum!'* they tell me.

I wish I could say I 'get it'. It's not for want of trying. I've spent five days a week for years doing work in various gyms, going for brisk walks, doing freestyle Pilates, stretching (and being stretched) on equipment definitely designed by a sadist. But, quite frankly, I've come to accept that I'd much rather go for a nice walk. Walking may not give me the drug-like 'high' people rave about but it's enjoyable, it's good for me and if I need to make business calls (and I do, daily), I can plug in my headset and talk on the move. Two birds, one stone – super!

Late in '95, with my big 5-0 looming on the horizon, I started toying with the idea of an epic walk – a personal challenge, maybe a fundraiser too. Mulling it over with Tony, I concluded that John O'Groats to Land's End seemed a good challenge. At just over 600 miles, we could do 10 miles a day and complete the whole thing in about three months.

Tony (in his innocence?) mentioned it in passing to someone at work and the idea was seized upon with such enthusiasm that before we knew it, managers from all over the country were calling Head Office inviting us to drop by their area en route. No one worth their salt misses a press-worthy opportunity at Slimming World.

This didn't seem like such a bad idea. We'd be able to raise money for charity, connect with managers, Consultants and members on our way and help our teams gain a wealth of newspaper editorials in the process. Pity there was no social media then but we did OK. *Three birds, one stone* – does it get any better?

Of course, it would be impossible to do this without zig-zagging – which would add thousands of miles to an already lengthy route. So we decided we'd hire a big Winnebago-style campervan, drive from location to location and then walk 10 miles a day, five miles in one area, and another five in the next. It would all amount to the same number of miles walked in the end.

Our chosen charity was Marie Curie Cancer Care. As you are aware, cancer distressingly touches all of us in one way or another. Back then, one-in-three people were developing the dreaded disease, and even more distressing is to know that those figures have increased. Now it's one-in-two people. Frightening to say the least. Thankfully, cures and treatments have also grown more numerous these days.

As it happened, Slimming World had recently hit its target of 5,000 groups in 1995 – much sooner than expected – and so the 1996 tour took on the celebratory name *Journey 5000* in celebration of that fact.

We announced Journey 5000, and our Head Office and field teams took on the huge job of co-ordinating the plans to organise the 12-week tour. Consultants and Area Managers all over the UK were hugely excited and keen to make the most of the opportunity. You wouldn't believe how people got behind the campaign (well, if you know Slimming World, then I'm sure you would) – or the brilliantly bonkers ideas that our teams thought up.

Not wishing to dampen their enthusiasm (and on the basis that I didn't believe any of it would actually happen), I risked agreeing to everything that was suggested, no matter how crazy. This involved anything from parading on horseback through the streets of Coventry, Lady Godiva style (although there was never any chance I would be naked wearing only a long wig – after all, it was winter in the UK!), to leading a bull through a West Country town, to riding the brand new 'Big One' rollercoaster at Blackpool Pleasure Beach (the park was closed for winter and I knew enough about logistics to know that they weren't going to go to the trouble and expense of opening it just for us).

My predictions were spot-on (thank you Lord) and the more ambitious stunts never came to fruition, although I did, at one point, find myself being thrown inelegantly by Tony over the chest-high basket of a hot air balloon at Aintree racecourse – much to everyone's amusement. And after all that, it was too windy to go up!

Journey 5000 began on 5th January 1996 in Aberdeen and we couldn't have wished for a warmer welcome, a more organised event or better weather for the time of year. It was chilly but sunny, as it continued to be through the whole of Scotland – with no rain and no snow to slow us down. How lucky were we? We were greeted by hordes of Consultants, members and Marie Curie representatives, many of them in full teddy bear costumes (the charity's mascot at the time). The press, too, was out in force.

That morning, the local team had arranged for a famous smokehouse in Arbroath to open specially and show us how they smoked their herring – and in the afternoon, it was on to another venue for yet more publicity for Slimming World and Marie Curie.

We followed a similar pattern as we worked our way south through Scotland, with two stops a day – one before lunch and one afterwards. Somehow, in among it all, we'd manage a few miles of walking each morning and a few more in the afternoon. In the evenings, we'd park our campervan in the car parks of various hotels – all of them incredibly kind, sometimes offering us a free room for the night (we politely declined. Everything we needed was in the camper). Even toll bridges would wave us through without charging – the generosity was genuinely heart-warming.

A few areas had gone the extra mile to raise even more money, organising fabulous ceilidhs and karaoke nights, with mad bands and dancers everywhere. Talk about community spirit. I never got blisters walking in my stout walking shoes but I did get them from all the dancing! And Tony and I raised quite a bit extra for charity by being persuaded to sing at karaoke sessions. Not sure who was bribing who there!

With members all over the UK getting sponsored for walking and for losing weight, it mattered massively to me that I dropped a few pounds and got fit as part of the adventure. Not as easy as you'd think – especially when all those lovely, generous and hospitable ceilidh venues were laying on (very beige!) buffets each evening.

Thank goodness for Little Chefs, where I could order a plate of beans on wholemeal toast (without butter) as a quick fill-me-up. And let's not forget Scan Bran (our high-fibre crispbread at the time), which I'd keep in the campervan with all sorts of salady bits, to fill me up when there was no time to stop. I must have been a great Girl Guide – be prepared!

One of my absolute favourite treats at the time was to spread a Scan Bran with a teaspoon of jam and then pile fat-free cottage cheese on top – it was a bit like very low-Syn cheesecake!

Over the course of the trip, I did indeed lose weight – almost three stones in fact – and we raised a not-at-all-shabby £500,000 plus for Marie Curie. It was an incredibly valuable experience from a business point of view too. Slimming World's growth spurt, it became clear, was a bit of a mixed blessing.

Journey 5000 shone a light on the positive spirit in many areas of the country – usually where management was strong and, therefore, so too were the teams of Consultants.

North of the border, everything had gone like a dream. Events were beautifully organised, we had super press coverage, huge turnouts of people every time we stopped and a warm and friendly reception to boot. People's attitudes were fantastic.

However, as we travelled the length and breadth of the UK, we discovered not every area was as welcoming, or as well organised, and the culture and commitment were nowhere near how we wanted them to be. Painful, but enlightening. We still had a lot of work to do on our training and selection processes, to meet the high standards we set ourselves.

On the brighter side, there were many, many positive experiences still to come. Who could forget walking the length of the Humber Bridge while unravelling a two-mile-long scarf knitted by Hull's Slimming World members? Or scrubbing the deck of a boat using just toothbrushes? So many fun memories and photo opportunities created by our amazing Consultants and managers.

The trip, as a whole, was a huge undertaking – something I'm still incredibly proud of and I hope that, so too, are all who made it the success it was. It was also a way for me to meet many Consultants and members en route who gave me invaluable and inspiring feedback, so I was even more committed to ramping up what was, already, an excellent training programme. I don't suppose we will ever rest on our laurels when it comes to training, no matter how proud we are of what we give already.

Based on the premise that you can take a horse to water but you can't make it drink, we constantly search for new and better ways to influence, persuade and inspire all our Consultants and managers, old and new, to take yet another leap forward in our quest to deliver effective help and support to members.

It was a relief to return to the office after our three-month road trip to find that the building was still standing and the business had come to no apparent harm.

As I lay flat on my back in bed one April evening, reliving the trip in my mind, I noticed something new about my now-much-slimmer stomach. Ask any previously overweight woman or man what it's like to feel their hip bones for the first time in many years and they'll tell you it's more delicious than any cream cake or cheese board. Exalted, I ran my hand across my stomach just below my belly button, only to notice something else – muscle! It was rock solid. Clearly a side-effect of all the walking we'd been doing. Marvellous!

A few weeks later, I started having a bit of tummy trouble, with some unusual pain I hadn't ever felt before. I made a quick trip to the doctor's surgery, expecting to walk away with a prescription for something to settle my tummy. The family and I had been seeing the same GP for years, so he knew me well enough not to beat around the bush.

Examining my stomach, he said: *'How long have you had this lump?'*

Lump? *Lump?!*

For the first time in months and years, Slimming World wasn't the first and foremost thing on my mind. It was my health – my existence.

'Can you feel something, then?' I asked.

'How long?' he insisted again.

'Well, I didn't really feel it as a lump – but I suppose it must be a couple of months now.'

'And I thought you were a sensible girl,' the doctor said, with oddly-timed humour (bear in mind I was nearly 50!).

He made a phone call to the hospital there and then, and booked me in for an ultrasound the following Monday.

Squeezing a blob of cold jelly on to my lower abdomen, the sonographer pressed and probed away, scrutinising the black-and-white apparition on the screen. Seeing for myself exactly what he saw (I've never been one to turn away from the needle), it came as no surprise when he told me there was a lump the size of a large grapefruit either on or inside my uterus, it was too big to tell.

'*I can tell it's not a cyst by the way it looks,*' he said. '*If it was a cyst, it'd be sort of spongy. So it's definitely a tumour.*'

I felt my throat constrict.

'*Is that a... benign tumour?*' I asked, desperately willing a '*yes*'.

All he said was: '*Hmmm, well, some people in my job like to think they can tell, but I prefer to leave it to the doctors to make a decision about that.*'

Just before I left, he came up to me, squeezed my shoulder and with a little frown, gave me a look of silent sympathy. First he'd avoided my question with a non-answer... now this.

I went home to Tony and said: '*I'm going to die. I'm going to die. The sonographer knows I'm going to die, and he doesn't want to tell me.*'

We held it together... just... as we waited the agonising 48 hours to see a specialist. The surgeon delivered the news: I'd need to have a full hysterectomy, and this was in order to diagnose the nature of the tumour. They scheduled my operation for that Friday – just five days after my initial scan.

Back home and back to holding it together... that was, until the Thursday night. Typical me, I'd spent every waking moment reading and researching everything I could about uterine tumours (on this relatively new thing called 'the Internet') – so by now, I was absolutely convinced I was already at Stage 4 and going to die. So convinced was I, in fact, that both Tony and I completely lost it. We were in bits. Terrified and in tears, we clung desperately to each other. I had already written letters to the children, both of us believing it was 'The End'. Eventually, we fell asleep through pure exhaustion.

Then... the weirdest thing happened.

I woke up next morning – on the day of my operation – feeling totally at peace. It was bewildering. I remember marvelling at how I could be so overwhelmed the night before and now experience this unbelievable calm. What had my brain done to help me in this way? Was it some special chemical that's only released in the most extreme cases of shock and emotional trauma? Whatever it was, the effect was miraculous. I wasn't frightened. I wasn't terrified. I wasn't panicked. I was accepting and prepared to let go of life.

In this unflappable frame of mind, I arrived at the hospital and went through all my pre-op assessments, before counting backwards from 100 into unconscious bliss.

If you've ever experienced the limbo of a hospital waiting room, you'll know that feeling of gazing at doors and down corridors for what seems like an eternity – waiting for the emergence of a stranger who, oddly, in that moment, you trust, revere and fear more than anyone else in the world.

When this person walked down the corridor in Tony's direction, it was the surgeon, Mr Clive Pickles. Clive was well known not just for his gynaecological expertise but also for his fairly eccentric style of dress. To complement his red dickie-bow tie that day, Mr Pickles was sporting a white shirt painted with a slightly comical-looking pair of bright red braces.

As Tony recounted it: *'I see the surgeon coming towards me and I'm thinking: "What a f#***!g stupid shirt to wear to tell a husband that his wife is going to die!" '*

'So we're all done,' says Mr Pickles. *'I've removed the tumour and although I've sent it to the lab to be checked, I've seen enough in my time to know that this one's benign.'*

*'What a f#***!g fantastic shirt!'* thought Tony.

*" The idea is to die young
– as late as possible. "*

CHAPTER TWELVE

a new outlook on life

Call me ungrateful, but you'd think after a day of nil-by-mouth, the extraction of a large grapefruit-size growth and most of my reproductive bits, I'd have lost a bit of weight, wouldn't you? I reckoned at least 11lbs (ever the optimist!).

Stepping on the same scales as I had done pre-op, I was shocked to discover that after my operation, I'd not only failed to lose my hoped-for 11lbs – but actually *gained* two! How very little it should have mattered in that moment, but I couldn't help chuckling at the outrage of my inner slimmer.

What I also discovered, re-discovered really, is that I would always be a Slimming World member at heart. We would always be '*WE*'. I would always be a slimmer. I would always be aware of how it feels to be just a tiny bit obsessed about my weight and size (can we be 'just a tiny bit obsessed'?). I can't imagine ever *not* being ridiculously happy when the scales are on an exciting downward trend.

My recovery was quick and straightforward and yet the effect on my psyche, the ordeal of the tumour and of the potential of cancer, was life-changing. Up until then, I'd been in the office seven days a week, working 12-hour days (and more) for as long as I could remember. Agreeing to leave the business entirely for Journey 5000 – for three whole months – had been a big deal for me. We had a fax machine installed in the campervan and I had a mobile phone so I could keep in touch with people at the office, but I was still worried to death about letting go for so long.

So having escaped what I'd thought would be terminal cancer – and now knowing from experience that the office wouldn't burst into flames in my absence (surely lightning couldn't strike twice!) – I decided (along with a now-retired Tony) that each month I'd take a week away from the office and we would do something with our lives other than me working long hours and many weekends. By now, we owned a boat – a very comfortable 51-foot motor cruiser – and I had become a competent helmsman and navigator thanks to Tony's brilliant teaching.

We made plans. Tony wanted to sail north into the Baltic Sea. After a winter living in a campervan, though, I'd had enough of cold weather and no sunshine, so I won the toss and we began a journey south. The lure of warm weather, blue skies and sunshine was just as attractive to Tony too, and as long as we could always finish our week at a marina near an airport, we were able to leave the boat and fly back home again. It was a superb arrangement.

We set off in the July of 1996, aiming for Brest – but some bad weather in the English Channel meant diverting to Guernsey, where we ended up stuck for four nights. No sooner had we left Saint Peter Port than we ended up at the mercy of more bad weather, diverting to Saint Helier in Jersey.

By now, I was fairly skilled at handling and manoeuvring boats. Tony, with his years of training and work in the steel erection trade (where people's lives depend on securely tied knots), had an incredible sense of balance and was, of course, fabulous at deck duties. So he'd deal with the lines and fenders, balancing on the front of the boat on choppy seas and lassoing the cleats. I much preferred being in the cockpit where it was safe and enclosed, so I was always the one at the wheel. We got along famously as a boating team. We trusted each other's abilities – although this division of roles came as a surprise to others. It was rare to find a woman in charge of a motor cruiser – it was generally seen as 'the man's job'.

It became quite amusing when we arrived in Saint Helier. Waiting for the tide to come in, we had moored the boat on the outer holding-pontoon and were met by a marina helper. He jumped on board to give us some help and, without acknowledging me at all, he addressed only Tony and ran all over the deck messing about with Tony's expertly prepared lines. I guess he assumed I'd tied them and so they couldn't possibly be correct!

All the while, Tony was standing on the front deck, nowhere near the helm, listening in great detail about the difficulties of manoeuvring the boat into the only tight space available. The gates opened and the boat moved off and into the marina, driven by me. Meanwhile, Tony, still on deck, nodded along in quiet amusement, while this chap – who *still* hadn't caught on that Tony wasn't driving – continued to give him a blow-by-blow account of how to reverse into the allotted space.

Tony just kept saying, *'No problem.'*

We reached our mooring and, positioning the boat correctly, the 'difficult' mooring caused us no problems at all and I took the boat astern with ease. To this day I don't think our 'helper's' brain ever computed the fact that it was a woman who'd taken charge of the manoeuvre.

Tony and I managed to fit in our wedding in August that year. We had, by now, been living together for five years and I decided it was time to get married. There's nothing like staring death in the face to make you realise what's important in life. When I started to draw up a list of wedding guests, I realised I had an impossible task on my hands. I wanted to invite half of Slimming World – and that's before we'd even started on our families. Not knowing how or where to draw the line, we made the decision to keep the whole thing a total secret.

We slipped away quietly to Chesterfield Register Office on Friday 16th August 1996 for a simple ceremony, witnessed by my dear colleague and friend, Sheila Hall, and her husband Brian – the only people in the world who'd known our plans. After we'd signed the register, we went to a village in the picturesque Chatsworth Estate for lunch, and then spent a beautiful afternoon walking around the grounds of Chatsworth House, residence of the Duke and Duchess of Devonshire. It was perfect (little did I know that many years later I would meet and dine with the Duke of Devonshire in a small restaurant in Derby – I'll get to that later!).

By October, we'd travelled south from Jersey, calling in at Brest. I had attempted to cross the notoriously challenging Bay of Biscay to La Coruña but as the seas became a little more wild, I changed course to make life a little more comfortable, taking us eventually to Bayonne, a tiny marina close to Biarritz. Biarritz was the famous playground of the jet set back in the day. Her faded glory is still very evident and we spent a delightful afternoon and evening there before moving on early the next day.

Our habit was to leave early every morning, arrive at our next chosen port, refuel and get ready for the following day's trip, then head off to experience the local town for lunch and maybe do a little shopping. As per our plan, we left Bayonne, travelling along the length of the north Spanish coast and thereby past the famous Basque region, lauded for its exciting, creative cuisine, with delicious fresh fish a staple.

The Basque Separatist movement ETA, formed in 1959 and disbanded in 2018, was creating alarm and destruction throughout Spain with their selective bombing campaigns, but thankfully we weren't affected.

As we left Bayonne, I had my first taste of the huge Atlantic swell in this particular corner of the Bay of Biscay. It was Tony's first experience of the phenomenon too. I've already told you what I'm like about reading and this was no different! My nose was stuck into a very helpful book that guided seafarers through these challenging waters. It explained that although these mountainous swells looked alarming (what an understatement), they posed very little risk.

Reassured by this trusty book, I was able to enjoy the unsettling experience of one second being at the top of a huge swell, with amazing views revealing other craft around us and the black flags marking sunken lobster pots, then the next second being in the valley of the swell and seeing nothing other than the sea towering over us. It was disconcerting to say the least, as the lobster pots are tied to their flags with lines that are dangerous to boat propellers, and a motor cruiser like ours relies on that propeller being free to do its job. The last thing we needed was to find ourselves disabled and adrift in the Bay of Biscay with its Atlantic swell.

We arrived in Santander – a huge, modern marina on that northern Spanish coast. In most of the French marinas, we'd moor up and be visited by crowds of locals curious to ask us about our motor boat (although a 51-foot motor cruiser isn't particularly large – just rare in those regions). I'd polished up my French to answer questions about the size of the motors and the range the boat could travel with no sails.

In Santander, however, our boat didn't raise so much as an eyebrow – she was in the company of many, many other fully motorised craft – plenty of them far larger than 51 feet!

We'd discovered that there was an airport at Santander which meant the homeward leg of the journey would be easy-peasy. However, with no Spanish in my vocabulary, simply having the remnants of my Latin classes to help me work out the possible meanings of some notices, I had no clues to guide me through the Basque language, Euskara, which is widely used in that part of Spain. Asking a waiter: *'Nongoa zara?'* (*'where are you from?'*) is one example of how clueless I was when it came even to understanding a menu.

Before we explored Santander, we thought it prudent to sort out our travel plans for the next day and were lucky to spot a taxi driving around the perimeter of the marina. I rushed off the boat and flagged him down. *'DO YOU HAVE A CARD?'* I asked slowly and loudly, waving my business card at him so that he would understand. *'Sure do, man!'* came the American-accented reply. 'Al the Taxi' had just re-homed after years in the USA. What a stroke of luck for us.

Al became our guide and took us to his favourite local restaurant for lunch and the Relais & Chateaux Hotel (part of a fairly well-known chain) we'd chosen for the evening. He offered to help us with the lunch menu and, thinking we'd be looking at Latin-based Spanish language, I thanked him kindly but assured him we could manage. WRONG! We chose a mixed salad and the speciality of the house. MISTAKE! It was the carcass of a baby lamb, literally skin and bone. Tony battled through, I could not. I was glad of the leafy salad and some bread.

On the flight over to collect the boat from France, I'd been reading about a Spanish restaurant that had won an award for its novel dessert – balsamic vinegar-flavoured ice cream with toasted cheese discs. It didn't sound too appetising to me and little did I know that, by chance, our chosen restaurant was the very one that had invented it. However, it was the starter chosen by Tony that caused us the most amusement and surprise. It was to be something from a pig – we couldn't understand what exactly – but Tony, ever the intrepid adventurer, wanted to try it. I stayed with the safety of a soup.

The first course arrived and, looking quite lonely on an oversized plate, was a small cube that wobbled and glistened translucently as it was presented to Tony with a flourish. We stared at it. I said: *'It looks like a lump of fat.'* Thinking of the price, Tony believed that was impossible. He cut into it and in the centre it was solid white. *'I rest my case,'* I said. So I called over the waiter to tell us as best he could, in his broken English, what exactly we had ordered. *'It is ze greez from ze angry peeg zat leeves in ze forest.'* So it was wild boar fat. Quite the delicacy, apparently, though I was so happy to be sipping my soup!

We have so many amusing memories of that trip, including arriving at Santander airport which was locked. I started laughing as we stood outside what looked like a house, only to hear my laughter coming right back at me. It was a mynah bird mimicking me exactly. Which only made me laugh more, which made the bird… etc.

On our return to collect the boat three weeks later, we left Al and our memorable gastronomic adventures to sail from Santander to our next port, Gijón, home to a delightful, traditional way of serving local cider. As described on the website atlasobscura.com: *'In Spain's northern region of Asturias, cider pouring is more performance art than table service. At local cider bars, known as sidrerías, servers pop the cork, then hoist the open bottle high into the air. One hand-tips the bottle, while the other catches the cloudy concoction in a glass held at waist height until it's roughly a quarter full.'* Quite a spectacle!

Our next stop was La Coruña. According to my faithful pilot's guide, it was a large, important port on the very north-west corner of Spain. I didn't envisage being turned away from a sheltered mooring within the marina, so it was a bit of a surprise when they said no! OK then, we'd just have to anchor off – but not before making a tricky manoeuvre into the fuel pontoon.

The tide was out, which meant Tony had to climb a tall ladder from the boat up to the pontoon to arrange our refuel. As you'll see from early photos of me, I have a mass of hair and it's naturally curly and unruly. Living on a boat meant I had to leave it to its wild ways rather than using a hairdryer to tame it. I stood on the deck, a long way down, and Tony called to me to say that the fuel man thought I was Bonnie Tyler. I raised my face (and my air guitar) to him and sang, *'It's a heartache!'* He immediately said: *'You can have a mooring!'* I waved, and bowed in gratitude. Thank you, Bonnie Tyler!

For the last few days, we'd been getting weather warnings – not good in this part of the world. We were leaving the Bay of Biscay and entering the Finisterre sea area, encountering Force 7 winds and wave heights of anything up to 19ft. Characteristically, this means that the sea heaps up and white foam, from breaking waves, is blown in streaks in the direction of the wind ('spindrift' is the technical term).

For a 51-foot boat this doesn't bode well. Off we went, seeking shelter before the storm took full effect. I remember passing Cape Finisterre. Yahoo! We were travelling at 36 knots (about 40 miles an hour), and thinking we were out of danger – but I forgot that the Finisterre sea area covers a vast area and isn't isolated to a few miles around the Cape. Thankfully we discovered a marina four miles up the entrance to the beautiful Ría de Muros e Noia, between dramatically high cliffs.

The storm came with its own drama. I'd never seen white tops on the waves *inside* a protected marina! We lost all contact with the outside world. No electricity. No GPS. No phone. No weather info. For four days. On the fifth day, we awoke to no white tops and Tony was itching to leave. Now Tony is fearless at sea – I am not. So he ignored my suggestion that we give the sea a couple more turns of tide (ie stay put another full day) before we ventured into what had to be a very rough Atlantic Ocean, still angry from the onslaught of the local winds.

I don't think I've ever been so afraid. I'll always remember Tony sitting with his feet up, cool as a cucumber, as we encountered towering waves, one after the next – me convinced our boat would be swallowed by each 'skyscraper' wall of heavy, grey water. Boy, was I happy to get into the Galician port of Baiona. I thought it was the prettiest place I'd ever been. And soon we would be into Portugal and moving closer to the Mediterranean.

We continued our 'work-three-weeks-and-cruise-one-week' pattern. About the only thing that could stop me thinking about work was having to concentrate on navigating, helming and getting us from A to B safely, enjoying the various towns we visited. It worked well. Each time I was back at Slimming World my mind was rested, refreshed and often relieved.

Apart from being stopped by Spanish Customs in the Bay of Gibraltar to search our boat for drugs, and apart from the relentlessly challenging seas even though we were now in the Mediterranean, we finally reached Moraira, a small, upmarket Spanish coastal town, 50 miles north of Alicante. Next morning, we left Moraira to leap to the closest of the Balearic islands, Formentera, next door to Ibiza and 60 miles from the largest of the Balearics, Mallorca.

It was a beautiful day. The sea was flat for the first time, sparkling as the sun created a million diamonds on the tips of its tiny ripples. Half a mile away a whale surfaced, spouting water, and in front of us, dolphins were playing, crossing our bows and having fun. We were making 36 knots once again, and it was so exhilarating. *'This is what it's all been about!'* I remember saying to Tony.

No sooner had the words left my mouth than the boat tipped violently sideways. One of the 'trim tabs', built into the boat to keep the bows straight and to be adjusted to cope with different sea conditions, had broken. Our only option was to make the other tab behave as if it too wasn't working, which meant the bows became very high and obstructed the view from the front of the boat. So it was that we limped into Formentera and the next day, Ibiza – and finally to Port Adriano, in the south-west of Mallorca, where there were mechanics who'd be able to fix our boat.

When we reached Mallorca, our lives were miraculously intact but our boat, and my nerves, needed major repairs!

My first impressions of this beautiful island were actually pretty dismal, despite blue skies and sunshine. It was late October 1996 and Puerto Adriano wasn't (still isn't in many people's opinion) the most uplifting of ports, especially as the winter beckons and the buzz of the season has faded. In '96 it was one of those places where out of season, when the English speak, heads turn and stare. We didn't feel the love.

Based on this first impression, we couldn't wait to leave Mallorca. One day, while waiting for our repair work to start, we met an English couple from the West Midlands, who understood our feelings completely. They enthusiastically talked of *their* marina, just a couple of miles further around the coast, in the Bay of Palma.

That evening they welcomed us aboard their boat and took us to Puerto Portals – a cosmopolitan, more magical port with fabulous restaurants and shops and plenty of friendly English people. Puerto Portals still benefits from a bit of that attractive 'buzz', even in November. Restaurants and shops were open, lights were on and the whole place felt warm and welcoming, especially when we were led upstairs to a restaurant called Wellies and introduced to a room full of British ex-pats.

When we returned to Mallorca some three weeks later, we found the port under attack from such huge seas that our newly repaired boat had been severely damaged. Living on the boat for the rest of that week, we dodged water and rocks hurtling over the sea wall. Thank goodness we were at least tied up and being protected from the worst of it. Unable to move the boat, we left for the UK again having been assured by the port authorities that the marina would mend all the damage. Before we left, we were able to move the boat to the far more sheltered Bay of Palma and the marina of Puerto Portals.

I remember turning to Tony and saying: *'I really like it here. I want to stay.'* *'OK,'* he said. He thought I meant for a couple of days or even a couple of weeks. *'No, you don't understand,'* I said. *'I want us to stay here – for good!'*

And that's how we came to settle and live in Mallorca – initially on the boat, permanently moored in Portals, with us flying to and from England every three weeks. It was while we were here in 1997 that we received the shocking news that Diana, Princess of Wales, had tragically died in a car accident in Paris. We were as stunned and shaken by this terrible incident as the rest of the world. Moments like that you never forget.

" Everyone should believe in something.
I believe I should go to the beach.
I'm done adulting.
Let's be mermaids. "

CHAPTER THIRTEEN

letting go… a little!

Learning to loosen my grip on the Slimming World reins – after so many years of unrelenting hard work – wasn't easy. But it was made easier by the fact that our Head Office was becoming, more and more, a well-oiled machine under the skilful leadership of Sheila Hall. Sheila, who you'll remember had been working for us since the dawn of time, was by now a director of the company. She headed up our field management for more than 20 years before her retirement in 2001.

As I've said before, the '90s saw an incredibly rapid period of growth (in the five years up to 1997 we grew by a staggering 600%). With the huge challenges that brought, Sheila had a lot of responsibility on her shoulders. We couldn't have been in safer hands. Her calm and incredibly focused approach during that period undoubtedly kept this glorious ship afloat at a time when many a lesser captain would have let go of the wheel, overwhelmed. Slimming World would not be where it is today without her dedication, loyalty, wisdom and sheer hard work. Sadly, Sheila died in the spring of 2019 as I was writing this book – and while she enjoyed a long and happy retirement, she will be dearly missed by her family and everyone who knew her.

At the same time as Sheila became our Field Director, we appointed David Rathbone (you'll remember he started working with us as our accountant back in 1986), as our Director of Finance. Meanwhile, Caryl Richards was making impressive headway looking after a great proportion of our managers in the field.

In many ways, it was a blessing that it wasn't until 1997 that I discovered a grim reality going on behind the scenes at our Head Office.

Although on the surface all had seemed tranquil, something underhand had been happening unbeknown to the management team. While we were at home in our secluded cottage, we received a disturbing phone call. An unknown man had discovered our private number and wanted money in exchange for information about a large-scale scam that was being perpetrated against the company.

The mystery caller told us he'd gained intelligence from his son – and that he would divulge the detail of what was happening if we paid him a large sum of money. It was, of course, a huge dilemma. A long-standing employee was suspected of being involved – a person I'd trusted for many years – but of course we couldn't go to *them*, even to ask questions.

In the end, we took a chance and paid the man, to be told exactly how the scam was working. It was a clever and complicated scheme run by a photocopier supplier who'd been fiddling records and overcharging us for years, to the tune of many thousands of pounds. We finally knew the 'whos' and 'hows', and I had to say an immediate goodbye to the member of staff involved. It was a terrible time – the sort of experience that dents your faith in people, yourself included. It's especially upsetting if, as in that case, your trust has been given to a person you believed had earned it. There have always been plenty of critics (is it my imagination or are there even more these days?) who want to blame and point the finger. I'm often accused of being too trusting. This time they were right.

The alternative, as far as I can see, could be to go through life trusting no one, which I think is a pretty sad state of affairs. Getting the balance perfect is a fantasy, so I'd rather err on the positive side of this dilemma and occasionally have my belief in others dented. Anyway, as I often say: *'We all make mistakes, as the Dalek said, climbing off the dustbin!'*

Looking back to 1990, when we were planning our little pitched-roof 'chalet' office (as it's come to be known), I thought we'd be rattling about like peas in a barrel. However, not long after we moved in, in 1994, we yet again found ourselves desperately short of space. Oops! Another Dalek and dustbin moment.

So we quickly constructed a new warehouse to accommodate the ever-increasing volumes of stock while we started planning, once again, to build even bigger offices. That early warehouse is now *'Hair and Beauty'* – our glamorous on-site salon, open to the public and subsidised for the beautification of our (already beautiful!) staff.

Our next big move – into our enormous, purpose-built new office and training facility next door to our original 'chalet' – took place in 1997. After the photocopier scam debacle and subsequent loss of a trusted colleague, Tony had stepped in to fill the gap and soon found Pam James – who'd worked in the printing business – to be his own ideal replacement. Pam became our company buyer, and it was through Pam that Tony also found Paul (Pam's husband), who became our on-site Foreman during the building of this huge new office. Paul is now our trusted Facilities Manager, looking after Slimming World's Head Office building.* (Pam's also now Tony's trusted and immensely loyal PA.)

Towering above our original building, the new Head Office incorporated a super reception area, a cavernous training suite, what seemed like miles of office space and a big restaurant – all connected to our previous home by a glazed bridge. Surely we'd never run out of space here!

The opening of the new building must have come as a relief to the many staff working in the chalet – not least our newest team,

* As I write in 2019, Paul and Pam must be in a state of déjà vu, or to be more accurate, déjà vécu, as they have been the key people involved, since 2016, in the more recently built extension to our 1997 offices. They have planned, sourced, negotiated and project-managed the whole enormous addition. This extended the building to incorporate a fabulous new multi-room training centre, a photography and film studio, underground car park, atrium, restaurant, meeting rooms and much-needed office space.

the members of which were crammed in the corner of an already tight, open-plan office. This was particularly undesirable given that these new members of staff had one mighty important task on their hands, the creation of a brand new magazine – our very own *Slimming World Magazine*.

I'd dreamed of this moment from the very earliest days of Slimming World. I'd already had a go myself at creating an inspiration-packed magazine in 1976 (back when we were still called J&M Slimming Club), approaching a printing company in Huthwaite to help me put together *The J&M Journal*. It was a one-woman production – just me, writing, editing and working with a printer, one Dick Sutton, in charge. Sorry, Dick. If you're looking down from that heavenly printing room in the sky, please forgive me for all my past publishing transgressions.

To be brutally honest, I was quite mortified with the result of our labours – a slim, mainly black-and-white newspaper was a far cry from the inspirational, high-quality product I had in my mind's eye. After much pulling-out of hair (mine), I took pity on our beleaguered printers and decided to close that chapter of the book of Slimming World's history. One of my redeeming qualities (and I do need a few of those) is that I learn quickly, especially from mistakes. Even faster from the unforgivable ones. This wasn't unforgivable, but it was caused by my ignorance combined with excessive optimism (not sure I'll ever lose that trait).

So I learned that producing even the simplest of periodicals was much more complicated than I'd ever imagined. I decided, there and then, that if I was ever going to bring out a magazine for members and the general public again, it would have to be something much, much more special. It would require an exceptional editor, a whole team of professional people, and some serious funds behind it. Until I had all those things, I parked the dream.

With the new building going up around us, 1997 was the year to bring that dream back to life.

Some years earlier, I'd met an editor of a famous and successful slimming magazine, based in London, and realised he wasn't the sort of person (and didn't have the sort of management style) that I would ever have trusted to care for Slimming World and our unique brand. Later again, I was invited to sit on the editorial board of another new slimming magazine. Again based in London (the centre of the media world, as it was at the time), the editor was male and the board was also predominantly so. In fact, I was the sole woman. After just one taste of the general attitude they had towards slimmers, I resigned. Again, it was a useful lesson for me. Slimming World was truly unique. Entrusting our precious brand to the hard-bitten cynics who seemed to dominate the publishing world in those days, was not the way to go. And, apologies as I don't want to offend *your* delicate sensibilities either, but you were, predominantly, MEN!*

So it was with no small degree of caution that, in the mid-1990s, we began the search in earnest for our own magazine team. Up until then, we'd made every attempt to find the right people – who would be based in Derbyshire, at our Head Office, and work with us, alongside us, with people who loved, and lived, the culture for which we're now so famous. This had proved impossible. We were told that the best magazine professionals were all based in London and wouldn't want to move house and home, leaving their media contacts and city life.

Like so many things, if you hold fast to your principles, often it works out well in the end. Surprisingly, I can be annoyingly stubborn. I'm aware that my mule-like attitude can be somewhat irritating and, for the less patient, downright frustrating. Call me old-fashioned darlings, but when you're right, you're right. Right? And creating our

---

* *Sir William Gerald Golding (1911–1993), who was a Nobel Prize-winning writer best known for his 1954 novel* Lord of the Flies, *famously wrote: 'I think women are foolish to pretend they are equal to men, they are far superior and always have been'. Source: https://www.snopes.com/fact-check/william-golding-on-women/*

own magazine was so important, it was vital that we got this spot-on. This was to be our 'shop-window' to the world.

Slimming World was, and is still, a nationwide company with just one Head Office. We hold most of our groups in rented rooms in local communities – somewhere with water and electricity (don't forget the kettle!), warmth, comfort and privacy, and with easy parking wherever possible. We use many types of venue, from church halls to private meeting rooms in *respectable* pubs.

I mention *respectable* after being unceremoniously chucked out of our Scout hut in Mansfield in the early '70s and urgently needing to move. We quickly found a new space – a private room upstairs in a local pub. Overnight, my group of 70-ish members diminished to 20-ish! I discovered that my lovely ladies, who'd recommended the pub because it was conveniently near the bus station with easy parking to boot, weren't aware of the pub's reputation. Their menfolk were though (I won't go into what it was known for), and they didn't want their wives to be seen even approaching the place!

While our Consultants have always done their best to give their venues a smart, warm and welcoming Slimming World feel, we ultimately had limited control over how our groups looked, and the image they projected of our brand. So our magazine needed to be the best 'shop window' ever. I wanted it to reflect the amazing warmth and compassion found in our groups. I wanted to showcase the success of our members, the exceptionally high standard of support available to all, and our deep understanding of the emotional, physical and psychological needs of people struggling with their weight.

I remember the day that we found the very person we could trust to pull together the right team. Her name was Claire Crowther (marrying to become a Barnham shortly after joining us). Claire, who'd been working for a London company editing another slimming magazine, approached us to let us know how much she admired our methods and to ask us if we wanted to launch our own publication.

After an initial chat, Anne Kirk invited her up to Head Office to meet me. Soon afterwards, I asked Claire if she'd be willing to leave her London life and come to Slimming World to create and launch our magazine. And she did! Claire brought with her Lynn Hayes, our first ever Art Editor – now the magazine's talented Creative Director – and we also gained an Advertising Manager to help us fund the project.*

Claire immediately began the tricky task of recruiting a top-quality Chief Sub-Editor, so she placed an advertisement in *The Guardian* – an advertisement that was to bring us one of our most treasured staff to date – Jan Boxshall (now our Joint Managing Director). Jan, who'd been a London-based journalist, had recently relocated to the Midlands and was working as a freelancer when she saw Claire's ad.

Jan has since confessed that when she saw the advert, she thought we must be bonkers – so unusual was it to be setting up a glossy magazine outside of London, let alone in Derbyshire! Intrigued nonetheless, she applied, came for interview and by the end of '97, was part of our tiny team of four working towards a launch deadline of January 1998 (all packed into that tiny corner of the office!).

I wanted *Slimming World Magazine* to be the best of the best. Claire, Jan and the dream team made it just that. They commissioned the most modern, sought-after food stylists and photographers. They pushed the boundaries and art-directed shoots in interesting locations. They found great writers, people with an instinctive understanding of our brand – creating articles that were warm, fascinating, funny in parts, and never patronising or 'telling'. And they brought it all together in a high-quality, glossy format – quite unlike any other slimming title of the time.

I was heavily involved with the first few issues, helping choose which members to photograph for our success stories and feeding

---

* *Claire Crowther is now a British poet and author of three full-length poetry collections.*

back on the written content. Getting the tone right was so, *so* important (and still is). I was determined that our magazine would speak to members as adults, just as our Consultants were trained to do in IMAGE Therapy. I wanted each and every reader to be inspired by the successes of their fellow members, and to finish each issue feeling ready to take on the world.

That tough brief paid off. Virtually straight after the first issue of *Slimming World Magazine* launched – solely within our groups to start off with and hitting news stands a year later – it became number one within what the industry call 'diet titles'.

By 2000, Jan had become Editor and Claire stepped away to pioneer another ambitious project – our very own TV channel on Granada Breeze. Digital Terrestrial TV had launched in 1998, making it relatively cheap and easy to buy and run a TV channel – and there was freedom to do what we liked with it (more or less). Despite the simplicity of its set-up, the channel was fairly short-lived. It didn't attract advertisers in the way that *Slimming World Magazine* did and it wasn't helping members in the way that we'd hoped it would – but it was an exciting experiment!

Slimming World has never shied away from experimental ventures over the years. Some of them have been a phenomenal success. Some haven't. Even after significant investment in a new product or service, we won't chase a financial return if it turns out it won't be in our members' best interests. We'd rather take the hit, move on and do something that will.

Thankfully, *Slimming World Magazine* has only ever gone from strength to strength.

It's attracted awards and accolades since it launched, steadily growing its readership year-on-year.

The strength of this arm of Slimming World comes not from luck or clever tricks, but from people – consistently brilliant people. Over the years, the magazine has been cared for by dedicated, loyal and hardworking editors who have always felt immense responsibility for the quality of their output. We've been very fortunate in this respect.

Today, in 2019, *Slimming World Magazine* is not only number one among 'diet' titles, but *the* number-one glossy magazine in the UK in terms of sales, and has been for several years. In fact, it's the third most actively purchased magazine of *all* magazines on the news stands in the UK. To say I'm proud of our magazine and our team would be putting it mildly.

If the launch of *Slimming World Magazine* had been our only major achievement as a business in 1997, I think I could still have looked back and been very proud. So you can probably picture me over here, glowing away, as I remember that '97 was also the year in which we launched our very own charity, SMILES. The acronym stands for 'Slimmers Making It a Little Easier for Someone' and to date, our members, Consultants, managers and staff have raised over £23 million for an array of good causes.

I've always felt an agonising sense of powerlessness when it comes to human suffering – and a compulsion to try to do something about it. The perpetual dilemma is knowing that, even when *our* intentions are in the right place, other people's sometimes aren't. For this reason, I've always been as cautious as I am generous in my donations to charity. If I've loaned or given money to people, I've done it to give them a leg-up, *not* let them off their own financial hook caused by irresponsible spending.

I do give private donations to overseas charities but I like to be as sure as I can be that the money won't be intercepted by a corrupt government. And when we did Journey 5000 in 1996, I made sure that Marie Curie saw 100% of the £500,000 raised. If we needed anything, we used our own personal money to buy it. We bought, sold and took the losses on our vehicle of choice for the journey. This seemed, to me, logical and right.

The frustrating part of working closely with big charities over the years was having so little control – and knowing that a lot of the funds raised would be ploughed into employees' wages and other business costs. That's why I set up SMILES. I knew we wouldn't drain the funds with administrative or staffing requirements (because Slimming World would absorb them); and I knew that it would enable us to donate significant sums of money each year – to causes of our choice; causes that are close to our and our members' hearts.

Over the years, SMILES has enabled us to make a huge difference through life-changing charities such as the NSPCC (a personal favourite of mine), Cancer Research UK, Great Ormond Street Hospital Children's Charity and Barnardo's to name just a few. We were Guinness World Record holders for staging the World's Biggest Hug for Sargent Cancer Care for Children (now known as CLIC Sargent), we've entered a team into the London Marathon every year since 2002, we donate money from every book sale to SMILES (this one included) and we run two huge fundraising campaigns each year through our groups. There's 'The Big Slimming World Clothes Throw' where members bag up their now over-sized clothes and donate them to Cancer Research UK shops (and Irish Cancer Society shops in Ireland); and then our summer fundraiser, usually an activity-based event, where members set their own personal activity target, commit to achieve it and get sponsored for doing so. Together, these campaigns have raised millions – £3.8 million in 2018 alone for Cancer Research UK. I couldn't even count the other, smaller collections – from the change collection boxes in groups and the donation envelopes on every table at our company awards ceremonies, to our Christmas card amnesties.

In 2000, a great honour was bestowed upon me (in truth on behalf of every single member, employee and Consultant of Slimming

World) when I was chosen to become a patron of the NSPCC, and presented with this accolade by Prince Andrew. Nearly a decade later, in November 2009, Slimming World received further huge recognition when HM the Queen awarded me the OBE (see, there are these little benefits of being the ageing founder) – making me an Officer of the Most Excellent Order of the British Empire (blimey!) for services to the health of the nation and to charity.

I was invited to Buckingham Palace, along with three guests, to collect the OBE. Standing directly before Prince Charles that day was, without doubt, one of the most special moments of my life. I wore a simple black trouser suit with gold embellishments and Tony, Caryl and my daughter Claire were my honoured guests that day.

I freely admit it's a huge personal privilege and I get a 'kick' signing off correspondence with those three special letters, but it's impossible to think of it as 'my' OBE. The medal, and all it represents, belongs to Slimming World. It's up on the wall in our reception area at Head Office, and that's where it will stay. I dearly hope everyone in our company – past and present – is as proud of it as I am.

66 *Society honours its living conformists
and its dead troublemakers.
How very weird!
I'm still alive and kicking!* 99

CHAPTER FOURTEEN

life in Mallorca

By the late 1990s, Tony and I were spending more time out in Mallorca – and less and less time back in the East Midlands. Claire was in her mid-30s and busy bringing up her twins, Joy and Harry (names I found bittersweet, of course), and Dom and Ben were by now young men.

Dom had moved out a few years earlier, when he was 19, and was living in a little bungalow, in the Nottinghamshire village of Old Clipstone, with a large double garage and plenty of hard-standing. He was (and still is) mad about cars – and loved nothing more than remodelling older cars, so needed this precious space. He achieved many accolades for his work in this area and now it's become his beloved hobby instead of his business. He's still in touch with many of his 'heroes' of the day who inspired him from as far afield as Japan. The respect is now mutual.

Ben was still living in our Mansfield cottage, working as a chef. Because he was still so young, I felt strongly that he should come out and live in Mallorca for a while, to meet a wider range of people than his local friends (lovely though most of them were), and stretch himself. I was ever-conscious of his tendency to shrink away from meeting new people, a result of his childhood health problems, and I believed that a change of scene would help him in his life (one thing I hopefully got right as a mum!). Eventually we convinced him and he moved to Mallorca, where he got a job working with an English builder called Colin – who was also a great friend and confidante to Ben during some tough times.

For years after we made our second home in Mallorca, life felt like a bit of an extended holiday – hard to stay in control of my lifestyle and my weight in that mindset, let me tell you! I joke about the fact that it took 10 years to realise I wasn't permanently on my jollies! That's the mode I automatically went into when anyone came out and visited us (which they frequently did), because *they* were on holiday. Finally I faced reality and told myself: '*This is your life, not a holiday. Deal with it!*'

I loved living on the boat in Puerto Portals. The inside of our little second home was cosy and outside there was always something happening or someone to talk to on the sunny marina. It was so easy and convenient to untie and sail into the local calas, with friends joining us on our trips. I wasn't at all interested in bricks and mortar. I had my real home in the UK and one was enough.

The only slight disadvantage was the Internet (rapidly becoming a major part of life) and my computer set-up on the boat. I wasted a lot of my time sitting next to a computer engineer – time I needed to spend sending emails, writing articles and training messages, reinforcing our brand and doing what I could to support our managers back at Head Office. My computer was my lifeline to Slimming World. I couldn't manage without it. That goes double today, so that wherever we are in the world, I can stay in touch, and I can see what's happening on the social media front. I say 'front' in the sense that – while it's an invaluable resource in so many ways, and a brilliant way to share stories far and wide – it can sometimes feel like a war, with many people and organisations trying to get their name out there by hanging on to Slimming World's coat-tails, even if that means 'fake news', distortion and put-downs. For me, social media is both a blessing and a curse. And yes, we are on the 'front line' always.

It was March 1999, and the same friend who'd introduced us to Puerto Portals told us he'd seen a house he was convinced we should buy as a good investment for our 'later life'. He'd arranged for an estate agent to show us around that very afternoon. We rather grudgingly agreed to go. To say I was not impressed with the house is the understatement of the month.

It was a poorly built 1960s bungalow, with an equally poorly built 1960s beige-tiled fireplace. All the attractive features of many Mallorcan villas were missing – no swimming pool, no sea views and no Mediterranean styling. If that wasn't our cup of tea, neither were the other dozen villas the agent subsequently showed us, for all sorts of reasons. Certainly we saw nothing that would tempt me to leave our cosy little boat or spend my hard-earned savings – but Robert, the agent, said that looking at all these properties meant he would be better able to understand our requirements and spot a suitable property ready for our 'retirement', which he was sure we would be needing (sooner rather than later, I think). Good line from a great salesman.

After we gave what we thought was the final thumbs down, we found that, unlike us, Robert had not given up. He had one more place up his sleeve (told you he was a good salesman!). *'There is one other villa but it's not to everyone's taste and the seller insists he won't move on the price which is probably out of your range. But would you like to see it anyway?'*

How could anyone resist?

An appointment was made for the Monday morning. We had flights home booked for the next day, Tuesday. Little did we know how much the viewing was to change our lives. The minute we walked in on that Monday – and I do mean the minute – we were blown away. The quality of the build was obvious. We had become immediate 'experts' on this in one afternoon!

The other houses hadn't had anywhere near enough love and attention during their construction. This house, on the other hand, had been built three years ago for a very demanding German customer.

The builders, overseen by this client, had done an excellent job. The owner had spent his days supervising every detail, including insisting that the wall cavities were vacuumed every night before the builders left the site. I can only imagine how popular that made him! The site was quite a way up on the western part of the Tramuntana Mountains. There were lots of things we loved, still do, but because of its elevated position, the views took the top prize. Just mind-blowing.

We made an offer. We weren't prepared to take on a new mortgage, so we offered virtually all our savings. The agent wasn't jumping for joy. It wasn't going to be easy because what we could afford was only two-thirds of the asking price – a very big drop and a big ask of him. I reminded him that he was a good salesman. His job was to get the house sold and he needed to convince the seller that this was a good, genuine offer, with no 'chain' involved and no mortgage to be organised, so he needed to just go and do his job.

We left Mallorca the next day. I didn't expect that our offer would be accepted. I thought I might be being too inflexible by refusing to borrow the remainder of the asking price. It was the only house I wanted to buy in Mallorca and my stubbornness could lose it forever. Then I did something I'd learned to do years before, to survive all those times when I couldn't afford even the simple things in life – I put it right out of my mind. I wouldn't torture myself by still wanting it. It would go into that special place in my head that stored impossible dreams, where I accepted that sometimes in life we can't have everything we would dearly love.

Back to our Mansfield Woodhouse home. Back to work. Back to reality. The week, as usual, flashed by. I arrived home from the office at 8.30pm that Friday to be met by Tony in the kitchen, just bursting with his news.

'I bought that house today.'

'*What house?*' I asked.

Tony paled and was speechless for a few seconds, in horror and disbelief that he'd just committed us to spend a *lot* of money on a house I'd already forgotten! The truth was my brain couldn't compute the information. That house was in a very well-guarded storage box in my brain. When he said, now sounding slightly desperate: *'That house in Mallorca!'*, the walls of my mental storage compartment fell away and it was *me* who couldn't believe it.

I can still see us hugging each other and dancing around the kitchen as he told me the full story of his superb negotiations, which were all conducted by phone, while attempting to focus on teaching his students the intricacies of manoeuvring a 42-foot boat into tight spaces in the marina and tying a bowline!

Pinching ourselves with disbelief, we moved into our beautiful villa some two weeks later, in March 1999, and it's still our Mallorcan home to this day. Honestly, you'd need a crowbar to prise me out of there.

On the cusp of the Millennium, I had left everything in the safe hands of Caryl and our managers at Slimming World and for the first time in many, many years, Tony and I were able to truly decompress. But it wasn't long before Tony became restless. He missed the Royal Yachting Association (RYA) training school he'd built up in Hull and he longed to get back to his great passion, which was teaching people how to enjoy motor cruising and become extremely competent in doing so.

So in 2000, we opened a new, small business, Mallorca Sea School and Charters, and it thrived. Private clients who wanted practical boat-handling lessons and the Certificate of Competence required to sail in Mediterranean waters (and up to the level of Day Skipper) were as much as Tony could deal with alone.

If there's one thing we can rely on in this life it's that nothing ever stays the same – and so it was with our little school. Large yachts, super yachts, mega yachts and occasionally 'giga' yachts (I know, vocabulary has changed forever!) would come into Palma's boat yard for maintenance over the winter months and many of their crew were looking to improve their skills and their rank. Soon we had more professional clients, looking for better qualifications to climb the ladder in their chosen careers. It was a much bigger deal. From classroom-based theory to practical courses like Ocean Master, it became clear that we needed to find a classroom and more instructors.

The world is sometimes very small, isn't it? The man who had originally trained Tony and persuaded him to become an instructor, John Hart, magically appeared in Mallorca – in our bit of Mallorca, too. John was one of the RYA's top instructors in sail, motor and power and he was, and still is, one of the most highly respected examiners – one who examines examiners! He is a specialist in everything you can think of, for every type of boat, from the rules of the sea to diesel engine maintenance and everything in between. Top man!

Within a very short time, our little school became the largest in the world when counting, for example, the number of Yachtmaster courses we ran. At our busiest, I remember issuing over 100 Yachtmaster certificates in just a month. As time went on, John and his wife Mags, also a top sailing instructor, were running the school with such proficiency, Tony became less and less involved.

It was quite a contrast to the set-up in Hull, where there were hardly enough private clients to keep one instructor fed and watered. Even so, many of our current friends in several corners of the world, including Mallorca, are the result of Tony being so very well-respected as a brilliant instructor. As a former student of his, I can heartily agree!

Back home in the UK, Caryl had agreed to become Slimming World's first ever Managing Director. She took some convincing, as she'd done at every stage of her ascent up the Slimming World career ladder. I'll never forget the look on her face when I popped the question and she responded: *'But Margaret, I don't know how to be an MD!'* To which I replied: *'Neither do I!'*

My theory is that with the right qualities, the right character and a ton of intelligence, you just get up and do it. Echoes of the bumblebee story here. There's no way a bumblebee can fly – its body is too big and its wings are too small, surely. But nobody ever told that to the bumblebee – so it just gets up and does it.

In an attempt to boost Caryl's confidence, I arranged a meeting between us and one of our trusted management consultants and trainers, Malcolm Thomas. At the time, Malcolm was working with the senior team to put a new, more effective management structure in place across Head Office and the field – so he was someone Caryl respected and could trust. In the meeting, he explained the role of an MD and helped Caryl to work through her stoppers.

At the end, I asked Caryl: *'So... do you think you can do it now?'* (fingers crossed behind my back). With apologetic eyes came her admission: *'I still don't think I can.'*

'Well, I need an MD,' I said. *'So if you don't want to do it, tell me, who should I choose?'*

'No one else!' Caryl replied, without hesitation.

In that moment, Caryl realised how deeply protective *she* was of Slimming World. And that, in fact, she knew *exactly* how to take the company forward. Focused like never before, she moved from a position of: *'I can't do this because it's your company,'* to *'I'm already doing this, I can continue to do this and I really want to do this.'* At first, I was Caryl's mentor and she'd ring me in Mallorca two or three times a day to seek my opinion – which turned into two or three times a week, which turned into two or three times a month until she virtually stopped. We're now very happy to chat occasionally, to have the odd meeting and to discuss those things that can drive a sane person over the edge!

So from 2001, my role at Slimming World became that of Founder and Chair (and so it remains today). This meant staying out of the way and letting Caryl and her teams get on with it! I still had input if and when it was needed. There were some major developments bubbling up at the time – not least the development of our activity programme, Body Magic, and the Slimming World website (which was originally named bodyOPTIMISE).

Body Magic came out of an idea I'd put forward after meeting the lovely Professor Ken Fox of Bristol University – now retired, but still a consultant and advisor in the field of activity. We have tremendous respect for him at Slimming World. A truly excellent man.

Early meetings with Ken gave us a clear idea of the best way to help people become more active, and the idea of gradual change, achievable goals and motivational awards came into focus. It immediately got Ken's stamp of approval and we worked collaboratively to create an activity programme that fitted beautifully into our existing strategy of supporting members to make lifestyle changes one step at a time. Caryl, Rebecca Robinson (now our Director of Communications) and Dr Jacquie Lavin (now our Head of Nutrition and Research) and their teams rounded out and polished the whole concept, so our Consultants could bring it to members in group – and they could reap the benefits.

A testament to the robustness of Body Magic as a concept is that very little has changed since we introduced it. Anything goes, from gardening or housework to walking, dancing, cycling or football. Members are encouraged to start with small steps, becoming less sedentary and gradually increasing the duration and intensity of their activity, and they're rewarded with Bronze, Silver and Gold awards as they gradually gain confidence and get into a great activity routine. Once it's a lifestyle – that magical point when being active most days is as natural as brushing your teeth – members reach Platinum status.

By this point, the shiny award means much less than the benefits they're seeing and feeling daily, from better sleep to reduced stress. Many members even tell us that the synergy of Body Magic and Food Optimising has enabled them to reduce medication for conditions such as type 2 diabetes and high blood pressure. Better still, there was never any pressure to join a gym or run marathons (unless that genuinely appealed). Body Magic busts the myth that you have to be 'sporty' to be fit, healthy and toned. It's all about gradually becoming more active in a way that you enjoy, and then keeping it up. Nothing scary about that!

Having completely handed over executive control of Slimming World, you'd think (as a woman approaching my 60s – or so it was alleged), that I'd be thinking about retirement. *You'd think?* To be honest, I'm not sure I'll ever be ready to retire completely.

Compared to the manic me of old – the Margaret who poured 16 hours a day into Slimming World for 30 years solid, for many of those years seven days a week – I'd already cut down my hours considerably by the time Caryl took the reins.

So getting involved in a new business wasn't a daunting prospect for me, or for Tony. In 2003, we were offered the chance to do just that – by buying a West Midlands company called Pearl Yachts, based in Stratford-upon-Avon. At the time, Pearl was managed by Iain Smallridge, a former skipper who Tony had bonded with over shared cigarette breaks at a few Southampton boat shows. The owner of the company wanted to sell and Tony saw an opportunity to be involved in his passion – motor cruising.

I was dead against the idea at first. I didn't like Pearl's boats for a start. I was into other brands – Sunseeker and Princess, which were beautiful and professionally styled – and I simply wasn't prepared to put our name to this style of motor cruiser. If we were to buy the company, it would be on the basis that I could reposition the brand (gosh, that sounds so grand! I mean, I just wanted them to undergo a complete redesign and move into the 21st century. OK then – a complete repositioning of the brand!).

Iain explained that Pearl boats were designed to appeal to a particular type of consumer – customers who identified as 'sailing people' who wanted to move to the greater comfort and convenience of a motor cruiser but steer clear (ha ha – puns abound) of those 'awful gin palaces' – my favourites! Far from the sleek styling and luxurious finishes of the biggest competitors in the motor-cruiser market, Pearl's interiors were deliberately simple with a 'homemade' feel to them. Iain, obviously alarmed by the enthusiastic ramblings of this mad woman (me!), warned that if we changed the styling to something more modern, we'd lose Pearl's entire customer base. When I asked him how many customers that was, he took his time to count them, and proudly announced that there were four. I nearly choked on my Diet Coke! To push home the reality of my non-negotiable changes, I announced: *'Well, if any of those four customers like what we do, then we'll have got it awfully wrong!'*

Tony wanted our boats to travel well at sea, so we employed one of the best naval architects in the business, Bill Dixon, who still designs for us to this day, to make sure the sea-keeping qualities of Pearl Yachts are among the best in the world. The over-worked Iain continues as MD, Paul Hannah (late of Princess) is our amazing Production Director, and, in recent years, we've brought in the celebrated interior designer Kelly Hoppen – who you might remember from the TV show *Dragon's Den* – to create cabin spaces that are every bit as stylish and sexy as the designs she's produced for many high-quality corporations, hotels and celebrities, including the Beckhams (to name-drop just one). I turned my attention to the marketing side of the business, working with designers to create a modern, stylish website and brochures for the brand, something I love to do.

This year, in the wake (can't get away from the puns) of our most recent model launch – the 95-foot Pearl yacht – we've already won two awards and continue to be nominated for more of these important industry acknowledgements. As I write, this stunning boat has been nominated for three more. I'm not sure what Iain's four original customers would make of our new-look Pearl, but the many dozens of discerning clients we have been able to count since then aren't complaining one bit.

With Pearl established and my writing skills no longer needed for the website and the brochure, in 2007 came another new business opportunity – one I was far more enthusiastic about from the off. I'd been introduced to Son Amar, a spectacular dinner show, soon after we moved to Mallorca, and I was fascinated by it. The business had started life in 1963 as a humble tourist attraction – an outdoor BBQ with entertainment, under the stars, set to the sounds of a Spanish guitarist, in the grounds of a Mallorcan country estate.

Since then it had grown into a full-on, singing, dancing, comedy and acrobatics spectacular, within a purpose-built theatre attached to the estate's imposing 16th century manor house, set in the foothills of the World Heritage site of the Tramuntana mountain range that stretches across the width of this amazingly beautiful island. It felt, to me, like something very special. I'd never dreamed of getting involved with it, until one day I was approached and asked to become a partner and buy a share of the business.

It came about through meeting someone in our local gym whose husband had run a dinner show in America called Medieval Times. Now relocated to his birthplace Mallorca, when Son Amar came up for sale, he'd been persuaded by a group of Mallorcan businessmen to go in on its purchase and asked me to be his equal partner – giving each of us a 37.5 percent share. His business friends shared the remaining 25 percent. By February 2007, the paperwork was ready and I was signing on the dotted line – excited to bits by the potential I saw in the place and the thrill of being involved in its future.

At around the same time, Tony came to me and asked: *'How do you feel about having a quarter share in a bar and restaurant? That place down by the sea in Costa d'en Blanes? The one with the terrific views?'*

'I think we need a bar and restaurant like we need a hole in the head,' came my reply.

Carlos and Graham, by now Tony's new business partners, owned a yacht brokerage, chartering and maintenance company in Puerto Portals called Baxter Marine and they'd been desperately trying to get hold of this well-located place for years – perfect for a beach club. It was in a very dilapidated state (falling down in some areas) but, with some investment, it could be something special. Another potential shareholder already had a little experience in running a bar. So, as a couple, Tony and I would be the fourth partner.

I'd known of too many people who had come to Mallorca with the fantasy of owning a little bar and restaurant, living the life in the sun – but 99 times out of 100 it goes bust within five minutes. It's such a seasonal business and you need hard-working, honest, bilingual people working for you – people who'll behave with professionalism – and good, strong managers to keep everything running like clockwork. Those qualities aren't easy to come by anywhere, let alone on a small island.

We'd been customers in bars and restaurants – but we'd never run one! One of the biggest mistakes you can make is going into a business that you know nothing about. I knew that much at least. *'Graham and Carlos have been waiting for years for this to come on the market. And they can't buy the lease unless we go in with them,'* Tony pleaded.

I reluctantly agreed, on the grounds that all four of us were equal partners. All four of us had to put in equal shares of money. I wasn't prepared to be 'The Bank'! That was agreed by all parties. Also (and you might have twigged this by now), I just can't resist an exciting challenge. The high you get from cracking something difficult to achieve is quite addictive. I can't say I enjoy the angst I get in the process (I'm not batty!), but when it works, the buzz of success is out of this world. We named the new venture *'Mood Beach Portals'*.

One by one, our business partners dropped out. It spread like the Spanish flu – and so, within a couple of years, we were outright owners of Mood Beach. By this stage, we'd invested thousands in doing the place up (it was, as I say, a wreck when we started out) and it was too late to turn our backs, so we spent the next nine years making a success out of it as the outright owners – 11 years in total.

Mood became the most glorious place. You could sit outside, under huge umbrellas, chatting and having a drink, looking out to turquoise blue waters, watching boats coming in and out of Puerto Portals, people kite surfing and paddle boarding, and become lulled by the gentle rocking of the boats at anchor in front of you. There was always something going on. We hosted beautiful weddings, swish corporate events and, in 2008, put on a huge American fundraiser called 'Playing for Good', when several major celebrities gave their time for free. *Warning: name-dropping imminent!*

We were joined by Goldie Hawn (I'm not easily starstruck but I adored Goldie!), Paris Hilton and Terrence Howard, who was so charming – modest, friendly, mixed with everyone – just gorgeous. We had a few photos together where I was obliged (it was a dirty job but someone had to do it) to have my arm around him – he said I gave the best hugs ever! Cristiano Ronaldo was there, and incredibly shy. Our General Manager at Mood Beach was an ardent Real Madrid fan and could hardly get his breath when Cristiano walked in. Somehow, I got wedged between these two handsome gents and I wasn't complaining (as you'll see in the photos section). The problem came when some disrespectful person called the paparazzi, who brought along an ex-girlfriend to trap him when he came out. Somehow we managed to sneak him into his shiny black limo and avoid any unpleasantness. For weeks later girls were calling Mood to find out if Cristiano would be in that evening. Excellent PR!

They were joined by Miss Universe (no less), Miss USA and Miss Teen USA (who not only towered over me, but made my 6ft tall Tony look small too). Many local celebs were there and this special event raised plenty of money for five charities worldwide. As you can imagine, it was one of the most memorable days of our life in Mallorca.

Since then, we've had the privilege of entertaining many other famous (and wonderful) people – Jason Donovan (none of us knowing that he'd host the Slimming World awards a decade later), Peter Stringfellow (a dearly missed friend we lost to pancreatic cancer in 2018), Sir Cliff Richard (such a lovely, genuine man), Calvin Harris (so tall), Rita Ora (yet to become an A-lister at the time), Idris Elba (grrr, I missed him three times and everyone was buzzing about him!), Pierce Brosnan (so polite and charming), Vernon Kay (what a nice man and another of our hosts at the Slimming World Awards) with Tess Daly (very lovely), Ainsley Harriott (yet another of our Awards hosts) and a raft of famous footballers and tennis stars.

Considering Mood was a business I'd never wanted, I became extremely attached to it over the years. I made it my own and poured my love and energy into bringing it to life, which made it all the more heartbreaking when, on New Year's Day 2019, we were forced to let it go because the landlord refused to give us another contract. As usual with these things, I prefer to remain mad rather than sad.

My heart has, thankfully, been lifted by three things. First, the amount of love and protestations of loyalty from our wonderful customers. Secondly, I managed to find and take over an old restaurant that used to be known as Samantha's, that we're in the process of refurbishing. Thirdly, we still have our beloved Son Amar.

Back in February 2007, when I signed the contracts for both businesses, I instinctively felt *this* would be the one that stood the test of time. And although Mood remained in our hands for far longer than I'd ever imagined it would, it's Son Amar, our cherished dinner show and country estate, that we can take forward into the next decade.

Keeping Son Amar alive and kicking hasn't been a walk in the park by any means. At one time, it thrived on the business brought in by tour operators filling charter flights with tourists on package holidays, who bought tickets for the show in bulk. But shortly after the Millennium, when the budget airlines started up in earnest and people began to tailor-make their own holidays, Son Amar lost a big part of its customer base. So when we took over, we had work to do.

Son Amar needed investment. We had to spend a great deal on the building itself, and also on letting holidaymakers and local residents know who and what we were. We invested in new branding, marketing, stunning lighting and sound systems, in a new stage and new screens, new choreographers, a brilliant show director and in the best performers worldwide. It's a spellbinding venue in every respect. We can now hire out the venue for weddings, corporate events, conferences and occasional TV spectaculars (if you watched 2018's *Love Island*, you'll have spotted Caz and Josh sharing a romantic meal on Son Amar's royal terrace). Our Mallorcan Show Director, Ricard, and his Russian wife Liubov (our Head Choreographer) are forever developing the dinner show to wow our audiences year after year, and every single year we have achieved Trip Advisor's Certificate of Excellence.

As I mentioned in an earlier chapter, Ben now manages Son Amar, the estate and our staff with incredible passion and care. The lengths he has gone to and the results he has achieved are nothing short of mind-blowing! Ben has much to be proud of.

In the grounds of Son Amar, Ben has designed and opened a new restaurant called El Castillo, which is well worth a visit. Virtually all the food served is plant-based (meat and fish are available for us carnivores), almost completely locally sourced and therefore referred to as 'Zero Kilometres', 'Farm-to-Fork' increasing the duration and intensity of their activity and 'Slow Food'. On site, thanks to Ben, we now have beehives, bat houses and a worm farm fed with compost made up of food waste and shredded cardboard to create an eco-friendly fertiliser for Son Amar's home-grown fruit and veg. Alan Titchmarsh eat your heart out!

Dominic, who moved out to Mallorca permanently a few years ago, has also been involved in Son Amar over the years – although not to the extent that Ben has.

Dom's business interests lie in another segment of the hospitality business – and in 2017, he became a partner, with Martyn Smith, in a fantastic beach club/nightclub, which sits in an enviable position in the middle of the Paseo Maritimo – the main road running along the seafront in Palma and overlooking the sea and the huge Palma Marina. In their first year, the Social Club Mallorca as it's called, became lauded as the island's premiere nightclub. Dom certainly has much to be proud of too.

Claire's family ties, meanwhile, have kept her happily at home in Derbyshire – and just as well when it came to putting this book together, because she's dug out and organised the treasure trove of old snaps you'll see on the photo pages. She's always been a terrific 'organiser'. Imagine my surprise when, upon turning 60 a little more than a decade ago (this *must* be a mistake!), Claire had co-ordinated a fun-filled party and *This is Your Life* style presentation, compèred by the affable actor Christopher Biggins. That's another day I'll never forget.

What's next for our family's lives and livelihoods in Mallorca and Derbyshire, only time will tell.

66 *Choose a job you love, and you'll
never work a day in your life.* **99**

Confucius

The endearing and enduring Sir Cliff Richard with our good friends Sara and Dennis Causier.

Cristiano Ronaldo's visit to Mood was the talk of the town for weeks!

Tony and me with our dear friends, actor and singer Jess Conrad and his lovely wife Renee at the Son Amar première.

This photo was taken at our home in Mallorca, just before we left for an evening show at Son Amar. I've always liked it because I felt happy and relaxed, because Tony was the photographer…and because I'd just had my hair done!

This is as close as Tony and I have come to staging a complete family photo (although it's a few years old now!), bringing together Tony's and my children and grandchildren (bar one, who couldn't make it that day). Quite a clan! Since then, we've added three great-grandchildren and there's a new grand child (number 11) on the way.

A poster for our dinner show at Son Amar — a true spectacle, set in the most gorgeous Mallorcan countryside, in the foothills of the Tramuntana Mountains, now a World Heritage site.

Tony and me meeting King Felipe VI of Spain at the Royal Palace of La Almudaina in Palma de Mallorca.

It was a true honour to
become a Patron of the
NSPCC, and to meet
HRH Prince Andrew
in the process.

Receiving my honorary
Master's degree from the
University of Derby, in
recognition of Slimming
World's compassionate and
highly supportive approach
to our members.

HRH Prince Charles awarding me the OBE in 2009 – a truly proud and unforgettable moment. I was proud to accept on behalf of our amazing organisation.

I was allowed three guests at Buckingham Palace to receive the OBE. Celebrating with me were (from left to right), my daughter Claire, my husband Tony and Slimming World's CEO (then MD) Caryl Richards. What a special day that was.

Ben with his wife Beatriz (Bea) and three brilliantly barmy boys! Joe (eldest), Samuel (middle) and Louis (youngest).

Dom and his partner Eva, with her son Max (and there's new baby due September 2019!).

Claire and her lovely twins, Harry and Joy, a few years back.

Friday 5th August 2016 – I remember it so clearly because it was the first time in an age that Tony felt well enough to leave the hospital and eat a proper meal in a restaurant. You can see, though, that by this point he was losing weight fast following his cancer diagnosis and treatment for raised calcium levels in his blood. He was extremely ill.

Tony and me at the Slimming World Awards in November 2016, two days after a liver biopsy and just before he started immunotherapy. His health was deteriorating rapidly following round after round of chemotherapy and this occasion was a struggle for him – yet still he found the strength to smile for a photograph with his wife. This is bravery. This is love.

Tony and me with Professor Christian Ottensmeier – Tony's life-saving immunologist, to whom we owe so much.

There are no such things as miracles, they say. Being rational about it, I'd probably agree – but it feels a lot like Tony and I have been blessed with one. This photograph was taken in 2019, some two years after immunotherapy wiped out Tony's Stage 4 terminal cancer. The look on our faces speaks volumes – the happiness of being together still.

CHAPTER FIFTEEN

Slimming World grows wings

If life dealt us nothing but good times and easy rides, would we ever appreciate real happiness? How can we know it, or feel it, if we never experience the darker side of life? So I tend to deal with regrets and missed opportunities with a fatalistic attitude.

This isn't to say I've never wished for something I couldn't have; or dreamed wistful dreams of what could have been. I've often wondered, for instance, how university and academic life would have changed me, my way of thinking, my future, my family and my friendships.

In my life, I've witnessed so many life-changing successes and our gorgeous, self-effacing members often say to me: *'I couldn't have done it without Slimming World.'* But the fact is, they did it. *They* did it! It's an honour to know our company gave them the tools and support to achieve their dreams and it's so important that *they* own their success.

So having read thus far – knowing me and my life now, as you do – you'll understand how personally meaningful it was for me to be awarded an honorary Master's degree from the University of Derby in 2010. I never sat in lecture theatres, took exams or ate (burnt!) cheese on toast in a student kitchen at 2am, but my years of hard work, my ability to analyse and understand the emotional and psychological, as well as the physiological, aspects of being overweight, and my downright persistence had been officially recognised.

The award came about after the University of Derby's Research Professor, Prof. Paul Gilbert, visited Head Office to witness our world-class Consultant training. Professor Gilbert is a psychologist specialising in the therapeutic benefits of compassion – something that's inherent in IMAGE Therapy, and always has been.

And it wasn't the first time that Slimming World's methods had attracted attention from academics. It had been over a decade since Doctor (now Professor) James Stubbs published that ground-breaking piece of research on macronutrients, energy density and satiety which I mentioned back in Chapter two. I always knew that the principles behind my eating plan were sound – based on good quality reading and analysis of my practical experience. And because it worked! But James's research, which has since been repeated and confirmed all over the world, gave Food Optimising important visibility and respectability in the scientific and academic communities. My honorary degree did the same for IMAGE Therapy.

Academic recognition opened up new avenues – enabling us to reach more members and help save more lives than ever before. With the credibility boost that such backing brings, we made greater progress than ever with our pioneering 'Slimming on Referral' scheme. We first piloted this ground-breaking idea in 2000 – creating a trial which allowed GPs to refer overweight patients to a local Slimming World group, at a fraction of the cost to the NHS of drug treatments or weight-loss surgery, and with total safety.

At that time there were very few partnerships between the NHS and commercial organisations, and our dedicated nutrition and research team had to work hard to build relationships with local GP practices. Because it had never been done before, they had to work out the practicalities of supporting GPs to raise the subject of weight with patients, how to give patients access to their local groups while ensuring they wouldn't worry about being seen to be different from other members, and how to monitor and report back on their progress

– because, of course, we had to be sure that patients referred by their doctor would be motivated enough to successfully lose weight.

That first pilot was a big success for patients and GPs alike. This enabled us to roll the model out all over the country, and to publish the scientific evidence, as well as presenting evidence to the government's Health Select Committee. Slimming on Referral (as it's now known) became an established part of the NHS's approach to tackling obesity – commissioned by an increasing number of health trusts and local authorities, and acknowledged to be an effective and cost-saving service.

This in turn gave us the confidence to go against general opinion and launch Free2Go in 2006 – a lifestyle-change programme geared specifically to 11 to 15-year-olds. Caryl Richards was the leading light in Slimming World for this project, and all of us were prepared to take any knocks that came our way for the sake of the young people who needed our care and guidance. At the time, few people were prepared to stick their necks out and give practical advice on managing childhood obesity. It was, and probably still is, a hot potato – understandable, because it's complicated. Free2Go is another example of Slimming World's willingness to make a bold move for the sake of its members and their loved ones.

Becoming 'noticed' by the academic world may have amounted to a few pieces of paper, but to us it was vitally important – robust scientific evidence of the power of Food Optimising and IMAGE Therapy. It was important that we could prove our effectiveness, not just for Slimming World and its employees and franchisees but for our members – for every desperately unhappy overweight person whose life changes when Slimming World groups open up in their community.

As the time grew closer to the University of Derby's ceremony, when I'd be awarded my honorary degree, I made a phone call to check that I wasn't expected to prepare anything special in advance.

No, they said – I simply had to turn up, collect my certificate and off I go. No acceptance speech? No. All I needed to do was say: *'Thank you'*.

The night before, I was invited to a dinner to meet some key figures from the University. One of them was the then-Chancellor of the University, Peregrine Andrew Morny Cavendish, 12th Duke of Devonshire, known to his friends simply as Stoker. What a truly, genuinely lovely man. Chatting to him after the meal, at just gone 11pm, I admitted how surprised I was that they didn't need me to make a speech the next day.

'What?' he said in amazement. *'Of course we want you to make a speech! You've been given an honorary degree for a reason. We want you to inspire other people!'*

Oh goodness me, I thought (or words to that effect!). So there was I, on YouTube at 2am, desperately scrolling for guidance, inspiration, divine intervention (anything!) from past honorary degree holders. The exercise may not have shown me what to do but it certainly showed me what *not* to do – and that was bore the audience of youngsters with my entire life story (I saved that for this book!).

My speech, I decided, should come from the heart. If that sounds familiar, it is. I don't know how to write or talk any other way. On the day, I talked about the fact that I would always have loved to go to university and hadn't had the chance. Everyone in that room had a qualification behind them from a fantastic institution – a great head start in life! So I posed the question: what would make them stand out? What got me through? It was absolutely all about attitude. If there's one thing I'd learned in life, it's that unless you have the right attitude and the right work ethic, you won't go anywhere – no matter how intelligent you are. I stand by those words to this day.

Through my honorary degree, the 'Miles-Bramwell Chair in Behaviour Change and Weight Management' was created – giving Slimming World's research specialists yet more opportunities to drill into the complexities of obesity and lifelong weight loss. We may never be able to give our members all the answers. But as always, we've got some really great questions.

The twenty-teens at Slimming World (ie 2010-2019) were about as far from adolescence as it gets – although there's no doubt we shot up in a very short space of time! Faster than any other decade, in fact. It was a dynamic, supercharged, risk-taking 10 years; a decade that saw the appontment of a four-strong board of directors. We already had Managing Director Caryl Richards and Finance Director David Rathbone, of course, and now we added Jan Boxshall as Marketing Director. Jan, who you'll remember was the Editor of our magazine, left Slimming World in 2000, and was tempted back into the business by Caryl in 2007 to become our Head of Communications. We also welcomed Lisa Salmon as our Director of Field Operations.

Lisa was something of an anomaly in Slimming World's history (in a good way!). For the first 30 years, we tended only to recruit managers for our field teams who'd started out as Consultants. For me, it was vital that everyone who worked with our Consultants understood the nitty-gritty of supporting members. So we liked them to have been a member, then a successful Consultant, before climbing the ladder to support teams of Consultants as an Area or Regional Manager. How else could they really 'get it'?

There was just one problem. Intelligent, vibrant, inspiring, motivated and organised Consultants didn't necessarily translate into vibrant, inspiring, motivated and organised managers. Maybe it's something to do with the natural creativity within all great Consultants – maybe this gave them a tendency to make up their own rules. Maybe we weren't training them well enough. Whatever the reason, we decided to try something entirely new to reinvigorate Slimming World's field management. And so, together with our trusted management consultant Malcolm Thomas, Caryl developed a new recruitment strategy that saw us wade into a much wider pool of potential management talent – our tens-of-thousands of members.

An advertisement went into *Slimming World Magazine* early in 2000 and by the end of that year, we'd welcomed an exceptionally strong cohort of high-quality, experienced managers into the business – managers who are still pushing the business forwards in their various areas of specialism to this day. Lisa was one of them. With a background in sales, Lisa loved a challenge from day one – and she quickly established herself as the best in the business when it came to helping others achieve goals. She was quickly promoted from District Manager to Senior Development Manager and later Field Manager, becoming National Manager a few years later and then Director of Field Operations (today she's our Joint Managing Director). In this role, guided by Caryl's steadying hand, Lisa has helped to drive unprecedented levels of growth throughout the business – helping us to change and, without exaggeration, very often save more lives than ever before.

This, as you know, was always the end game for me – growing not for growth's sake, but for the sake of all those millions of people who struggle with the multiple demons of excess weight. There's the physical and psychological pain, the shame, the guilt, the frustration and the sheer effort of dealing with all that while trying to have a life! The Slimming World members who have successfully conquered those demons – from our stunning competition winners over the years to the many Slimming World success stories I read about in the papers and on social media – never fail to inspire me. You'd think that after 50 years in this job, these very personal, transformative tales might start to lose their power. But they don't. Each and every time I meet or hear from a Slimming World member who's changed their life (and I always encourage them to own that success completely – *they* did it!), I still feel the same awe, the same fascination and the same massive respect that I always have and always will. Each and every story is new and special. Each and every story moves me to my core.

So as proved by Lisa and the cohort of managers who joined around the same time, sometimes it's worth taking a risk. It's worth trying something new. It's proof that – as every slimmer knows in their head and heart – nothing changes if nothing changes. And during this pivotal period in Slimming World history, change was everywhere.

Our Sin-a-Day plan had been renamed 'Food Optimising' in the year 2000. You'll remember that I quickly adjusted the original plan in 1969 when I discovered just how many high-fat foods some members could consume. After this, the basic eating plan encouraged members to fill up on unlimited lean protein, plus plenty of fresh vegetables, while limiting carbohydrates. My early research led me to develop a list of foods that were (and still are) great for slimmers – foods that are low in energy density, highly satisfying, healthy and hugely helpful in reducing calorie intake without counting a single calorie.

We designated these foods as Free Food, and in a bold and brave move that revolutionised weight loss at the time, we let members know that they could eat Free Food in unlimited amounts – without weighing, counting or measuring at all. At any time of the day or night. Ridiculous! We also pioneered something we call the Personal Achievement Target (PAT) – whereby the member (not their Consultant) chooses and sets their own target weight, with free attendance at group after they achieve it. Also deemed pretty ridiculous by some when I first introduced it many moons ago!

Over the years, we streamlined the eating plan as our understanding of nutrition, and of our members, developed. We added daily portions of calcium-rich and fibre-rich foods, initially called Two for You, then renamed Healthy Extras, to make sure every member was getting a healthy balance in their diet.

We also added fruit and fat-free dairy products to our designated list of Free Food. In 1991, we introduced an alternative plan, initially created for vegetarians, which allowed members to enjoy unlimited carbohydrates like pasta, rice and potatoes, while limiting lean protein (and they absolutely loved it!). We called the two plans our 'Original' and 'Green' plans, but members tended to refer to them as 'Red days' and 'Green days' – you still hear people talk about them in groups now.

Both the Original and Green plans enabled members to enjoy a varied, well-rounded diet week on week – each super-effective for weight loss. There was just one issue. 'Food Combining' was a popular diet fad at the time – and although Food Optimising was most definitely never a Food Combining programme – a misconception began to develop that it was. So in 2009 we made another major change.

Under the guidance and expertise of Dr Jacquie Lavin and her team, we launched Extra Easy – an idea based on our Free2Go eating plan developed for young adults and bringing everything our members loved about the Green and Original diets into one, simple, streamlined eating plan (yes, by now the 'D' word had been well and truly outlawed!).

Members couldn't believe it. Non-members couldn't believe it. The nutrition establishment couldn't believe it. The press couldn't believe it. With its extensive list of Free Food, Extra Easy seemed too good to be true – impossible to lose weight on. Insanely generous! But guess what? It was another risk that paid off because – with decades of experience and in-house nutrition expertise behind us – Extra Easy was never going to fail. It was based on robust scientific research (which I've always, always been committed to funding) and a deep understanding of the way slimmers think and feel about food. It was a revolution – and it's since been imitated by our competitors all over the world.

The science behind Food Optimising – that of energy density, satiety and satiation – sounds a bit technical, but it's actually incredibly simple. Energy density is simply how many calories a food has per gram. Cheese (mmm, who said cheese?) is very energy-dense, for example, packing loads of calories into a very small space. Right at the other end of the scale would be a food like celery, which packs hardly any calories into the same space – so you'll get full from the sheer volume of the food before you've eaten enough calories to pose a risk to your weight loss (clever!). That's why we love our fruits and veggies at Slimming World – they're a slimmer's best friend!

One thing I never, ever wanted, though, was for Food Optimising to be a rabbit food diet (perish the thought!). Foods like lean meat, fat-free yogurt, eggs, pulses and pasta are relatively low in energy density too, so when you're Food Optimising, you can also eat them freely. These foods (and there are loads more) are also highly 'satiating' – so as well as filling you up in the short term, they keep you feeling full for longer (and that means you're less likely to go scavenging for snacks – which are so often those foods posing the greatest risk to our weight loss, like biscuits or crisps).

I've always found that people understand energy density and satiety best when you ask them to think about eating four apples versus drinking a medium-sized glass of apple juice. To eat four apples, there'd be a lot of bites, a lot of chewing, you'd eat the skin, the flesh and it would take you bloomin' ages to get through them all. Chances are, you'd stop after one or two anyway – jaw ache would set in… and you'd probably get a bit bored! Think, instead, about a glass of apple juice – taking more like eight apples to make and containing many more calories than those four whole pieces of fruit, and in a different, much easier-to-consume format. How likely would you be to drink that whole glass of juice? And how long would it take? How full up would you feel afterwards? And do you think you'd still feel full in 10 or 20 minutes?

You see where I'm going with this!

That's why apples are Free Food – but apple juice isn't (nor any other pure fruit juices). It can take our members a bit of time to get their heads around that (especially because juices seem like a 'healthy' choice) but when you think about it, it makes complete sense.

Psychologically speaking, Food Optimising's generous synergy of Free Food, Healthy Extras and Syns also helps prevent that vicious cycle of shame and overeating which scuppered me in virtually every diet I tried as a young woman – and that scuppers many, many other slimmers too. With so many unlimited foods to fill up on when you're Food Optimising, there's no need to feel guilty about eating as much as you like until you're really, truly satisfied. With measured Healthy Extras and Syns, no food is banned – not one. Food Optimising – which had never been simpler, as the name Extra Easy suggests – took away the sense of deprivation that makes so many other weight loss programmes miserable and unsustainable. And for the rebels among us (I count myself firmly in that camp), it took away the 'fight'. If there's nothing to rebel against, there's no urge to rebel!

It was also during this action-packed period that we formalised our relationship with The Royal College of Midwives, becoming one of their Alliance Partners. We'd worked with them previously, particularly in the late 1990s, when they helped us develop our policy to support mums and mums-to-be to maintain a healthy weight during pregnancy and breastfeeding (in fact, we're the only national weight management company to offer this vital help). Our new partnership allowed us to strengthen and formalise that policy, and to spread the word to midwives and other health professionals about our unique support.

It wasn't about weight loss. The policy allowed us to help women – women who wanted and needed our support – to manage their weight safely and develop great healthy eating habits at a key time in their lives. Oh to have had that kind of help during my own pregnancies!

It's no coincidence that with the rise of technology – giving our Consultants a whole new landscape in which to promote their groups and new ways to communicate with members – the last two decades have also seen our digital service move in leaps and bounds. In 2004, the year Facebook was founded, Slimming World still ran much as it had when I opened my very first group in 1969. Operating out of village halls and Scout huts, Consultants used a pen and paper to record all their member information. They took cash only and sent copies of their accounting paperwork in the post each and every week to our Head Office, where the hundreds of brown envelopes were opened, and the contents diligently transcribed onto a computer.

By 2011, our in-house IT development team (which included Paul Siddall, Sean Chapman and Liz Bullimore – all still with us today!) had created a complete group management system which did away with all of this. We named it *XpressWeigh*. This software allowed Consultants to gather important member information, payment details, weight loss progress records and IMAGE Therapy support all in one place – making the group experience and the after-group administration slicker, smoother and more professional than ever.

In the same year, we modernised, re-branded and re-launched *bodyOPTIMISE* as 'Slimming World Online', and our global and members-only websites and social media pages have been continually refreshed and refined ever since, to give members the essential between-group support and inspiration that was once only available through magazines, newspapers or a cup of tea with fellow slimmers.

In 2015, with Slimming World well established as a trusted household name, we took another plunge – launching a range of frozen Slimming World meals, in partnership with Iceland. I'll always remember Caryl wringing her hands with anxiety, worried about whether it was the right thing to do. We'd been on the fence about it for years. Members had told us – frequently! – that they'd love to be able to buy ready-prepared Free Food meals – something to help them stay on track with their weight loss on those busy days when there's no time to cook (and when the temptation of the takeaway looms largest!).

What worried us to death was putting out a mixed message. The last thing we wanted to do was to undermine the importance of cooking healthy meals (which is what Food Optimising is all about – and always has been). We didn't want members to think that it's not possible to make healthy, fast, satisfying, Free Food meals from scratch – it most certainly is, even for someone like me who isn't the world's best cook (understatement of the year)! And we didn't want them to *rely* on our frozen meals – because then we wouldn't be helping them to change their lifestyles at that deep, lasting level so essential to keep weight loss off for life. It was a real 'do-we, don't-we?' dilemma.

In the end, because we found the right manufacturer to partner with, who was able to meet our (very exacting, let's be honest!) demands, we went for it! We saw an opportunity to genuinely help those members in their all-important first few weeks, before we've helped them develop the vital recipe and cooking skills that will carry them through their weight loss journey to new, healthy routines in the kitchen. And of course, everyone – even homecooking maestros – benefits from a handy, healthy back-up in the freezer for really busy days. Our range at Iceland was developed and marketed with scrupulous love and care by a team led by our Head of Food and Publications, Allison Brentnall. Allison started work with me way back in the summer of 1990 at the tender age of 18. She didn't come to Slimming World for a career – in fact, she was temporary cover for my PA at the time, Margaret Tryner, when she broke her leg! But I liked Allison a lot – we hit it off – and so I offered her a permanent position, building our food database.

Twenty-five years down the line, Allison's deep understanding of Slimming World's philosophy, and her passion for good food, made her the perfect person to develop our food brand with Iceland. The range was intended, very importantly, not as a 'solution' to weight loss, but as a fall-back for busy days. Uniquely, the recipe was (and still is) printed on the packaging – so members could create the same dish at home when they have more time. The ingredients were painstakingly selected by Allison and the Iceland team to ensure each meal was completely Free, as well as delicious and nutritionally balanced. And at every opportunity, we steered members to serve our meals with a third of a plate of very low-energy-density veggies, to fill them up by volume, while reducing their overall calorie intake.

The range was an immediate success, becoming the UK's largest frozen ready meal range within the space of just a few weeks. We (not to mention a stunned Iceland) could barely believe it as freezers full of Slimming World meals emptied all over the country – in many cases, within just an hour or so of the stores opening. Talk about panic. Reminds me of that night back in the sports hall in Barnsley in 1971, with all those members queuing out of the doors and up the stairs, eager to get a slice of the best weight loss club in town. Thankfully, Slimming World's logistical capabilities have come on a little since those days!

Although I've overseen this era of Slimming World from a distance (often graciously keeping my nose entirely out of anything that's better left to our IT-savvy new generation), I look on with enormous pride. It's like planting a seed, tending to it, watering it, supporting its fragile stem to see it through rough weather, checking up on it as it fares each season – and then knowing you've done enough to walk away and let it grow. The culture I instilled at Slimming World – upheld and cared for by managers and staff at every level – remained alive across the business when Tony and I moved to Mallorca, and has done ever since. It would be too much to ask for an eternal springtime – but at Slimming World, I like to think you can smell blossom all year round.

66 *To succeed in life you need three things. A wish bone, a back bone and a funny bone.* **99**

CHAPTER SIXTEEN

the lowest of lows

How strange life can be sometimes. One minute we're jogging along as normal, having a giggle (or a niggle) at the ridiculous, and taking for granted that life will continue in much the same way, and then wham! Our lives are capsized, and we're drowning in fear, helplessness and hopelessness.

I think I used to be an optimist, teetering on the edge of realism. Now I'm a realist barely hanging on to optimism with aching fingertips. Many nights, I've looked across at Tony, sleeping soundly, wondering how many more years we have together, comfort and company for each other. Then I'm gripped with a feeling of impending doom. I dash away the tears, and castigate my silly self for wallowing in such thoughts – before unnecessarily allowing myself to do more of the same.

Our lives were going well – Slimming World, Son Amar, Mood and Pearl Yachts were all thriving, our families were happy and largely settled. And then one day along came a strange ache in Tony's hip. We joked about the pain in the backside and Tony put it down to a 40-year-old injury plaguing him once again (or the three different mattresses we'd been sleeping on). But then the ache spread down his leg – so badly that he needed a walking stick, then crutches, all within a matter of days towards the end of April 2016.

We were in Mansfield at the time, so we visited a reputed physiotherapist just a few miles down the road from Slimming World. He wouldn't touch Tony, he said, until he'd had a scan. Maybe this guy knew something we didn't. Either way, it gave Tony the push he needed to make a hospital appointment, a few weeks later back home in Mallorca.

After a day of X-rays and MRIs, that night Tony swung his legs around to get out of bed and his femur snapped. He was in excruciating pain. Tony is one of the toughest men I know, but this pain had him screaming. I rang frantically for our doctor, Marcus Fisser – a man we hugely respect. No answer. Tony wouldn't allow me to call an ambulance, preferring to wait – in agony – until the morning so he could see Dr Fisser.

That night was like watching someone being tortured – an experience I never want to go through again. Morning came and our doctor arrived, knowing by now (following a phone call from Tony's radiologist) that there was a tumour in Tony's bone. Eventually, an ambulance arrived, Tony was given the strong pain relief he needed and he was whisked off to hospital for hip replacement surgery.

The surgeon told us he'd seen enough tumours in his time to be 99 percent sure that this one was benign – but he'd send the tumour tissue away for analysis, just to be sure. Last time we'd heard those words, it was in 1996, from the surgeon in the ridiculous red dickie bow. The tie belied his expertise, because *my* tumour did, indeed, turn out to be benign. I had no reason to believe it would be different this time, for Tony.

For the next 10 days we lived in a fool's paradise. That is until Marcus came to tell us the devastating news. The tumour was malignant and it wasn't the primary tumour, but a secondary one – one of many – originating in the lung. The cancer was NSCLC, Non Small Cell Lung Cancer, Stage Four – and that meant it was terminal.

Tony hadn't been short of breath. He hadn't had a cough. There had been no warning signs at all. All this took a while to process – Tony remaining calm and strong, trusting me to know how best to proceed. Life as we knew it stopped. We were aware that everyone was worried for us, and also that life must go on outside of our personal nightmare. It had to. Friends, family and employees rallied around us.

As it turned out, I was a great nurse – much to Tony's surprise, I think. I'd had plenty of practice with my mum and dad and with Ben in babyhood and childhood, with so many hospitals and operations. So, with Tony, I would have no problem dealing with personal care, with dressings and injections, with communicating with hospital staff – and I had a perfect excuse to cuddle him whenever I liked.

Our super-duper doctor Marcus joined us to some degree in our distress. It must be really hard, as a doctor, to be at once empathetic and at the same time sufficiently distant. To be able to steer clear of the intense feelings of the sufferers and their loved ones so that the best decisions can be made is, indeed, a very special skill.

My immediate thought was to find a miracle. That was what was needed and it was up to me to find one. So where best to look? Well, Slimming World had been doing some great work supporting Cancer Research UK, sending them millions via the 'Big Slimming World Clothes Throw', thanks to our amazing members and their Consultants, so maybe they could give me advice. I just needed to know where was the best, most cutting-edge cancer hospital to be found in the UK for lung cancer cures – or, if not the UK, then Europe, or if not Europe, the world!

My logic went something like this: 'Cancer Research UK get billions of £s every year and they decide how best to spend it and who best to give it to, to find cures for the previously incurable. They must know where the best researchers and the best clinicians are. They must know where the clinical trials are happening. And, for sure, they must know a hell of a lot more than I did, because I know a big fat NOTHING about cancer and my husband is DYING!'

The message came back that a senior clinician would call me without delay. That call never came. Apparently, it was handed down to someone else, who did call. She didn't appear to be listening to my request. I was, I believe, pretty clear. I was looking for some miracle, some cutting-edge science that would give my husband a chance to live. So where was the best place for me to go, the best hospital with the latest trial, or whatever else would be the best way of finding this miracle?

She told me that all cancer hospitals were very good. *'No, they are not,'* I said. Well yes, she insisted, they all give very good palliative care. At the time, I wasn't entirely familiar with cancer terminology. *'Palliative care? Isn't that what they give to patients in a hospice?'* I asked. Her haughty reply came whistling back to me: *'He can't go into a hospice until the last few days of his life.'* As I started to protest that I didn't want him in a hospice – I wanted to find a cure – I stopped and realised I wasn't talking to the right person, so I thanked her and ended the call.

Marcus was as desperate to help as I was. Together we searched for the 'best' treatments, the 'best' trials, and the 'best' hospitals in the world. It seemed to boil down to three – number one for adults was said to be the MD Anderson Hospital in Houston, Texas. Dana Faber in Boston was also high, number one for children and not far behind for adults, and then there was the famous Mayo Clinic in New York. Marcus had a contact at MD Anderson, so that seemed like our best option. After hours of Googling, I booked us into a fairly basic three-star hotel in Houston, near MD Anderson and with a shuttle bus for regular hospital to-ing and fro-ing – and we needed that as appointments were certainly not planned for the convenience of patients. Former patients online said the hospital had performed miracles. I hoped upon hope that this was true, because we needed one.

An extract from my diary
July 2016

*We've arrived at MD Anderson and the doctors are
very positive about Tony's general state of health.
He really is one of the most clean-living people you
could wish to meet. He doesn't drink, smoke (it's
been 14 years since his last cigarette) or take drugs
and he exercises regularly when life is normal. Just
walking, or swimming or stretching – simple stuff –
and his diet is great. He eats salads, vegetables,
fruit, fish, wholemeal bread and potatoes – nothing
too sweet and negligible fats. The doctors say this
will help him a lot in this fight ahead.*

*They have a team to look after Tony, specialist
nurses and radiologists under the experienced Dr
Blumenschein. He told us he'd be using what he
calls multimodal, multidisciplinary therapies.
Chemotherapy is certain to be one of those, but he
can't use that until he knows the genetic make-up of
the primary cancer. That could take a few weeks of
pathology. In the meantime, he is going to zap the
tumour in Tony's leg with radiotherapy, stopping
any future growth of residual cells, along with what
he thinks is another tumour in the same femur.*

*We have our family doctor, Dr Fisser in Mallorca,
to thank for moving things along so fast. He has a
contact in this hospital and has been
incredibly supportive.*

We seem to be coming to terms with the hospital regime.

The brain scan results were clear – a bit of much-needed good news. Apparently cancers of the lung metastasise downwards to bones and the liver but can also go upwards into the brain. I think that Tony is actually beginning to believe that he has cancer. His brain has been taking in all the masses of information coming at him, all the tests and scans, but in his heart he hadn't really accepted it because he has been feeling so well. Now we're being told some specifics of the treatment and I can sense he is seeing the reality of the situation. In addition, his appetite is dwindling, he's losing weight rapidly, and his muscles are weakening, and he's so tired, sleeping much of the day and then suffering from insomnia at night.

The wound from the hip replacement is still giving him some pain but much less now, and he still relies on his crutches, but walking is getting better. Now all he has to do is work at eating. That is his job, and everyone else will do theirs.

It's the last week of July and Tony started his radiotherapy this week – a five-session treatment to clear up the cancer cells lurking in his leg and hopefully stop any more tumours developing. His last one will be on Tuesday. It's quite a high dose but it shortens the length of time by half. There's no discomfort, he's not in any pain, but he's terribly tired and very, very nauseous.

He was sick after eating just a little of the only thing he fancied last night, which was some fresh sea bass with lots of lemon. I cooked it in the hotel room, in which we have a small kitchenette. The fridge is filling up with foods I keep buying to tempt him to eat, not very successfully.

The next stage has been decided. We'll be talking to the research nurse next week and Tony will be put on a clinical trial, using a new immunotherapy drug, atezolizumab, which has been showing some remarkable results, combined with chemotherapy.

We don't know when this will start, but sooner rather than later I hope. It will last for 18 weeks, but if things go really well, maybe only 12 weeks. I can only imagine how bad this is going to be, but Tony swears he'll tolerate anything they throw at him. He may not be physically robust at the moment, but I hope that stubborn streak of his stays strong.

People ask how I'm doing. I'm OK. Terrified, but OK 90% of the time.

I'm trying to prevent my emotions taking over by finding things to do, like writing this diary or shopping for Tony, or doing the laundry here in the hotel. All the people Tony touches and has touched in his life are finding out about this ordeal and sending so many lovely messages.

It's as heart-warming as his condition is heart-breaking.

Two weeks ago today I wrote that Tony was losing his appetite and feeling nauseous. Well that turned from bad to worse, with hallucinations, vomiting (even water), sleeping, confusion, weight loss – all after just three radiotherapy treatments, with two left to go. Somehow, we managed over the weekend (why is it always worse overnight or on Saturdays and Sundays, when all Monday to Friday 9 to 5-ers aren't there?) but I was getting very stressed – frightened actually – and not sure what to do or who to call for help.

Ben saw my emotional state on a Facetime call, and decided it was time for action to support Mum. Since then, we've had Claire over for a week and now Pam James, who is still here for another couple of days.

August 2016

We were at the hospital early, at 7am, for the next radiotherapy session. We should have seen Tony's doctor of radiology that afternoon, but I decided not to wait and, without an appointment (how daring was that!), I wheeled him off to another department where we'd met the doctors and senior nurses at the outset of his treatment, who are there for general support.

They decided pretty quickly that he should go straight to Emergency, where he was tested thoroughly and, by midnight, admitted to a hospital ward. Dr Blumenschein was on a three-week holiday, which was somewhat alarming.

The medical team were absolutely fantastic. After observation and tests, he had visits from at least three different doctors every day. One was Dr B, who had popped in even though he was on holiday. It transpired that the cancer had sent Tony's calcium levels so high, he was at the point of not just hallucinations but seizures, and there was a risk of death.

It wasn't an easy week, but by Friday they had the calcium levels under control – so much so that he was discharged and on Friday evening we were out at a restaurant, eating salmon and toast! That same Friday, August 5th, we signed the documents agreeing to the trial. Things were far from normal, but coming out, together, to an actual restaurant brought us some relief from the hospital routine, from watching him suffer day after day.

The order to eat and eat and get away from the hotel room and hospitals and try to live a more normal life.

Dr B said he wanted to know that Tony was back to living as normal a life as possible, as this would help him with his eligibility for the clinical trial.

To that end, more tests start next week.

So onwards and upwards, and let's fight this evil, disgusting disease with every fibre of our being.

––––––––––––––––––––

Well, we've had another very hectic few days. This weekend I could see Tony deteriorating again, and the symptoms looked very much as if the high calcium levels had returned. After a blood test on Monday, the hospital confirmed this was the case.

They sent us to ATC (Ambulatory Treatment Centre) for an intravenous infusion of more meds to reduce the calcium levels.

We returned to the hospital yesterday, Tuesday 16th August – our wedding anniversary. I'd shopped the day before and bought no less than three anniversary cards (weeping buckets in the middle of the supermarket as I read the words inside). They all seemed to say things I wanted and needed to say – but couldn't possibly – to Tony. Far too emotional.

It's been a long day, but the good news is that our strong Tony is still strong in many ways. Caryl and Jan from Slimming World are visiting us this week, and seeing them has helped enormously. However, in between the scans, Tony came back to the waiting room and his speech was slurred. This is a recognised alarm bell. After contacting the doctor on call, we went, this time by ambulance, back to

*the Emergency department at MD Anderson. And
finally, after more blood tests, they gave him more
meds intravenously and decided it was worth the
risk to let him 'go home' to our hotel instead of
admitting him to the hospital once again.*

*You'll probably think I'm mad, but coming back to
the hotel together – instead of him in hospital and
me travelling back to the hotel alone – has been one
of our best anniversary moments ever.
Pure happiness!*

September 2016

*The cancer was growing and multiplying, and
nothing was working – until they gave up on the
trial and gave Tony chemotherapy. The type of
chemo he's on, a double whammy of Carboplatin
and Permatrexed we're told, is intolerable for some
people and they have to stop. But for Tony, it seems
to be giving the cancer a good smack – and has
knocked it back enough to see some real
improvements. He can eat a little and keep his food
down. It's knocking back the high calcium levels too.*

*I've suggested we go back to the UK where this type
of chemotherapy is readily available, as MD
Anderson can offer us nothing better now, no
miracles, no trial drugs, nothing. As a last chance, I
asked our Slimming World team to contact CRUK
again and plead with them to give us some advice
and hope. This time, it bore fruit and we were
recommended to contact a Professor Christian*

Ottensmeier, a melanoma and lung cancer specialist who works at Southampton University Hospital.

From that point on our lives changed forever!

Prof Ottensmeier called me immediately, via WhatsApp. He kept me involved in every part of the loop between Dr Blumenschein, Dr Fisser and himself. I knew what was happening, I knew the chemo was doomed to fail and I knew he was already planning what next for Tony. This was a first. No one else had believed there was a 'next' for Tony.

October 2016
We're back in the UK. Slimming World's November Awards ceremony is coming up soon and Professor Ottensmeier wants Tony to have a liver biopsy on the Wednesday before the event. The surgeon was asked to take one of the tumours from his liver for analysis. He actually took four, explaining that there were so many and they were so easy to reach, it would give the Professor more material to work with.

5th November 2016
Somehow we made it to the Slimming World Awards. But Tony was far from well.

The chemo has stopped working and Tony is back to not eating. In fact, he's fading fast and my hope is dwindling. The cancer is rampant again, the chemo is failing as predicted, the tumours are growing and he's barely able to get out of his wheelchair, so he's mostly bedridden. Today we've decided on some new immunotherapy treatment in place of the failing chemo. Christian explains the pros and cons and the lack of guarantees. And really, to work, they needed the tumour to have a biomarker called pd-ll, which tests had shown Tony didn't have. But Christian has a feeling, he says – he has hope. He explains that our BUPA cover will pay for one of the drugs he wants to try but not the other – and asks if we'd be willing to fund it ourselves. Yes, of course!

The proposed trial, a combination of immunotherapy drugs called ipilimumab and nivolumab, had, so far, only been tested on patients with skin cancer – not lung cancer. Christian describes the likely side effects – all very similar to chemo, with one little difference. There will be a rash. This appears by the 12th week, in most cases.

New Year's Eve, 2016

We're back in Mallorca and I wheeled Tony into Mood. He'd been pottering about the bedroom as we got ready and, maybe it's wishful thinking, but I'm sure he could have walked in tonight. I think he might be getting a bit better, but how can that be? He only had the ipi-nivo combination 12 days ago.

6th January 2017

We've come back to Southampton for the second infusion of the immunotherapy drugs and today I

*shared my thoughts with Professor Ottensmeier. I
hope I'm not imagining it, but I really feel as if I'm
seeing a difference in Tony. Not only that, but the
rash he'd said would appear after 12 weeks has
already emerged in less than three. So, I reason,
tentatively... if the side effects are there early, could
that suggest the drugs are starting to work earlier
than expected? 'Possibly,' came Christian's answer
– and a glimmer of hope lit up my heart for the first
time in weeks. He smiled. 'But cautious optimism,
cautious optimism,' he warned.*

27th January 2017

*The improvement in Tony is now obvious to
everyone. It's 42 days since his first treatment with
these wonder drugs. No one is imagining anything.
We visited Christian today and I couldn't help but
pick up on a suppressed excitement in his manner
– though again, he recommended cautious optimism.*

17th February 2017

*Back to Southampton and Christian could no longer
contain his joy – he was punching the air (and so
was I!). He showed us his research charts – with
Tony well and truly at the top of the class, having
had one of the best responses possible to this
combination of immunotherapy drugs. The surgeon
did another liver biopsy and declared that he had
never seen anything like it. He couldn't find a single
tumour. He declared Tony was a miracle.*

I'm still pinching myself.

Within just eight months, Tony has gone from a diagnosis of late stage terminal cancer to scans showing that most of the tumours had gone and the rest were rapidly dying. Could this be a miracle? I didn't dare believe it at the time, but it felt a lot like one!

What happened next wasn't plain sailing, as the side effects Christian had mentioned started to reveal themselves. They could actually have been from the chemotherapy or the immunotherapy, as both can have similar side effects. The immunotherapy miracle needed to be controlled as Tony's colon had become inflamed, so he needed more immunotherapy to reverse the efficiency of the ipi-nivo combo. This, I believe (though I have no concrete evidence to support my belief), led to a tiny recurrence of the cancer, in one lymph node in the following October, which we caught early.

Twenty days of radiotherapy sorted that. At the time of writing, all side effects seem to have disappeared and Tony is as well as is possible at 78 years of age. No cancer. It truly is a miracle. Professor Christian Ottensmeier is a miracle-worker. Everyone else, apart from Christian (and me and our Dr Fisser), had given up on Tony – albeit for perfectly realistic reasons.

Professor Ottensmeier is a scientist and clinician extraordinaire. He really does deserve a medal, and I hope one day he is awarded the highest honour possible. He has earned it, and continues to do so. The world needs more Ottensmeiers, that's for sure. I hope that the research he and his team conduct, with such dedication and passion, receives its necessary funding from Cancer Research UK and other bodies.

66 *I always wake up smiling.*
I think that's your fault.
I want to be naughty with you
for the rest of my life.
And that's your fault too.
I just want you to be happy.
And naked.
That's your fault again. 99

CHAPTER SEVENTEEN/EPILOGUE

now and next

The amazing organisation I am proud to have founded continues its upward and onward trajectory. It's fulfilled virtually every dream I ever had for it. If we could help 100 percent of our members to achieve their dreams, then that would be mine completed.

We will never stop researching ways to help every one of our members to achieve their weight loss dreams. We will never stop looking for new ways to help them be super-motivated to change their lifestyle forever, bringing them the lasting health and happiness and that sense of pride and self-esteem that inevitably emerges from their choices and actions.

We will continue to engage and employ the very best people we can find. We will continue to invest in those people and in our treasured Consultants, who carry out truly life-changing work. New ideas will be devised and tested, new ways to motivate and encourage, new ways to make those important lifestyle changes even easier, new ways to bring interest and joy to making those changes – and all of this as we find ways to integrate and adapt to the new realities of a digital age.

We will continue to develop our nutrition knowledge and filter out the 'fake news', replacing it with the practical truth.

Through all of these things – healthy eating, healthy living, showing mums and dads a healthier way for their families to live – we know we're making tiny steps every day towards a healthier population and that will eventually result in fewer cases of diabetes, fewer heart problems, fewer cancers and a far greater chance of not just survival, but a quality of life that at the moment seems terr bly threatened, just as our planet is terribly threatened by our pre: ent-day choices.

Building a healthier future is paramount if our children, and their. are to survive. I therefore hope and pray that in future, as now, ou profits will be used to promote caring for those in need, and to sup port all organisations which fight the evils of the world long afte I've left it.

So my wish for my own family, as well as my other Slimmin, World family, and for all my friends, is to continue to work with true kindness and compassion in the way you do, and to continue to se and follow the right path. I know it's not easy. Sometimes it's incred ibly difficult. Be very proud of yourselves for your achievements and know just how proud of you I am and how much I love you.

Yours, always and forever,

ACKNOWLEDGEMENTS

Writing an autobiography, I've discovered, is a bit like raising a child (or three) – it takes a village!

In no strict order, I'd like to thank the following people, who were an enormous help in dredging up memories past, organising and recording them, fact-checking, typing, photo-hunting, designing, reading, re-reading, re-re-reading (can't hurt) and making this whole thing look just like a real book.

Jane Love – one of our Senior Writers – for working with me side by side to help me pull my story together. I truly couldn't have done it without her.

Jan Boxshall, who's edited this book alongside her day-to-day role as Slimming World's Joint Managing Director.

All those who have contributed to the research process: David Rathbone, Sheila Hall, Anne Kirk, Jacquie Lavin, Sue Ashton, Janet Marvell, Dave Armstrong, Denise Kimberley and of course, my darling husband Tony Whittaker.

Caryl Richards, Rebecca Robinson and Jenny Caven – for your eagle eyes and sound guidance as guardians of our brand.

My daughter Claire, for finding the gems in our family photograph albums.

Flixx Wedgwood-Walker, Kathryn Briggs and Andy Warburton – for your design and image wizardry.

Schillings, London – for your help with the legal bits and bobs.

Sterling Creative, Edinburgh – for your patience and flexibility with ever-changing briefs and deadlines.

Sterling Solutions – for your ever-reliable service and high-quality output.

Did you know?

10p from the sale of this book goes to our charitable foundation
SMILES (Slimmers Making It A Little Easier for Someone).
Our charity partners have included the NSPCC, Cancer Research
UK and Great Ormond Street Hospital Children's Charity, and
each year we donate around £100,000 from recipe book sales.

FROM THE HEART

a selection of the articles I've written for *Slimming World Magazine*

Ever since *Slimming World Magazine* launched in the '90s, I've penned a letter or article to feature in each issue. I love this regular opportunity to share my thoughts directly with members and potential members. In some, I give my (usually strong – I've had to be censored at times!) opinion on a hot topic in the weight loss world. In others, I'll delve deep into the psychology of slimming, always drawing on my lifetime's personal experience. Here's a selection of the articles that have resonated most with our Consultants and our members – dating all the way back to Issue 2, in 1998.

1998

March/April, Issue 2

freedom from guilt

Turn down the volume on that harsh, critical person telling you that you're useless. Turn up the volume on the warm, kind, understanding voice of someone who really cares. It's time to forgive yourself.

It's a huge subject and couldn't possibly be covered in one article but the place to start is for you to understand about guilt and shame, and the need to forgive yourself regarding your weight. Without forgiveness, the same patterns that have led you unerringly to each slimming disaster will simply repeat themselves time and again, no matter how generous and easy the eating plans, no matter how many recipe ideas you read. Nothing changes if nothing changes. Learning to forgive yourself and shed the burden of shame (and excess weight) is a change that those of you who have suffered long enough need to make right now, today.

This is also a subject which very few people truly understand. Many psychologists, who understand the theory, appear to be unable to relate to reality when it comes to weight/body/food issues. Because since 1969 I have studied these issues, because since 1969 I have been privileged to talk to and to help many thousands of overweight people and, perhaps most importantly, because since childhood I too have suffered these problems, I can assure you that I am one of the few who truly understand. One of the key things that I have learned is that forgiveness is paramount to your success.

let go of pain

Guilt or shame is possibly our biggest and most effective self-sabotage technique. When we feel guilty or ashamed, we are in pain. So much so that sometimes we can go into a denial of reality. We deceive ourselves. We convince ourselves that we've been 'good', we haven't done a thing to deserve it, but those damned scales say we haven't lost weight, we've put it on. Because we are so convinced we, in turn, become convincing. Those who might have been able to help may be deceived too. If so, they become unable to help us. When we don't lose weight, we can become angry – with ourselves, our parents, our Consultant, Slimming World, nature, God, anybody! Or we become passive and defeated and don't have the energy to make the effort any more. Or we pretend we don't care anyway, it's all a big joke.

Whichever way, we give strong, hidden messages to people who could help us through this to 'back off', 'leave me alone'. We don't follow the advice in the eating plan, we don't count Syns properly, we don't bother to exercise, and we have a long list of excuses as to why it isn't our fault, although deep down we really believe it is. We don't stay for the real help in IMAGE Therapy, we just weigh and go. Matters deteriorate even further, we start to regain weight we have lost, and finally we stop coming to group.

When we feel guilty, we dislike ourselves. We may even despise ourselves. The conversation we have in our heads about ourselves goes something like this: 'You idiot. You're so weak. You're hopeless. Useless.' It's as though we are two people; one is like a severe and over-critical parent, harsh, cruel and judgemental, while the other is childlike, vulnerable and believing.

The sneaky part is that we often have this conversation without realising it. It happens subconsciously – outside our awareness. The subconscious mind is not like the conscious one. With our conscious mind, we are able to reason, use logic and sort fact from fiction. Compared to that, our subconscious is a pretty simple affair. It does not have the same reasoning and logical powers.

It accepts and stores messages about us, true or false, that we may have mistakenly believed at the time to be fact. It is very, very powerful. This power can be harnessed in a very positive way (many of the techniques used in IMAGE Therapy enable you to tap into your subconscious this way) or it can be a destructive force in our lives. If we tell ourselves often enough (or others tell us) that we are useless, weak, stupid etc, we actually start to believe it at this deeper, powerful level, in our subconscious. These messages that we store about ourselves may have been formed very early in our lives, before our brain was even fully formed. And they can become a kind of script for the way we play out our lives. Without knowing, we tend to be selective about the things we hear, and only remember those which reinforce these early negative messages.

So, when we start to tackle the difficult problem of changing some well-established habits, for example eating in a different way, we may already believe we are destined to fail, and this belief becomes a self-fulfilling prophecy.

Shame about past failures only serves to reinforce this destructive self-belief. Your self-esteem is diminished, the confidence you have in your ability ever to succeed as a slimmer is battered. This pain is real. It may not be a physical pain but it is no less debilitating. Sounds terribly depressing, doesn't it? And it would be if there were no escape, if you were helpless – powerless to change. The good news is that you aren't helpless. You can change. You may not be able to change other people's minds but one thing's for sure – you can certainly change your own! And therein lies your power.

Let's talk about those past failures. Do you believe it was all your fault? Do you believe that it's because you are weak, stupid, useless? Read on.

food becomes an issue

In our society today, rich by world standards, it's the easiest thing in the world for someone to become overweight. Imagine a child raised in a loving family. The child is given food by loving parents, sometimes inappropriately, when the child is not actually hungry for food. In other words, those kind, well-meaning parents mistakenly believe that more food is required when the baby or child is hungry for a hug, or is simply thirsty. And this mistake happens many times until the child believes that it's food that is required to satisfy this need it feels. Or the child is given sweets, chocolate, crisps, fried food – all the things that the parents have come to believe are treats, naughty but nice! If the child becomes overweight, this same concerned family start to withhold food and 'treats'. Sheer torment begins.

Food becomes an issue, a battleground. Maybe you've had a weight problem since childhood. Maybe you can no longer read your needs correctly. Or perhaps you reached adulthood as a slim person. But as you became older and your lifestyle changed, you probably became slightly less active. You started to eat out more, and eat more convenience foods. You never even realised that you were taking in far more calories than you used to, yet you were using up fewer. At first the change in your weight may have been hardly noticeable. By the age of 35 or 40, the effects had become clearly visible.

the vicious circle

At some point, for all of us, the first serious attempt to lose weight is made. We embark on our first ever diet. By this stage in our lives we have been bombarded with information and advice – often confusing, contradictory and inaccurate. The most common advice is: 'If you want to lose weight, you simply must eat less.' This is often supported by 'Calories count – so count calories!' It's nearly right – but 'nearly right' ends up sending us so awfully wrong.

So we go 'on' a diet. For days, weeks or even months. And life becomes a miserable existence. We're hungry! Permanently hungry. We do, however, feel martyred and good about our iron will for as long as we can survive the torture. If you didn't have issues around food in childhood, you'll certainly get them now. The hunger, the deprivation, the torment! And then we stop. We go 'off' the diet. Bliss!

But, horror of horrors, the weight goes back on.

Who in their right mind is going to put themselves through that nightmare scenario again? Someone desperate, that's who. Because what so often happens is that we then put on more weight than we lost and reach a size and weight we have never experienced before and most certainly do not like. Pure fear then drives us to start the vicious circle all over again. No wonder some people give up the battle permanently. They are sick of the guilt and shame of repeated failure and appalled by how big they think the sacrifice has to be in order to lose weight.

Slimming World's Food Optimising is so generous, as you know, and so effective, that many people feel they've found a miracle. That alone can be enough for some of us, especially if we have a relatively small amount to lose. But others, whose journey to success will take longer, or whose negative messages about themselves are stronger, can still self-sabotage using a pattern rather like the scenario described opposite.

stop the self-sabotage

This is an example of a pattern of long-term self-sabotage, which would be completely outside a slimmer's awareness:

When I am slimming, I put myself on a very tight deadline to lose weight. I want to lose weight fast.

This means I have to be very strict with myself, with no room to manoeuvre.

My life becomes dominated by my diet.

Eventually I can't stand it any longer, life has become miserable and so I stop counting Syns altogether.

The length of time I abandon my diet varies from several days to months/years.

I feel very bad about myself – I see myself as a complete failure.

I lose all confidence in my ability to slim, even with Slimming World's plan, which I know is the easiest of all.

Knowing this makes me feel even worse so I 'kick' myself even more and as a result my self-esteem gets even lower. I am now in great pain because I do not like myself.

I cannot face starting yet another nightmare scenario of slimming.

Then I get so frightened by how much weight I am gaining that I find the necessary strength to start the whole process all over again.

Many people put themselves under this appalling pressure without even realising it. They are afraid of 'flexible' Syns, afraid to do anything they believe will slow down their weight loss, in fact terrified of the very things that will mean long-term success.

The scenario varies in content, but the process is the same – a life of sufficient misery as to make the rewards (losing weight) not worth it.

No one can sustain this misery indefinitely. But there is a way to break the cycle – and that is to forgive yourself.

break the cycle, forgive yourself

No normal healthy person enjoys suffering. Instead of criticising yourself for deciding not to suffer any longer, congratulate yourself on being normal and healthy.

When you make a mistake, when you're not as perfect as you'd intended, instead of telling yourself that you've ruined everything, that you've 'blown it', say to yourself, *How fascinating! I wonder what chain of events led me to stop counting my Syns?* (or whatever your heinous crime has been). If you can work on understanding that, you can give yourself some advance warning and protect yourself better in the future.

Begin the healing process that is so deserved, and so necessary, by forgiving yourself. It wasn't your fault. You did all this to yourself outside your awareness. You didn't know this was what you were doing.

You can now stop blaming yourself for past failures. Tomorrow is a new day. Let your sense of humour work its magic. Take yourself more lightly and the task in hand more seriously. Let the success come. Allow yourself to imagine, to revel in the pure, unadulterated joy of achievement and the ecstasy of success.

1998

May/June, Issue 3

have you fallen into the sabotage trap?

There's a rebellious teenager inside every one of us, fighting against authority and sometimes sabotaging our attempts to change. But you can make friends with the rebel inside you.

Have you ever wondered why when you want to lose weight so badly, you seem to lack willpower? You know that you can eat really well and never go hungry and yet still you don't stay with the eating plan. You know that if you keep eating too many Syns you won't lose weight. Yet rather than make better choices, you choose to take the path of slimming destruction.

Please note I use the word 'choose'. In fact, you don't feel as though you're choosing anything. You just feel out of control. You feel so out of control, it goes beyond a simple lack of willpower. It's more akin to feeling driven to eat those high-fat, high-sugar foods. When you want to lose weight so badly, it nearly feels like a form of temporary insanity. Take heart. You aren't batty – you aren't even weak-willed. In fact, you're just the opposite. All that's happening is that simple but sneaky subconscious is at it again.

teenager mode

As a mother of three and adopted mother of one – the youngest is 17 – not to mention stepmother to two already grown-up, I speak from the heart when I agree with one comedian's definition of a teenager – God's punishment for enjoying sex! You'd think that by the time I got to number three I would have learned how to handle them. But no, I press on regardless, lighting the blue touch paper – and I have the emotional scars to prove it!

I am merely getting my just desserts. As a child, I was too afraid to go against the authority of my parents, although deep down I resented their restrictions. I was a good little girl. But as a teenager, well, now that's an entirely different story. As a teenager I was as horrid as they come. Margaret the teenager was on a mission – a rule-breaking, authority-snubbing mission! Rebellion – with bells on!

Unfortunately, we don't leave rebellion behind when we become adults. Our subconscious is like a tape recorder which records all our behaviour patterns, whether they're helpful to us or not. And so we still have a tendency to go into 'teenager mode' and rebel against anything that sounds remotely like the voice of authority – even when that voice is inside our own head. Every time we hear, or even think, words like 'should', 'must' or 'ought to', we can easily slide into teenager mode without realising what we're doing. When it comes to slimming, this can become a real pain in the posterior. Self-sabotage – with bells on!

Because our unconscious self-sabotage processes are exactly that, below our consciousness, out of our awareness, it leaves us very little chance of protecting ourselves when the danger arises. So the first key step is to bring them into our consciousness – then we can make plans to protect ourselves from them.

There are various ways to do this and one that I've found useful is to create your own 'For and Against' list. The procedure is simple. Find a private spot where you won't be overlooked or disturbed. Take a blank sheet of paper, draw a line down the centre, and label one side 'For' and the other side 'Against'. Then write down all your reasons for and against being slim. The reasons are yours, for your eyes only. If you believe that someone else will see what you are writing down, you are likely to be less honest with yourself. You may find that you don't allow yourself to access some of the deeper reasons which are so important to your success. Even when you've completed it, keep thinking and feeling about Fors and Againsts. Quite often you can build a much fuller list over a period of time.

rebels with a cause

If you think that teenager mode sounds silly and immature, that this kind of self-sabotage doesn't exist, and you're saying to yourself, *'I certainly don't do that!'*, the chances are you're in denial. In my experience, we all can – and do – get there. Some of us more than others!

Teenager mode is one way we deal with the issues left over from childhood. When parents are too strict, a child can develop problems with control which linger into adulthood and form the basis for future rebellion. When that subconscious tape recorder starts to play and we hear our own parents' voices (now disguised as our own) trying to control our eating, we still react to the message and often do exactly the opposite.

The more controlled we were, or felt we were, the more we are prone to rebelling as adults. Rather than denying that this kind of self-sabotage applies to you, it's more useful to say, *'I do this. When do I do it? How often do I do it?'*

Drawing up your 'For and Against' list can be a way of recognising your own sabotage techniques, and tapping into the deeper reasons which have shaped how you behave today and which may make you resist being slim. My own reasons were so deep that when I did access them, they came as a complete surprise.

setting the patterns

When I was about eight years old, two things happened that led me to make decisions that affected the rest of my life. I belonged to our chapel youth club, which had members ranging from my age to about 18. I longed to be part of this 'in-crowd'. So I decided that as all of them were such beautiful people, the only way someone as fat and unattractive as me (which was how I saw myself) was going to be accepted was if I was fun to be with. In other words, it had to be for my personality and not my looks. Thirty years later, when I did my 'For and Against' list, I discovered that one of my fears was that if I lost my excess weight, then I would lose my personality.

The second decision I made probably had an even more profound effect. I had two aunts, Aunty Laura and Aunty Elsie. Aunty Laura was large. She was like a well-stuffed settee. She had a large family. She was always to be found in her kitchen, along with at least two of my cousins. There was always a fire burning in the kitchen stove, always the kettle simmering away and always something cooking. It was, literally and metaphorically, a warm place to be. The whole atmosphere was relaxed and cosy and loving. I remember staying with her for a whole week once. She turned Uncle Charlie out of the marital bed and I was allowed to cuddle up to her each night. Conspiratorially, and promising she wouldn't breathe a word to my mother

(her sister), she would give me a Nuttall's Mintoe each night as
climbed into bed beside her. I thought this was deliciously naughty
I loved my Aunty Laura.

Aunty Elsie, on the other hand, was just about the opposite in
every way. She was small and thin. Her mouth seemed to be for
ever pressed into a thin, disapproving line. Her house was always
immaculate, but cold and empty of life. Looking back, I can see how
faulty those memories really were, but these were the impressions
that stayed in my mind. Now, when I grew up, who do you think
wanted to be like most? Aunty Laura, of course! It's as though deep
down I believed that to be surrounded by a loving family, to love
and be loved, I needed to be sofa-shaped.

a brand new message

Realisation can be an emotional experience. I felt amazed and sad
Once I knew, though, I could at last do something to protect myself
I needed to let my subconscious know that I could be like Aunty
Laura without taking on board the whole package, excess weight
and all!

A tried-and-tested way to do this is to give your subconscious a
new message that is completely positive – no negative words in it at
all. The wrong message to give my subconscious would have been
'I don't have to be overweight to be loved and loving'. The subcon
scious misses out the 'don't'. My positive message went something
like this: 'I can be loved and loving and slim'. Saying it out loud
repeatedly, so your own ears can hear, helps the subconscious to take
it in. Write it down, stick it in places where you can't miss it, turn it
into an affirmation (use the present tense, ie 'I am loved and loving
and slim') – all these things can help to overwrite the old tape-re
corded message and replace it with a far more useful one.

1999

Jan/Feb, Issue 5

the motivation miracle

Losing weight takes commitment, and your chances of success soar when you enjoy the support of a group of like-minded people. That's exactly what you get at Slimming World, and that's why we're convinced that this year is the year when you can turn your new year's resolutions into reality.

Good intentions abound as we resolve, yet again, to face the new year in a new way. Can we sustain that initial determination? Will we stay the distance this time?

The world of the slimmer sometimes seems hopeless, with the odds simply stacked against us. Eating habits that make us gain weight are reinforced by a billion-pound food industry. The fast food chains who specialise in serving high-fat meals are multiplying, and eating out in them has become a convenient part of modern life. How on earth can we break out of the vicious cycle where overweight and unhappiness lead to more overeating, which in turn causes deeper unhappiness – and occasionally despair? The good news is that there really is light at the end of this very dark tunnel. At Slimming World there's more at work than an incredibly generous and healthy way of eating. Even though it's the easiest slimming programme ever, it still needs you to play your part, and we can help you there too. Food Optimising means you never have to go hungry again to lose weight. That's a fact. But it's also a fact that changing your eating habits requires effort. And the energy to power that effort depends very much on your state of mind.

At the beginning of your slimming campaign, enthusiasm is high, commitment is at a peak and you're filled with hope for a new tomorrow. But sooner or later – and it becomes sooner rather than later if we have a few failed attempts under our belt – the motivation begins to crumble.

Overeating is simply taking in more energy (in the form of calories) than we use up. That can happen if our activity levels have reduced over the years or our intake of fat-rich foods has increased slightly. The imbalance can be quite small, but it still adds up to excess weight.

Losing that weight is one of the hardest challenges we ever have to deal with. People who have never experienced that struggle, never experienced the pain of failure, simply do not understand the emotional and psychological upheaval and distress that is part and parcel of trying to correct the results of overeating. Anyone who has tried it on their own knows that empathy is in short supply and it can be a very lonely and miserable journey. And so, often, a very short and fruitless one.

group support – does it really work?

Yes, it does. There's no longer any question about this. We know this after 36 years of success at Slimming World, and the medical establishment agrees, that groups have worked where individuals have failed. It's not foolproof – there can be no guarantees – but without a doubt, your chances of success soar when you have the support of a group of like-minded people.

Even a poorly organised group may be better than no group at all but at Slimming World we turn ourselves inside out to give you the best group support there is – bar none. And the whole thing works so well because underpinning every Slimming World group is a basic belief, a philosophy, born of a deep understanding of the burden of excess weight. It's about respect, and holding overweight people in high regard. There's no humiliation, no disapproval, no critical judgements, no put-downs of even the most subtle kind. Instead you'll find warmth, praise, support, understanding and sharing. Sharing what? A joke, maybe, or a little light relief. Or it could be a recipe that's easy to cook, or a kind word, or an experience that helped, or an insight, or a lift to the group or the phone number of someone who can help between groups.

allowing the magic to work

Group therapy has long been recognised as a powerful way of supporting people who are going through change in their lives. Nowhere is its power seen more clearly than in a Slimming World group. It's particularly effective when there is a common goal, because then a kind of team spirit emerges. Implicit in joining a Slimming World group is the commitment not just to getting help for yourself, but to giving it where you can. And a kind of magic begins to work. The more involved you allow yourself to become, sharing ideas and thoughts with others, the stronger your own motivation becomes.

MAGE Therapy

We call this special brand of care and support IMAGE Therapy. You can feel it. It's like a warm blanket that wraps itself around you, comforting and strong. IMAGE stands for Individual Motivation And Group Experience. Every single person has, in just a few short minutes, the combined power and support of the whole group working for them. And the focus is not just on you, but on your future rather than your past. It's like a magic spotlight that shines and illuminates the way forward in a completely positive way, so that when motivation starts to flag, instead of sliding down the slippery slope into hopelessness, you find your footing and the climb gets easy again.

For some people, it means they never lose that initial determination. It burns just as brightly throughout their whole journey to their target weight and keeps them there forever. When it comes to motivation, it's positively miraculous.

Let me give you some examples of how Slimming World's philosophy and IMAGE Therapy work in real life. We believe that to make a mistake, slip a little, or to have a bad day or a bad week is only human. It's not a crime. It doesn't require forgiveness. In fact, if you put on weight between meetings, rather than a tut-tut when you come back to your group, you'll get a pat on the back. Why? Because we know what it's like. You didn't have a very good week and you knew you'd probably put a little weight on. You could have stayed at home and hoped to do better next week. Of course, you'd probably have just slipped further. But you didn't do any of that. Even though you weren't feeling too good about yourself, didn't really want anyone to know that you'd gained a pound (or more), you came anyway, to refuel your motivation, to get the support and help you needed. That took a great deal of courage. That's why you deserve praise and why you'll get it.

someone cares

Or maybe you've fallen into the trap of thinking that the less food you eat, the quicker your weight will go down. Without even realising you've 'adapted' Food Optimising to a plan of your own. You start feeling hungry. And you start snacking on high fat, high sugar foods to compensate. But they don't satisfy you and now you're getting hungry but still not losing weight. When you come to a Slimming World group, you'll find that not only is your Consultant genuinely interested in your success, but your fellow members are too. They'll listen to your problem and soon see where you're going wrong. Many of them will probably have been in the same boat at some time. From then on, you'll be back in the right gear for charging ahead.

At Slimming World, your Consultant is always there for you. They too probably struggle with their weight. They have probably lost several stones themselves, and have enormous empathy with their members. Every pound you lose is a step in the right direction, every half stone you lose is a major milestone. Your Consultant will be every bit as thrilled as you are with your success. It matters to them – and it shows. Every week they'll probably tell the group how much you've lost (though your actual weight is never announced).

Should you have a gain and arrive with a heavy heart, they'll make sure you remember how well you're doing and help you keep it in perspective. You'll leave feeling a lot lighter than when you arrived and ready to forge ahead the next week. All our Consultants, with the help of your fellow members, will share with you great ideas, help you plan the week ahead, help you identify your most difficult times and work out a strategy that will see you through them. And when you're having trouble getting refocused, maybe after a major holiday or Christmas binge, they have a complete 'toolkit' of strategies they can share with you.

support that's firm

Moral support, like a good bra, needs to have an element of strength about it, otherwise you don't get the necessary lift! Occasionally we need a little nudge to get us over our own personal hurdle, a touch of gentle confrontation. I don't mean the aggressive kind that is more an excuse for criticism – that doesn't help anyone move forward. Gentle confrontation is like someone holding up a mirror so that we can better see ourselves and look more closely at what we are thinking, feeling, doing, achieving. Some examples of this gentle kind of confrontation include:

Discussing your weight change with the rest of the group without anyone passing judgement on you.

Chatting thoughtfully and with genuine concern, about questions and problems over weight loss that you all face – the times you find it harder to keep going, or your own personal pitfalls, for instance.

Committing yourself to achieving a target that you have chosen – with a plan of how you're going to achieve it.

Gentle confrontation is about being helped to appreciate our own power. It's about en-abling, not dis-abling. That's why tea and sympathy don't work. They just help us wallow in self-pity. True support is enabling and active. And being in a group multiplies your power. No longer is the support from one person – it's from 50!

a laughing matter…

In IMAGE Therapy, having fun is all part of the process. In fact, no laughter is no laughing matter! Laughter relieves stress and burns calories, and if that isn't enough in itself, laughing at ourselves with people in exactly the same situation is one more form of that gentle confrontation.

Empathy and laughter work incredibly well together. Imagine the sort of week when you know you've had a bad run. You know you're going to have put weight on. It's the night of your group. Decision time. It's raining. To go or not to go? That is the question. If going to the group is more of a tonic than watching a funny TV programme, if you know that everyone there understands about that sort of week, if you know you'll emerge with a lighter heart and a new determination, then you're more likely to make the right decision and go.

Having fun, taking ourselves just a little less seriously means our self-esteem continues to climb, not dive. Lightening the burden of excess weight is part of the Slimming World philosophy and it means far more than losing the physical stones and pounds.

2005

Aug/Sept, Issue 49

get the picture!

We've all heard the expression 'think thin!' and when we hear something so often it can become a mere platitude, maybe a bit of a joke, and not something we give much thought to. Yet thinking thin, or in Slimming World language, using visualisation as an aid, is well worth the effort. This is one of the greatest exercises you can do and you won't even break out into a glow, let alone a sweat. So give your weight loss a tremendous boost, give yourself a distinct advantage and go for this in a big way. You're going to love how you feel, how you think and how you act. So bring on the new thinking and watch yourself transform more easily than you ever thought possible.

OK, we're going to start this little exercise with the unprecedented step of taking ourselves off to a nice, quiet, relaxing room and sitting (or lying) down while we let our minds take us to a place where we are exactly the person we really want to be.

Take a good look at yourself. You are slim. Maybe you're stylishly dressed for a special night out or maybe you're in jeans and a figure-hugging top. You see yourself living your life as a slim person. It's no problem whatsoever to turn down offers of biscuits, sweets and chocolate – you'd much prefer a sweet, juicy orange or a crisp apple. You're drinking plenty of water and particularly enjoy sipping it chilled. You take your time when eating food, savouring and enjoying each mouthful.

You love nothing more than going out into the fresh air for a walk and you delight in physical exertion and getting your heart pumping a little harder. Swimming feels marvellous too; so does gardening, and knowing you've done really well strengthening your heart, your lungs and toning those muscles.

You have the odd day when you slightly overindulge like any human being, but that doesn't faze you because most of the time you eat well and within your limits. You have more energy than ever before and although you are extremely organised, you're flexible and give yourself space to adapt and enjoy new experiences as and when the opportunity arises. You feel fantastic. You feel really good about yourself. You look great and you revel in the knowledge that people notice just how good you look. You're confident, you have poise, you're calm, you're at peace with yourself and you're in control.

Get the picture? Well, don't make another move until you do, because from this moment on, this is how you are going to live your life, as a slim person.

2008

May/June, Issue 68

the positive power of 'no'!

Many years ago, when I had my own group, I would have a joke with my members and get them to practice saying the hardest word in the English language – 'no'. I'd pretend that 'no' wouldn't emerge from my lips no matter how hard I tried. Yes, it was silly (typically), but the silliness made a point and I think it's one well worth making again.

'No' is one of the most beautiful words in our language – because saying 'no' has a profound effect on our own beauty (inner beauty and outer beauty). There are some fairly obvious reasons for this. Saying 'no' to our old eating habits when they leap into action to tempt us into old ways is clearly an extremely good move on our part. But learning the 'no' habit won't just help us to lose weight, it can also ensure that we lead happier, healthier lives day-to-day.

Whether we realise it or not, our waking moments are littered with opportunities to say 'no'. Every minute we make decisions – tiny decisions that shape our lives, even more than the big ones. Here are some of the tiny decisions we make every day:

Shall I let myself become upset with:

* *the shop assistant who isn't being very efficient?*

* *the waitress who seems slow?*

* *the driver who's driving badly? Shall I grow this somewhat negative situation into a big deal? Shall I dramatise and exaggerate this until I'm really outraged?*

Shall I have one of those:

* *biscuits/cakes/pastries?*

* *packets of crisps/chocolate bars/bags of sweets?*

* *chips/burgers/pies?*

* *beers/wines/spirits?*

Because you, my highly valued reader, are a most intelligent person, by now you get my drift!

OK, so things happen. But small things happen to all of us. Life doesn't pick us out to be mean to, we all get our fair share of small irritants and setbacks. It's how we handle those that define us as a person and that can make us either an ugly person inside or a beautiful person inside.

Saying 'no', whether it's 'no' to the temptation of giving someone a venomous tongue-lashing (deserving though it may be) in order to vent our frustrations, or saying 'no' to something that means breaking a promise we made to ourselves about food, is a really great way to inner and outer beauty.

Each time we use 'no' in this positive way, we not only save ourselves from wrecking another week's weight loss, we reinforce our confidence, our self-esteem, our belief in ourselves that we are indeed capable of saying 'no'. We prove to ourselves that we can do it, we just did it – again! And we can do it again, the next time! This reinforcement is the most important thing we can do for ourselves – ever. Instead of feeling just a bit irritated/disappointed/annoyed with ourselves, we can start to like ourselves, be proud of ourselves, and appreciate what a great person we really are.

So altogether now, 'N.. n.. n.. no!'

2016

Aug/Sept, Issue 126

let go – and lose weight

Let go – and give yourself a much better chance to lose weight and achieve your dreams. Let go of what exactly? Actually, of quite a few things that are holding you back. It's a lot to do with what you believe about yourself. It's your life script, your story, those things you say to yourself, that secret story about yourself that you've created and that plays over and over again in your mind. It's things you decided about yourself at some point in your life – sometimes when you were much younger, sometimes even as far back as your early childhood. It's your past – it's not your future.

Your story may go something like this:

- *I'm not a physically active person.*

- *I'm no good at sports – not swimming, nor dancing, nor even walking.*

- *I'm hopeless at losing weight – I'm just no good at it.*

- *I'm the sort of person who starts well, then never finishes anything.*

- *I'm not a great achiever – I usually fail if it's something a bit more difficult than I'm used to.*

- *I'm the sort of person who hates change – of any kind.*

- *I'm not a fruit and vegetable lover.*

- *I can't get by without my crisps and chocolate.*

- *I can't survive without my wine, beer or Kahlúa and cola (or whatever your favourite tipple is).*

- *I'm not a fan of drinking water.*

You've probably got the idea by now and can add your own unique story, your own unique script. It's a tape that plays constantly and has done for a long time – and by now you actually believe it. And, of course, you have loads of evidence. Of course you have. There's plenty of proof that your story is absolutely right – you only have to look at your failed attempts to lose weight. This way, you are able to live your life in a way that constantly proves you are right about you.

Well, I have some great news. All you have to do is write a new life script. One that says the opposite of all this negative stuff, because all that negative stuff about you is completely wrong. And here at Slimming World, we have plenty of proof of that. It's easy to say and, actually, easier to do than you think. First, you need to identify your story. Identify that false voice that is so very wrong about you. And, once that light-bulb moment happens, replace it with all the things that you are more than capable of doing. It's a very powerful switch. It's life-changing.

Slimming World – and our knowledge, our beliefs, our experience, our methods, our Food Optimising system, our understanding and our unique support – is here to help you have your 'aha' moment. It's all here to help you write that new story and to help you make that story the one that is you, now and forever. It is our great pleasure and privilege to be here for you throughout your metamorphosis. We have the sensational satisfaction of knowing we help thousands of people every single week to have their light-bulb moment, and help them to keep that light shining dazzlingly bright. It feels like a miracle, but it's just you letting go of the past, and finding your superhighway to being all you really can be. Thank you for allowing us to play our part in your personal discovery – that you are, without doubt, truly amazing.

2016

October, Issue 127

rollercoaster slimming

One minute you're riding high, the next you're plummeting to the depths... Sound familiar? Here's how to keep your weight-loss journey on the up!

Slimming sometimes feels a bit like being on a rollercoaster. One minute you're up and the world is a wonderful place, the next you're plummeting down. Those ups can feel like a long haul, yet the downs seem to happen with startling speed. You're filled with happiness one week, despondency the next. The experience is deeply emotional.

In fact, if you've ever had the privilege of being in love, you'll recognise that the similarity is amazing. Maybe it's because when you're on a high, you are in love – with yourself. It's the most warm, delicious feeling. You become beautiful from the most vital perspective of all – from inside. But we know that when it comes to losing weight, it can be hard to hang on to that 'in love' feeling. If losing weight is something that, in the past, you've found difficult, then it's little wonder that you have no confidence. We could describe this feeling as being 'out of love' with yourself. It's a painful place to be. In this psychological state, your emotions are prey to every negative nuance, and you can be tipped on to that downward spiral quite easily.

stay on the rails

At Slimming World we want to help you hold on to that special feeling, and the surest way of all to do so – and I know this from experience – is to attend group regularly, allow IMAGE Therapy to work its magic, stay with the plan and lose weight. But I also know all too well that there are danger zones that can send your emotions careering downhill. Working out what they are is the first step towards avoiding them.

One of the most common danger zones is stepping on to the scales, either at home or at group. Just one week when they register no loss or, worse still, a gain, can send you plummeting. Feelings of confusion, despair and frustration sweep through you. Anger and fear wreak their havoc. The world isn't a wonderful place.

And although it seems to the outside world that you are angry with them, deep down you are angry with yourself.

Most of us who are working hard to lose weight are extremely susceptible to this. And of course, if you are impulsive and impatient (who, me?) then the practise of daily weighing can take its toll.

One day I would step on the scales and be delighted with the drop. Without being aware, I would ease off and allow myself to stop counting, cockily overconfident that I knew what I was doing (me? never!), and didn't need to be so careful. So a few days later I would step back on the scales to discover an unexpected zero loss – or worse a slight gain – and be plunged into gloom. At this point thinking and reasoning fly out the window. In this vulnerable state you're at risk of coming off the rails altogether!

When we feel in control, we find it far easier to stay on track, and the key to staying in control is making the right choices. The correct decisions are those that will, sooner or later, lead us to achieving our goal. I'm talking about those small daily decisions that affect every action we take.

Deciding to weigh yourself just once a week, rather than every single day, is one such decision. But even before we step on the scales if we've been making the right decisions, each meal, each change becomes a positive reinforcement of our self-worth.

Examples of decisions that may help your weight loss include:

- *Deciding how many Syns you are going to have for the day and sticking to it.*

- *Deciding to jot down your Syns lest you develop temporary amnesia.*

- *Deciding to fill up on lots and lots of veg because they're Speed Free Foods.*

- *Deciding to make a plan for the week ahead and shopping accordingly.*

- *Deciding to use the recipes from the wealth on offer in this magazine, online or in Slimming World's many recipe books.*

- *Deciding to watch a little less TV and build exercise into your daily routine.*

- *Deciding to make yourself aware of those patterns that might lead to poor-quality snacking.*

Even before we have lost any weight, we can immediately and justifiably feel good about ourselves and if it doesn't show up on the scales that week, it doesn't matter. It will show eventually.

virtuous circle

With positive decisions like these, success is inevitable and you'll even find yourself making friends with the scales! Instead of a love-hate relationship, the scales can become a tool, rather than a tyrant taking over your life.

With a longer-term and broader based view, you can and should feel very good about yourself, and the general pattern of the figures on the scales will, inevitably, be downwards! One week at the same weight or with a small gain need never put you off track again and, at last and for ever, you'll be controlling the scales, not being controlled by them.

Being in control is a marvellous feeling, but it's different for different people. How do you feel? Are there any physical changes – an un-knotting of the stomach, maybe? For me, as well as feeling pleased with myself, I gain a deep sense of calm, as if I've stopped fighting. I feel less tense. Before, I wasn't even aware that I was actually feeling tense.

The opposite occurs when we're not feeling good about ourselves. We make the wrong decisions. Each mealtime becomes an opportunity to reinforce our negative feelings about ourselves. We enjoy the moment of rebellion. Yet at that moment, when we eat the foods we feel guilty about, at another level we're saying to ourselves, 'See! I knew I was weak and useless', creating a vicious circle.

The easiest route to getting out of the vicious circle is to decide you want to. Follow that with a good decision the next time you're faced with choices about food. Then simply let one good decision lead to another. And realise that every time you've chosen well, you've put yourself more firmly on track to success. That's an achievement of mammoth proportions and you deserve many congratulations.

put it in writing

Another way to hang on to the high is to capture your feelings at the point when your self-esteem is high. Write them in a list. Keep that list confidential, keep it handy, and turn to it at times when you feel your self-confidence flagging.

Add to the list all the positive points about yourself that you can think of.

Add the good stuff that other people have noticed that you might have missed. Even when you think they're wrong, add it to the list anyway. Chances are they are right and you've been setting yourself impossibly high standards. For example, I know someone who is extremely organised. She plans well and is very efficient. Yet when I admire her for being so organised, she denies it! I'm all for having high standards and can be a bit of a perfectionist myself, but having standards that are unreachable can be harmful. Preferring to think badly of ourselves might seem like modesty and humility, but in actual fact the damage we do to our self-esteem is serious. So learn to acknowledge the positives.

pat on the back

Achievement in any walk of life brings with it a massive boost to self-esteem. Without doubt, losing weight is a great achievement. Changing eating habits that have been well established for many years is no mean feat. Taking time to look after yourself when you are under pressure to fit so many things into your life deserves congratulations. At the end of a busy day, when exhaustion hits, replacing activities like watching TV and comfort eating with something more useful like exercise deserves a pat on the back. No wonder you feel great happiness. It's the surest way to fall in love with yourself – and those highs will just last and last.

2016

November/December, Issue 128

be a quitter –
and lose weight!

*I know it sounds so negative – nobody wants to be called
a quitter. Yet sometimes it's the very best thing to be – well
actually, the very best thing to do. If you've ever quit smoking
you'll know what I'm talking about. Well, here are some
great things to quit that are going to spell your absolute,
total, ultimate, long-lasting success in being the master of
your weight issues once and for all. You are in the driving
seat of the most exciting journey of your life.*

quit – *asking why did this have to happen **to** me and instead ask why did this happen **for** me?*

It's a much more useful and searching question and I'm sure if you've been a member of a Slimming World group, you've already learnt a lot about yourself and others in the same boat. All our wonderful, caring Consultants joined us because they had that oh-so-special quality, that much-needed empathy for others.

quit – *those old habits that made you gain weight – using high-fat, high-sugar foods to appease your appetite.*

Instead, find your personal route to enjoying all the good stuff – clean, healthy vegetables and whole fruits, giving yourself a fibre boost and crushing your appetite, and adding an electrifying protein boost with lean meat, poultry and fish, cooked in a low-fat, healthy way. Learn this system, this clever switch, of making 90 per cent of your daily food intake like this and not only will you lose all your extra weight, you will, I can guarantee, keep it off forever.

quit – *over-reacting to having a bad meal, or a bad day.*

This is nothing in the grand scheme of things. You are filling up on Free Foods as your standard, daily way, so there's no need to have a major panic when you slip for the briefest time. Remember how far you've come. Remember when every day was like this in your life. Remember you can continue to be amazing.

quit – *kicking yourself.*

You absolutely don't deserve it and it is so very destructive. If you find yourself saying bad things about yourself, then be aware this negative self-talk will simply send you spiralling out of control. You can be in complete control. It's only this unfair, untrue rubbishing of you, this truly amazing person, that is preventing you from taking charge of the most important person in the world – YOU! You are human, you are not a robot, you are perfectly imperfect. So take back control right away. You can do it.

When you think about quitting things that are holding you back, make your own list and add to it every time you analyse what went wrong and how it happened. Then never leave it at that. Think about your replacements, think about what you can do instead, of what led to the situation and how you can be kind to yourself in other ways that will eventually lead to a happiness that's lasting. This is a new and exciting habit that you can make. Together, you and Slimming World can achieve miracles.

Together, we can do it.

2010

July, Issue 83

togetherness makes a real difference

We all know that 'people who live in glass houses shouldn't throw stones' so I'm hoping that you'll be in a forgiving mood as I prepare to risk all and stick my head above the parapet. I do this in the hope that you'll take these observations to heart and do a better job than I ever did. Do it in the hope that you'll find a way to have a great relationship with your family, set them up for a happier, more satisfying life, help yourself lose weight in the process and help them not fall into the obesity trap. Not only that, we (you and I), could actually have a profound effect on society as a whole, something that successive governments have failed to do. (No surprise there then!) So what's going

*to bring about this important transformation in our lives?
What can we do as ordinary mums and dads that has the
potential dynamite to blast the past and change the future?
Now don't fall off your sofa just because the answer sounds
too easy. The core ingredient to kick-start this change is...
home cooking!*

Stop laughing and think about it. Imagine a family, preparing a meal together, sitting down together, eating a well-balanced meal and talking – actually having a conversation, you know, where somebody talks and somebody else listens. And then doing the clearing up together. Imagine the implications of that! Think about the example you are setting for your family. Think about the bonding. Think about the potential weight loss. Think about the money saved. Think about this pain-free way of teaching personal responsibility and self-discipline.

All too often we talk the talk, but expect someone else (usually our kids) to walk the walk. The age-old adage, whether we like it or not, is so true – actions really do speak louder than words. Round the dining table, with the whole family, you actually have the time to focus on family members and give each of them the positive attention they (we) all crave and need. This could be the only time in your busy day that you can get everyone together at the same time. And let's just push this a bit further. What if you started, or finished, this daily get-together with an activity that everyone enjoyed? A team game (of whatever favourite ball game suits you) creates so much fun and laughter, is so healthy compared to the normal rut that so many of us fall into, that everyone benefits in so many ways. Think about what you've achieved in that deceivingly simple, family evening spent at home:

- *You've shown your children how to cook healthy meals that are also tasty and satisfying even for the heartiest appetite.*

- *You've benefitted from eating loads of good, clean, healthy Free Food and helped yourself lose weight in the process, as well as helping everyone in the family do the same.*

- *You've created an atmosphere in your home that's more loving, sharing and caring, and that teaches self-reliance and a sense of responsibility.*

- *You've initiated a healthy activity habit that everyone can enjoy, at home.*

- *You may even have started a trend that other families want to emulate. Could this actually lead to less drinking, less drug taking, less angry behaviour and a more caring society?*

I know togetherness makes a real difference. Just like losing weight at Slimming World – together we really can do it.